The Human Soul
in a World of
The Neurological Sciences

The Human Soul
in a World of
The Neurological Sciences

Editors
Job Kozhamthadam,
Roy Pereira

Indian Institute of Science and Religion
(IISR)
2021

Laser typeset by
ISPCK, Post Box 1585, 1654, Madarsa Road, Kashmere Gate, Delhi-110006 • *Tel:* 23866323

e-mail: ashish@ispck.org.in • ella@ispck.org.in
website: www.ispck.org.in

Contents

Acknowledgements

This volume is indebted to many persons and organizations for their generous support and active collaboration. The chapters of this book are the modified version of the papers presented at IISR International Symposium on "Developments in the Neurological Sciences and the New Interpretation of the Spiritual Dimension of Humans," organized by IISR (Indian Institute of Science and Religion), Delhi, in collaboration with St. Xavier's College, Mumbai, on 9-11 February, 2018. The editors extend our wholehearted appreciation and gratitude to the Principal and his team of St. Xavier's College for their invaluable support and encouragement. We remain grateful to several others for the preparation of the text of this book. Particularly we are indebted to K.T. Thomas, SJ, for going over the whole manuscript with meticulous care, and making valuable corrections and suggestions. Mrs. Preethi George very generously provided all the secretarial help, and we remain grateful to her.

ISPCK most graciously agreed to co-publish this volume with IISR Delhi. We appreciate this valuable collaboration and express our gratitude to ISPCK.

Editors

Introduction

Today the field of the neurological sciences is at the forefront of scientific study and research worldwide. The findings these investigations bring to light assure us that this trend has come to stay for years and decades. Almost every week researchers are coming up with very valuable data and information that are bound to rewrite many past views and ideas about the human brain, mind and even some of the activities of our innermost self. Many long-held myths have been exploded, bringing self-esteem and dignity to many past victims, many new insights and techniques are appearing on the horizon assuring hope and solace to those still living in anxiety and fear. The medical science perhaps is the greatest beneficiary of this rich inflow of information, invention of new diagnostic methods, production of effective medicines, introduction of new techniques, etc. There is every reason to be optimistic that our world will be a better and happier one, thanks to these unprecedented achievements of the neurological sciences.

Today it is becoming clear that developments in science and technology are no mere carrier of welcome amenities and comforts. Their impact goes deeper and wider to touch and transform many aspects of human life and activities, particularly in the social and religious fields. Not only our meaning system and value system are being reshaped, but also even our way of thinking, our personality itself, is being re-formed and reoriented. How are the recent developments in the world of the neurological sciences impacting men and women of today? What are some of the changes that have already taken place, and many more yet to come? How should religion and society respond to these developments so as to maximize the benefits and minimize the harm they entail?

Echoes of this neurological revolution are perhaps most seriously felt in the field of spirituality or the spiritual dimension of humans, which is usually referred to as the human soul. As we know, the brain, consciousness, mind and the soul have been intimately interlinked from time immemorial, although clarity with regard to this interrelationship still remains elusive. We can be glad and grateful that many findings in recent times have contributed considerably towards clarifying these important concepts and their interrelationship. In the past these areas, particularly of the human soul, were deemed outside the purview of hard sciences, and were left in the hands of philosophers and psychologists. But today, owing to the developments in the different branches of science and technology, scientists are in a position to study these matters empirically and *in vivo* – while they are in normal operation – and come up with new ideas and insights with regard to their nature and activities. Detailed brain mapping is no more part of science fiction. We have far better and more reliable ideas about the plasticity, powers and limitations of the brain, etc. In light of all these developments, many past beliefs have been challenged. For instance, till the beginning of the 20th century, it was believed that the brain cells could not change. But today research has brought the good news that the brain cells can change and further develop, can repair themselves, and even find new pathways when the natural ones are damaged, etc. Also, it has been pointed out by researchers that the brain is not able to distinguish between real events and imagined (e.g., in dream) events. More importantly, doubts have been raised with regard to the existence and nature of free will. Some researchers claim that the free will is nothing but a trick the brain plays on itself.

Another area that has attracted the attention of scientists and scholars is the genesis of the spiritual dimension or soul of humans. Although in most religions and cultures the existence and attributes of the soul occupy a central place, none of them seems to have paid any attention to the genesis of the soul. All of them take it for granted that the soul has a divine origin, is directly created by God and has a superior status compared to the body. It is also assumed that no material agent could have given rise to this immaterial and superior being. However, this situation is also changing, thanks not only to developments in the neurological sciences, but also to the new findings in other branches of science, particularly the dynamic and creative character and potentialities of matter. For Newton and his followers matter was inert and incapable of moving by itself, having no energy of its own. However, special theory of relativity has revealed the revolutionary idea that matter (mass) and energy are inter-convertible, and hence matter can be a source of immense energy. The general theory of relativity has revealed that spacetime, although inaccessible to our ordinary senses, is real, and matter is capable of interacting with and curving it (new understanding of gravitation). Quantum theory also has brought to light many new features and capabilities of matter. Matter has dual nature. Newton thought that matter could exist only as point particles. But quantum theory has shown that it can have wave nature also, and hence be dynamic. Quantum entanglement is a very strange phenomenon, but reveals a remarkable property of particles. According to this phenomenon, once two particles are entangled or twined, that unity does not go away even when they are separated by a long distance. A change in one of them is reflected in the other and the other responds accordingly. All this happens instantly, at a speed faster than light. Again, it has been found that at least in the quantum world the same atom can be in two different places at the same time. Dark energy and dark matter are still vastly an unexplored world. One can confidently expect more surprises about the capabilities of matter when this dark world becomes bright enough to be accessible to detailed scientific study.

Furthermore, many scientists today question the justifiability of the superior status accorded to the spiritual world traditionally. After all, one of the traditional arguments Plato, Aristotle, and others gave for the superior status of the celestial (spiritual) over the terrestrial (material), founders in the sea of the data and information contemporary science is revealing. For instance, for Plato and Aristotle, the celestial was superior because it was the paradigm of order and immutability, whereas the terrestrial faired very poorly in both these criteria. Also according to them, being at rest assured stability, whereas being in motion or in a state of change foreclosed all possibility of stability. Modern science has exposed the hollowness of such claims. For instance, for Plato, Aristotle and others the celestial world could not be stable if it changed and moved. Today we know that movement or change is necessary for stability; once the bodies in the solar system stop moving, the system will collapse. Furthermore, in the past it was believed that the spiritual was indestructible, whereas the material was destructible. Today science tells us that matter-energy is indestructible. In light of these scientific findings, it seems that the traditional claim of the innate superiority of the spiritual and corresponding inferiority of matter needs to be reconsidered or at least reinterpreted.

Given the above observations and related developments, particularly the findings about the inherent, Creator-given, powers of material reality, philosophically-minded scientists and other thinkers have come up with several proposals – theistic and atheistic – and new understanding of the soul. These developments also have given rise to new disciplines like neurotheology. The points discussed above and related issues were critically studied and reflected upon by a carefully chosen team of international &national experts, and their findings were presented at the International Symposium on "Recent Developments in the Neurological Sciences and the New Interpretation of the Spiritual Dimension of Humans," organized by St. Xavier's College Mumbai and Indian Institute of Science and Religion (IISR) Delhi, at St. Xavier's College Mumbai on 9-11 February, 2018. The fifteen papers of this volume are modified and revised versions of these papers. They are divided into two principal sections: Those from a scientifico-philosophical perspective (the first 10 chapters) and those from a scientifico-religious perspective (the last 5 chapters), in the sense that the first principal section dwells mainly on the philosophical aspects and the second section on the religious aspects of the impact of these recent scientific developments.

The first paper, "Neurological Developments & the Spiritual Dimension of Humans," by Professor Job Kozhamthadam begins by discussing some of the inadequacies and flaws of the traditional views of the human person, particularly that of the Aristotelian-Thomistic tradition, and points out that with the help of the latest findings in the different branches of science, particularly in the neurological sciences, better light can be shed on the enigma of the human soul and the human person. In his view contemporary science favours a unitary view of the human person, and illustrates this point with the help of a detailed study of the view of Teilhard de Chardin. The second paper, "The Soul – Entangled Wave of Potentiality," by Professor Heidi Russell, taking her cue from Karl Rahner's insight that the human soul is "the capacity for the infinite," presents a unitary view of the human person by interpreting the human soul in terms of two key quantum mechanical concepts of wave-particle complementarity and the phenomenon of quantum entanglement. According to this view, the soul is our "wave of potential which is collapsed in our embodiment." Taking the analogy further, she presents the view that the human person is formed when the soul, understood as the infinite potential, is limited by the inherent relationality of human existence. The third paper, "The Soul of the Matter and the Matter of the Soul: A Scientific Perspective," by Professor Vincent Braganza points out that reality is dual without duality, in the sense that we do notice different aspects in reality, but these aspects are not different entities. Following the Teilhardian intuition, this paper points out that this differentiation without separation occurs at all levels of reality. At the level of humans the spiritual aspect is traditionally referred to as the soul. What is particularly original about this study is that it supplies an empirical basis for its findings in the experimental study on the worm *C. elegans,* which the author and his team conducted in their lab at Xavier Research Foundation, Ahmedabad, India. The fourth paper, "Developments in Neuroscience and Their Impact on Spirituality: A Critical Perspective," by Dr. Roy Pereira navigates the reader through the world of neurosciences and makes a critical study of what conclusions these developments can lead to. More specifically, he critically examines whether these findings can establish the spiritual dimension of humans. Furthermore, he gives a few valuable suggestions for building up a robust neurotheology. The fifth paper, "Neurosciences-Religion Dialogue – Towards a New Domain of Neurotheology," by Professors František Mikeš and Geraldine Edith Mikes introduces the reader to the new emerging field of Nuerotheology – reflective study of the linkage between the brain/mind and religion/theology. More specifically it studies the nexus between neural correlates of the brain and religious/spiritual systems of beliefs, experiences and practices. Special emphasis is placed on the pioneering and ground-breaking empirical studies conducted by Eugene d'Aquili and Andrew Newberg.Furthermore, it gives a rather up-to-date highlights of the current literature on the matter. It discusses briefly the phenomenon of psychedelic substances and neurotransmitters and how the operations of these can produce behaviour patterns that are usually associated with the human soul. At the same time, it emphasizes the fundamental metaphysical point that similarity of effects does not lead to sameness of cause. These phenomena and related experimental studies may point to correlation, not to causal relation. The sixth chapter, "Does the Brain Make God? A Philosophical Analysis," by Dr.ChackoNadakavely, while lauding the achievements of recent findings of the neurological sciences, points out that a mere materialistic or mechanistic explanation of human cognitive phenomena falls far too short to do due justice to the complexities and subtleties of human mental activities like cognition, semantics, intentionality, etc. Hence he concludes that the neural correlates of spiritual activities involved in religious experience, as revealed by developments in neurology, need to go beyond the capabilities of matter. The seventh paper, "Neurology and the Soul: Exploring the Story of Spiritual Dimension of Human Existence," by Professor Kuruvilla Pandikattu attempts to explain the problem of the human soul in terms of the narrative self and spiritual self, following the ideas of the French philosopher Paul Ricoeur. The eighth paper, "Can Science Essentially Estrange Spirituality? Philosophy of Science Perspectives," by Professor Stephen Jayard challenges the traditional, popular view that science and spirituality belong to two different domains. He argues that recent developments in the different branches of science and the new insights on spirituality point out that they can productively and fruitfully collaborate with each other, particularly in light of recent revelations concerning the limits and limitations of these two comprehensive disciplines. The ninth paper, "The Soul – The Missing Link: A Psychiatrist's Perspective on Avenues of Interfacing the Soul, Psychiatry and Neuroscience," by Dr. Sally John, a practicing psychiatrist, brings a psychiatric and clinical dimension to our theme. After serious study, reflection and practice in the field, she has come to the conclusion that, despite the major advances in the field of neuropsychiatry, there is an apparent "soul-loss" or missing link in the current approach to understanding and managing mental illness. In her view, there is need to look for new vistas to discover an interlink between the soul, spirituality and neurobiology. The tenth paper, "The Biology of Violence: An Ethico-Philosophical Response," by Professor Victor Ferrao points out that one of the consequences of the developments in the world of neurology and related fields is the emergence of the view that human actions are biologically or genetically determined. It takes a critical view at this view as it refers to the field of human violence. It points out that this situation raises very serious ethical and social issues, and we need to develop clear and effective principles to deal with it.

The essays in the second major part of the book approach the principal theme from a scientifico-religious perspective, in the sense that they focus on how the various scientific developments interact with religious views. Thus the eleventh paper, "The Spiritual Dimension of

Humans in the Light of Sri Aurobindo and the Limitations of Science," by Professor Ramesh Bijlani focuses on the ideas and insights of Sri Aurobindo. He exposes the fallacy of the traditional view that mystic experience is alien to science. In fact, the paper points out that research in physics, neurophysiology and medicine has observed facts and phenomena that are consistent with the corollaries and implications of mystic experience. Deeply steeped in the Indian tradition, the philosophy of Sri Aurobindo is not only non-dualistic but also world-affirming and life-affirming as well as evolutionary. Although not all these aspects of the vision of Sri Aurobindo come under the purview of science, some of them are, which are discussed in this well-thought out and highly scholarly paper. Furthermore, it points out a very striking contrast between the Indian spiritual perspective and the scientific perspective: for the latter consciousness is an emergent property of ever complexifying matter, for the former it is primary, brain being only an instrument to channelize consciousness. The twelfth paper, "*Chan* Consciousness and Enlightenment & the Spiritual Dimension of Humans," by Professor Jijimon Alakkalam Joseph sheds valuable light on our theme from the Buddhist tradition. Although Buddhism does not believe in the existence of the soul in the usual sense, this tradition is replete with spiritual ideas and ideals. This paper is an attempt to look at *Chan* consciousness and enlightenment from the spiritual dimension of humans. *Chan* is often called the meditation school of Mahāyāna Buddhism. The thirteenth paper, "The Human Soul: A Biblical Perspective," by Dr. Thomas Karimundackal is a very scholarly textual study of the biblical perspective of the human person. On the basis of a detailed study of the relevant texts of both Old and New Testaments, the paper points out that the original Hebrew view of the human being is not bipartite but unitary. The Hebrews were well aware of the different manifestations of the human person; yet they did not consider it necessary to postulate two different parts – body and soul. According to this view, a person "does not *have* a soul, but *is* a soul." Today this unitary perspective takes on special significance since contemporary science is very strongly favouring a non-dualisticview, and so the basic Hebrew, and hence the biblical, view is closer to the findings of modern science. In the fourteenth paper, "The Concept of the Mind, Body and Soul in the Sikh Scripture (SGGS)," Professor Hardev Singh Virk presents the perspective of the Sikh religion on the theme of the human soul in the context of the developments in the neurological sciences. He points out that although Sikhism accords great importance to the human body, considering it the temple of God (*HariMandir*), the human soul is given supreme importance since the human soul (*Atma*) is ultimately responsible for giving the body its life-force. In the fifteenth and final paper, "The Near-Death Experience," Dr. Mehra Srikhande who has done extensive study and research in the field of "near-death experiences" shares some of her important findings.

This book and the international symposium that gave rise to it are part of IISR (Indian Institute of Science and Religion) Delhi's attempt to attain its goal of blending together the latest findings of modern science and deepest insights of religions to build up a better humanity and a better world, particularly in the multireligious, multicultural and multiracial fabric of India. IISR believes that, just like religion, science is also a gift from God, although in the case of science the human contribution is more substantial. It also believes that science and religion are not contradictory, but complementary to each other, in the sense that science brings in something important, which religion is not able to, and vice versa. It also believes that this complemenarity relationship is a mediated one – there is a third party in and through which the interaction takes place. In the case of the complementarity relationship between science and religion the mediator is the human person, particularly the lived life of the human person. Science brings something precious and necessary for humans, which religion cannot. Similarly religion brings something precious and necessary for humans, which science cannot. Thus here the human person becomes both the mediator and the beneficiary, and an enriched humanity ushers in. With regard to the spiritual dimension of humans, religious traditions have given very valuable insights. With the developments of science, particularly neurological sciences, certain new ideas have emerged enabling us to have a better understanding of the human person. The different chapters of the book by well-established scholars attempt to give the readers this enriched understanding of the human person. It is my hope that this book will serve as a catalyst for more such initiatives so that humanity becomes richer and happier.

Job Kozhamthadam,
3rd July, 2020

Chapter 1

Neurological Developments & the Spiritual Dimension of Humans

Job Kozhamthadam

Abstract

This paper is an attempt to shed some new light on the age old enigma of the human soul. Belief in the soul is fundamental to all religions and traditions from time immemorial. It begins by briefly exposing and critically analyzing the nature and activities of the soul, as propounded by eminent scholars and established religious traditions in the past. It points out that these views were not the result of any direct observation, rather they can be looked upon as instances of "inference to the best explanation," in the sense that these brilliant thinkers noticed certain behaviour patterns and manifestations in humans, and tried to account for them by inferring that deep within humans there must be some being responsible for them. They also attributed certain qualities and capabilities to this inner being, which was usually referred to as the soul. This gave rise to the dominant view that the human being is made of two parts – an external, material body and an internal, spiritual soul. In most traditions it was also believed that the soul or spiritual component was superior, whereas the physical inferior. This was particularly true of the Aristotelian-Thomistic tradition which was very dominant in the West. In the East also similar traditions could be found. Being committed to a static cosmology these traditions subscribed to a static worldview, according to which change was considered a sign of imperfection and inferiority. The body which belonged to the material realm was subject to change, and so it was inferior, whereas the soul which belonged to the immaterial did not change, and so was superior. However, with the arrival of modern science many of these ideas and claims were questioned, and some of them were shown to be unjustifiable. For instance, with the success of the theory of evolution to explain many phenomena in the biological and physical world (now in the neurological also), evolution began to be accepted as a universal phenomenon governing the developmental process of practically all phenomena. Consequently the dynamic worldview began to replace the traditional static worldview, with very serious consequences, particularly for the Christian tradition and teaching. In the static worldview change was looked upon as a sign of imperfection, but in the evolutionary, dynamic worldview change is something positive and is understood as an opportunity to seek better ways of becoming more perfect. Also, modern science challenged the claim of the superiority of the spiritual over the material by showing that matter also had many of the capabilities which the spirit was claimed to have. Furthermore, the traditional dualistic view of humans was shown to be full of insoluble problems, and a non-dualist view was shown to be possible. The recent developments in brain study and neurology posed even more serious challenges to the traditional body-soul combination of the human person. All these and many related to them became a serious threat to the traditional understanding of the origin, development and nature of human being, and new theories which could do better justice to our understanding of the human person, particularly the soul, were proposed. One such attempt was the view developed by Teilhard deChardin. This paper discusses his view in some detail, and points out some of its merits and demerits. It is hoped that with further developments in the different branches of science, particularly those related to the neurological and computer sciences, more light will be shed on the matter, and the mystery of the human soul will become less enigmatic.

Keywords: The soul, static and dynamic worldviews, neurology, Teilhard de Chardin

Introduction

Although hardly any serious scholar doubts the existence of a spiritual dimension (or soul)in humans, mystery has been a constant companion of this aspect of humans. This matter has been rendered even more perplexing by two principal beliefs closely associated with it. Firstly, the spiritual dimension is very different from the material or physical dimension. Since it belongs to a totally different domain, it becomes inaccessible to the usual methods of investigation, particularly scientific method. Secondly, it was thought that the spiritual is superior to the material or physical. Hence it was considered by many that ordinary scientific tools and means are inadequate to deal with this world of the spiritual. However, in recent times contemporary science has challenged all these traditional views and presuppositions. Tremendous research and study has been done to fathom the depths of the world of the spiritual, and the results have been amazing with far-reaching consequences. The decade from 1990 to 2000 is rightly called the "decade of the brain" since it brought in very valuable information and technology into the field. The following years were even more eventful and revealing. Today we know a lot about the human brain and the spiritual world closely associated with it. In light of these developments, many old misconceptions have been exploded and new scientific facts have been discovered, bringing much hope, joy and consolation to many afflicted by various brain or psychological maladies. This paper will go into some of these encouraging and promising developments.

Another important spin off from all these new findings is a new understanding of the origin, nature and activities of the spiritual dimension in humans, or what is traditionally called the human soul. Although practically all religions and cultures believe in the existence of the soul, none of them has given a satisfactory theory about the origin and development of the soul. In recent times several scientifically-minded thinkers like Teilhard de Chardin in the West and Sri Aurobindo in our own India, have delved deeply into this area and have shared their findings with us. In this paper I give a brief outline of the Teilhardian view which has been modified by recent findings in the neurological sciences. Using the ideas of evolution, scientific view of emergence, the intrinsically dynamic nature of our universe and the understanding of the power and capabilities of matter as revealed by The Theory of Relativity, Quantum Theory, Chaos theory, etc., I present a proposal concerning the origin, development and destiny of the human soul. Following the footsteps of Teilhard, I hold the view that in the beginning the creator created elementary unitary beings, the initial stuff, which had two mutually interacting and mutually enriching aspects. In accordance with the law of theistic evolution and the law of complexity-consciousness, they developed into different beings, culminating in humans who are self-conscious and self-reflective (they know that they know). I also point out that the neurological sciences are very much in their infancy, and we can expect many more surprises and promises, hopefully for the good of humanity today and years to come. I end the paper inviting all to be part of this ongoing progressive process, and make their valuable contribution towards it in whatever way possible.

The Soul: Its Importance and Attributes

Humans, undoubtedly, are the most advanced and complex of all beings in the universe. They have two noticeably distinct dimensions: the immaterial/spiritual and the material/physical. What marks out humans from all other beings is the spiritual dimension, as is clear from the fact that, although genomically they differ from chimpanzees by less than one per cent, they show vast differences in their capabilities and behaviour.

Some Philosophical Views on the Soul

The Greek Tradition

Plato

Although the idea and interest in understanding the nature and operation of the soul are as old as the human race itself, credit goes mostly to Plato for having given a rather clear and definite view on the soul. According to him, the soul is the essence of the person having three parts: logos (mind), thymis (emotion) and eros (desire). This view lasted for quite some time. In fact, even now many people essentially subscribe to this view. It believes in the separate existence of the soul. In fact, at the time of death the soul departs from the body and carries on an independent life. Thus Plato presented a dualist view concerning the nature of the human person.

Aristotle

Aristotle who was, in many ways, the most well-known disciple of Plato accepted most of the ideas of Plato on the human soul. However, he was uneasy with the sharp distinction Plato made between the body and the soul. For Aristotle the relationship between the body and the soul was like the relationship between substantial form and prime matter, as explained by his theory of hylomorphism. Hence he opposes a separate existence for the soul, and in this sense he was trying to dissociate himself from the dualist view of Plato.

The Jewish Tradition

Unlike the Greeks, the Jewish tradition concerning the nature of humans was non-dualist. Scholars point out that nowhere in the Jewish scriptures do we find the notion of the soul existing apart from its embodiment in the individual person, and thus the Jewish tradition supported a unified view of the human person.

The Christian Tradition

Christianity, as it was developing its view on the human person, borrowed heavily from the Greek tradition, although its original roots were Jewish. Jesus Christ was a Jew, and so were his apostles and early followers.

St. Augustine

St. Augustine was one of the first most important philosopher-theologians of the Church to delve deeply into the nature and behaviour of the human person. His thinking was very much along the Greek tradition. In his view the soul was a special substance, endowed with reason and adapted to rule the body. Thus he gave a preeminent place to the soul, and the body was reduced to a secondary accompaniment.

Thomas Aquinas

St. Thomas Aquinas in the 13th century took up the issue of the human soul very seriously, and presented his view, which became very prominent in the centuries to come. According to him, the soul was the first principle of the body. It was not corporeal and could subsist without the body. He also emphasized the immortality of the soul. Concerning the relationship between the body and the soul, his view was that the soul was extrinsically dependent on the body, that is, the body was required for the soul to begin to exist, but once the soul began to exist, it could continue for ever without the body.

Roman Catholicism

Roman Catholicism basically accepts the ideas of Augustine and Thomas and has added to them some further aspects of Christian belief and tradition. It teaches that the soul is the innermost aspect of humans. Taking the Biblical view that humans are created in the image and likeness of God, it points out that the soul enables humans most especially to be in the image and likeness of God. Furthermore, it emphasizes the need for a special intervention of God to create and infuse the human soul into the zygote at each time of conception.

Buddhism

Buddhism advocates the impermanence of the soul. It believes that there is no unchanging and abiding substance in humans.

Hinduism

Since Hinduism has many lines and traditions of thought, it presents many views concerning the human soul and the nature of humans. One of the dominant views is that the human soul is part of Brahman.

Islam

As in the Book of Genesis, Islam talks of Allah breathing souls into humans. It emphasizes the non-physical aspects.

Critique of the Traditional Views

Although many of the ideas of various religious traditions are being challenged today, we need to give credit to the scholars involved for venturing into this field and giving us certain insights into the reality and activities of the human soul. The following points are of special significance, and I highlight some of the inadequacies of the old, traditional views.

Vague and Controversial

The views advocated by past scholars on the human soul have been vague and controversial. It is evident that no one seemed to have a clear perception of the matter based on reliable data.

Phenomenological Views

The ideas expressed on the soul were not based on any direct, reliable observation and study. Rather they were attempts to make sense of certain observed features of human behaviour and activities. Scholars and thinkers observed certain features in humans, which could not be explained mechanically or in terms of ordinarily known forces and processes. Hence they seemed to have inferred that there must be some non-physical or non-material dimension in humans, which they called the soul. The observed phenomena were looked upon as the manifestations of this indwelling, spiritual entity. In other words, according to these scholars, the soul was the cause of these observed manifestations. It was very much an "inference to the best explanation."

Certain Scientific Observations and Challenges to the Traditional Views

However, with the development of modern science and observations based on it, challenges began to be posed to the traditional view. For instance, it was shown that some of the features attributed to the action of the indwelling, spiritual being can be accounted for by the action of certain chemicals and material substances. For instance, the drug LSD could induce some of the feelings and behaviour patterns traditionally attributed to the soul. Again, it was found that oxytocin (love hormone) and some other chemicals could explain phenomena like sympathy, spirit of caring for the loved ones, etc. Some agnostics and theistic-minded scholars began to argue that, with further developments in science, all the phenomena or behaviour patterns traditionally attributed to the spiritual soul could be accounted for in terms of different chemicals and activities associated with them. Some of these are tall claims made by diehard supporters and admirers of science. Yet, as we shall see later in this paper, some of the traditional claims regarding the human soul will have to be reconsidered in light of important developments in various branches of science.

Some Basic /Foundational Ideas of the Traditional View of the Soul

Dualism

It is quite clear that at the foundation of the traditional views on the human soul, particularly in the Greek tradition of Plato, Aristotle, Augustine and Aquinas, was the sharp distinction between matter and spirit, physical and spiritual, body and soul, natural and supernatural, etc.

Superiority of the Spirit or Soul over Matter or Body

Not only did the traditional views make a sharp distinction between body and soul, and related items, they also attributed superiority to the spiritual and related world over the material. Here one can see the overpowering influence of Plato who was primarily responsible for initiating or at least popularising this view.

Immutability a Sign of Superiority, Changeability a Sign of Inferiority

The traditional view justified its claim of superiority of the spirit by arguing that anything that changes was inferior, whereas anything that remained immutable was superior. The line of argument of the promoters of this view was simple and straightforward: a thing changed because it did not have something it needed. It had to undergo change to get that missing item. On the other hand, a perfect thing had everything it needed, and so was not in need of any change.

Inertness or Lack of Dynamism a Mark of Inferiority

Another justification the traditionalists used to undermine the status of matter (material/physical) was the criterion of dynamism. In their view matter was inert, lacking dynamism and self-activity. On the other hand, spirit was dynamic. The soul was dynamic. It was considered the principle of activity of the human being. This absence of dynamism became a demeaning factor for matter.

Order a Sign of Superiority

Another argument for placing the spiritual over the material was the claimed order in the spiritual world and disorder in the material world. The material world of our experience was found to be disorderly. On the other hand, the spiritual world, as represented by the heavenly world, was orderly. It may be noted that the ancients considered the star-studded heavens the paradigm of order and regularity. In fact, 'cosmos' originally meant 'right order.'

Immortality or Imperishablility a Sign of Superiority

Another reason why the traditionalists considered the soul superior and the body inferior was the criterion of imperishability. According to them, whatever is perishable is inferior, whereas whatever is imperishable is superior. Matter was deemed perishable, and so inferior. The soul was immortal, and hence superior.

The traditionalists got further support in the initial stages of neurological studies. It was found that the brain cells were different from other cells of the human body, in the sense that these cells stop multiplying and growing at a very early stage. Also it was thought that adults could not grow new neurons or brain cells. This meant that if an adult brain is damaged through accident or in some other way, there was no way to come back to normalcy.

Developments in Modern Science & Erosion/Banishing of Many of the above Claims

Theory of Evolution & New Understanding of Change

Today evolution is accepted not merely as a theory of the biological world, but a general, fundamental feature of all material reality. The basic insight of the theory of evolution is that change is a fundamental characteristic of all beings. Thus the Big Bang Theory tells that the physical world has been evolving. The Theory of Biological Evolution says that the living world has been evolving. Evolution is found to be active in the neurological world as well. All these considerations lead us to conclude that change is not a sign of imperfection/inferiority, but **an opportunity to seek better ways of becoming more perfect.**

Change and Stability – Dynamic Equilibrium

In the past, it was thought that change and stability were incompatible; change upset stability and the normal functioning of a system. Today with the development of science and the expansion of our knowledge of various dynamic systems, a new understanding of stability has emerged. In fact, it is becoming clear that certain changes, far from disturbing stability, ensure it. For instance, take the mechanism involved in the stability of our solar system. Here motion, which is a common form of change, is found to be necessary for stability. In fact, we need to make a distinction between static equilibrium and dynamic equilibrium. In the latter case change or some form of motion is necessary, and this brings about equilibrium.

Dynamism/Energy of Matter Affirmed

The discovery of the energy or dynamism of matter is another important development in contemporary science, which has serious repercussions on the status of matter. In Newtonian science in the beginning matter was considered inert and inactive; it would move only when force is applied on it. Later on with the discovery of the Law of Gravitation, in a way, this view had to be modified since this law showed that matter was capable of exerting a force on other material bodies. Einstein's Special Theory of Relativity went much further when it showed the equivalence of matter and energy. The inter-convertibility of mass (matter) and energy means that matter is a huge source of energy and dynamism. The General Theory of Relativity went still further when it argued that matter could influence even four-dimensional spacetime continuum, as was validated by the discovery of gravitational waves in 2016.

Certain Spirit-like Properties of Matter

Quantum Entanglement

Entanglement is a phenomenon involving a pair of entangled or twined particles. They remain so connected or correlated that an action performed on one of them affects the other also even when they are separated from each other by a long distance. Here information about what happens to one particle is communicated to the other instantaneously, defying the limit imposed by the Special Theory of Relativity which stipulates that the velocity of light is the highest velocity possible. Such instantaneous communication usually happens only in the world of the spiritual where there are no space-time limits.

Multi-Dimensionality of the Universe

We humans understand very well space as 3-dimensional and time as one dimensional. However, Relativity tells us that our universe is really 4-dimensional spacetime – not space and time, but spacetime, all the 4 dimensions, including time, having the same ontological status. Actually, we humans are not able to experience by ordinary means this spacetime. But today, in the post-gravitational wave era, we know that spacetime is indeed a physical reality accessible to empirical science. In M-theory advocated by Stephen Hawking and others, there are 11 dimensions – 9 space dimensions, 1 time dimension and 1 energy dimension. Current string theory has 10 dimensions. It may be noted that at present string theories remain at the hypothetical level. Many theoretical scientists believe that in course of time some form of string theory or M-theory may be shown to be not just hypothetical, but physical. But there seems to be hardly any possibility that they will be accessible to direct observation like 3-dimensional space and one-dimensional time. This will take us to a situation where something is real and physical, but not accessible to direct sense observation. This is a situation very much akin to the world of the spiritual.

Towards a New Understanding of the Human Person or the Body-Soul Relationship

Developments in Science and Challenge to the Traditional View

Several developments in modern science challenge many of the claims made in the past, on the basis of which the world of the spiritual had been glorified and shown to be superior, while that of the material had been vilified and shown to be inferior. Since the traditional pair of spirit and matter is intimately linked to the pair of soul and body, these developments become a serious challenge to the old ideas on the nature of the soul and body and the relationship between the two. The traditional sharp distinction between soul and body is challenged. Also the claim to the intrinsic superiority of the soul over the body is questioned. At this stage of scientific development what is questioned is not the distinction itself, rather the traditional *sharp* distinction. With regard to the matter of superiority, at this stage of scientific study and data what is questioned is the low status that was accorded to matter and material phenomena in the past – matter has to be given greater dignity and importance. What further developments in science will bring about only the future can tell.

Relationship between Body and Soul – Complementarity, not Competition

Another important consideration in this context is that in the case of body-soul relationship what is involved is a relationship of complementarity, not of competition. Complementarity implies that the different aspects contribute to complete the case under consideration. An absence of any complementary aspect leaves the final product incomplete. What is important is not which contributing factor is superior or more important, rather whether all the contributing factors are present or not. It is possible that the spiritual or, in this case, the soul aspect may have greater intrinsic merit and value. But whatever be the intrinsic merit of the soul aspect, without the body aspect the human person remains incomplete. Hence any focusing on superiority/inferiority consideration is not very relevant here.

The foregoing discussion calls for a reconsideration of the traditional understanding of the nature of the human person. It also calls for a new look at the nature and status of the human soul. Although several views have been proposed by many scholars, I will focus on the view of Teilhard de Chardin that has been modified in light of recent scientific developments.

The Teilhardian View of the Human Person or Body-Soul Relationship

Some Important Elements of the Teilhardian System/Worldview

A Unified View

Faced with the problems of the traditional view of the body-soul relationship and several other problems associated with it, many scholars – particularly those who subscribe to an atheistic or scientistic[1] view – have chosen a materialistic reductionist view. They propose a unitary or one- substance (matter) view in which whatever were attributed to the spiritual or soul in the past can now be reduced to mere physico-chemical phenomena that can be analysed and accounted for in terms of scientific laws and methods. The Teilhardian approach does not accept this view. It steers clear of such new atheistic view and the traditional Platonic dualist view. Differences are acknowledged, but they are of different aspects, not of different individual parts. Such difference in aspects does not lead to separation, but to mutual dependence and enrichment.

Evolution as Fundamental

Teilhard was a convinced believer of evolution. He subscribed to a dynamic view of the universe, according to which God created the universe imperfect so that through the evolutionary process it may gradually become more and more perfect. In this process the different items in the universe appeared, starting from the less developed moving to the more developed ones. Teilhard time and again affirmed that the fundamental principles of his system were evolution and Christ. In fact, the very last sentence he wrote in his diary was "The universe is centred-evolutely (upward and forward); and Christ is its centre."[2] However, unlike Darwin, he subscribed to theistic evolution. For him God is the Alpha and the Omega, origin and end, of the evolutionary process. He also believed that evolution had a direction. His scientific evidence for this directionality of the evolutionary process was his study of the brain and nervous systems of living beings. In this study he found that the more developed a living being, the higher its level of consciousness – thereby showing a directionality towards greater complexity and corresponding higher level of consciousness.

The 'Within' and the 'Without'

The 'within' and the 'without' pair is a fundamental concept in Teilhard's system. In his view all beings have two different, but mutually related aspects – the 'within,' which refers to the immaterial, conscious dimension and the 'without,' which refers to the material, measurable aspect. Also he held that the more developed a being, the more dominant its 'within' dimension. This would mean that even a stone has a 'within' aspect, albeit being too little to be noticed.

The Law of Complexity- Consciousness

This law is often referred to as the Teilhardian Law. It states that there is a direct relationship between the complexity of a being and its level of consciousness. The more complex a being, the higher the level of its consciousness. Thus the complexity of the brain/nervous system of an earthworm is rather low compared to that of a chimpanzee. Correspondingly, its level of consciousness also is low.

It is obvious that the 'within' and the 'without' pair and the law of complexity-consciousness are closely related. In fact, we can talk of mutual dependence and enrichment between complexity of matter and the level of consciousness. The more the complexity of matter, the higher the level of consciousness attained by the resulting system of reality,e.g., the human brain is the most complex of all realities in the known universe, and humans have the highest the level of consciousness. Also, the higher the level of consciousness, the more the complexity the resulting system attains, e.g., a robot with higher intelligence is able to produce systems that are more complex.

The Mechanism of Evolutionary Development

Although the full mechanism of evolutionary development is not clear, the phenomenon of emergence is presented as one of the agents involved in this process.

What is emergence?

Emergence is a phenomenon whereby larger entities arise through interactions among smaller or simpler entities such that the larger entities exhibit properties the smaller/simpler entities do not exhibit. For instance, water is hydrogen and oxygen compounded, sodium chloride (common salt) is a chemical compound produced when sodium and chlorine form a complex compound. In both these cases we know that the compound produced exhibits higher properties which the components individually or in isolation are unable to exhibit.

Emergence, Property of Matter like Gravitation –Evidence for Inner Richness of Matter

What is the source of emergence? What enables a substance to have this property? History of human thought tells us that a similar question was asked in the case of gravitation, particularly in the Newton (Samuel Clarke)-Leibniz debate. Emergence seems to be a property of matter quite akin to gravitation.

In my view, the property of emergence, like that of gravitation, can be looked upon as one of the inner resources of matter. At present there is no satisfactory scientific explanation for it. We can hope that, just as Einstein in 1905 showed that energy is an inner resource of matter ($E = mc^2$), some reliable explanation will be found with regard to matter-emergence relationship.

Life, Intelligence, etc., Emergent Properties

Many scholars have proposed to look upon life, intelligence, self-consciousness, etc., as emergent properties. When simple constituents form complex compounds, at a certain level of complexity, the system thus formed becomes capable of manifesting properties associated with life – response to external stimuli, self-maintenance, self-repair, etc. Similarly when living systems become more complex, the resultant system begins to manifest properties associated with rationality – intelligence, ability to make choices, etc. Some critics may point out that this process involves more than emergence. Science is not yet in a position to decide on this matter definitively. What is claimed here is that the property of emergence is one of the factors involved.

Process of Evolutionary Development – Creation of Life, Intelligence, Self-Reflection, Etc.

The "Initial or Primeval Stuff"

In the beginning the creator created the "primeval stuff" or beings which were simple but pregnant with numerous, almost infinite, potentialities. According to the Teilhardian insight these primeval beings had two dimensions – material/physical and immaterial/spiritual. Teilhard calls the two aspects "the without" and the "the within."They were endowed with the potentialities for complexification, emergence, etc. Evolutionary in their mode of development and growth, they were also governed by the Law of Complexity-Consciousness.

Formation of Different Beings

The evolutionary process was set in and following the path of complexity-consciousness, emergence, etc., the universe followed in the course of overall development a general direction, and in the process the different items we see in the universe came into being. At one stage living beings appeared, and differentiated themselves into various forms. At a later stage rational, intelligent beings and finally humans with self-reflective, self-knowing abilities appeared.

Special Divine Intervention for Human Soul?

Teilhard's system is fully theistic since for him God is the Alpha and Omega (beginning and end) of all evolutionary processes of creation He does not see any necessity for a special divine intervention for the creation of the human soul or spiritual dimension, although he is not opposed to it.

Human being, the Net-effect of Both the Physical and Spiritual Dimensions

As mentioned earlier, the process involves mutual dependence and enrichment from both physical and spiritual dimensions.What a person is at a given stage is the result of the combined contribution of both the dimensions. What a person is at a given moment is determined by both his/her physical and spiritual dimension at that moment. What a person is at the time of death is the net product of this mutual enrichment. Hence death can be looked upon not as the separation of the physical and the spiritual, but the cessation of this process of mutual enrichment.

Critique of the New View

Many Difficulties and Unclarities

Although certain elements of Teilhard's thinking and system can be found in earlier thinkers and traditions, particularly in French intellectual and scientific traditions, many of the ideas were original to him. In some ways, he was blazing new trails, particularly in his attempt to blend harmoniously the latest scientific ideas and intuitions and the time-tested religious teachings and insights. There was no pre-set method or procedure in this field. In such an attempt ambiguities and unclarities are a forgone consequence. I discuss very briefly some serious ones raised by different critics.

Vagueness of Ideas and Claims

A persistent criticism of Teilhard has been that his ideas and claims are couched in vague and ambiguous terms. His frequent use of neologisms is presented as a clear illustration. Also his style of writing is heavy, convoluted and laborious.

Modernist Tendencies

Teilhard has been accused of following the path of the Modernists at the beginning of the 20th century. According to Arthur Vermmersch, Modernism was an attempt to transform human thought in relations to God, human, the world and life in light of humanistic, philosophical and scientific developments prevalent at the time. In the early part of the 20th century some of the prominent proponents and promoters of Modernism were George Tyrrell, Alfred Loisy, Maude Petre, Friedrich von Hügel, etc.[3] The Church authorities at the time thought that the views of Modernists had gone too far, and Pope Pius X condemned this movement. Several scholars today point out that there were valuable elements in this movement, such as that religion in general, the Church of Christ in particular, is a living and dynamic community of believers, and hence should respond responsibly and creatively to the developments taking place all around it. In my view this is exactly what the Second Vatican Council, under the charismatic leadership of Popes John XXIII and Paul VI ventured to do. However, even now there are people, scholars included, who think differently, and count Teilhard among the Modernists, and argue that his system should meet the same fate as of the Modernists in the time of Pope Pius X.

Relativism

Another serious criticism levelled against Teilhard is that his view leads to relativism, and hence the absolute truths of the Catholic religion are in danger. Since Teilhard takes evolution as fundamental, his system is positively committed to change. In a constantly changing world, the place and relevance of absolute principles and values become a serious issue. Also it is argued that such a state of affairs will lead to anarchy and lawlessness. The traditional eternal truths like important Catholic doctrines and dogmas will be in jeopardy.

Pantheism

Pantheism basically identifies the universe with God. According to critics, Teilhard gives so much importance to matter and the material universe that his view easily slips into pantheism. Teilhard's well-known book,*Hymn of the Universe,* has its first chapter titled "The Mass on the World." There are also many statements wherein he extolls the universe exuberantly. According to critics, all these are subtle signs of pantheism he himself has cultivated, and to which he invites others. Also for Teilhard the many astounding developments in science and technology are all an integral part of the onward, progressive march of humanity and the cosmos to the Omega-Point, who is Christ. Such theories also smack of pantheism, say the critics.

Some Observations and Responses to the Critics

Some Comments on the Vagueness and Lack of Clarity in Teilhard's Thought

It may be noted that there are many more objections raised by critics. Since the present work is not a theological or technical paper, I will remain somewhat general in my response to these and other objections. First of all, it must be kept in mind that the primary purpose of Teilhard's mission was to respond to the difficulties raised by scientists and other highly educated and critical-minded persons with regard to our Christian religion. He was not attempting to write a formal, theological treatise. Nor was he addressing the ordinary, church-going, simple Christians. He took the findings of contemporary science very seriously and made a serious attempt to understand and interpret some of the deepest beliefs and insights of the Christian tradition in light of these findings. Then he tried to share these new experiences and ideas with the intelligentsia in a language and idiom intelligible to an open-minded, but demanding and critical-minded group. While going through the remarks and observations of a number of critics, even recent ones, I get the impression that most of them have missed this important aspect. The vast majority of Teilhard's critics seem to be approaching the subject with a background of Thomism/Scholasticism or Neo-Thomism. As far as my knowledge of contemporary science, particularly its philosophy and history, goes neither Thomism which was developed in the 13th pre-scientific era nor Neo-Thomism which is a modified version of the same in the early part of the 20th century is able to deal with contemporary science in any fruitful or helpful way without making serious modifications on many of their own fundamental presuppositions and ideas. It is not at all my position that whatever science says is right and whatever these traditional philosophies say is not right – that will be very irresponsible from my side. What I notice is that there are serious differences between some of the basic ideas of both, and hence appropriate adaptations and modifications will have to be made by both sides to find a platform where a meaningful dialogue can take place. Teilhard is trying to make such a platform and in this process he has to tread unchartered paths. This explains why, on the one hand, many scientists, especially the atheistic minded ones, are dissatisfied by him, and, on the other hand, many religious scholars, especially those with traditional or fundamentalist leanings, are unhappy with his system of thought. More open-minded, better-informed dialogue and reflection can certainly help. The spirit of the Second Vatican Council, especially its call for a genuine Aggiornamento, and some of the important statements of the Documents of the same Council, as well as the statements of popes like John XXIII, Paul VI, John Paul II, Francis can be of great help in this context. On the other side, the spirit and attitude of openness and humility shown by many contemporary scientists like Francis Collins, late Allan Sandage, late Freeman Dyson, etc., can also set the stage for a healthy and fruitful dialogue. My own personal view on this matter is that ambiguities and unclarities in the Teilhardian system arise, at least partly, from the newness of the field and the complexity of the issues involved. "Big questions" like what religion is, what science is, how they can interact meaningfully and creatively, etc., cannot be settled by any simple method or by a single discussion. It is a rather long process and can be achieved only gradually. But it has to start, and the present atmosphere of both science and religion seems to be an opportune time for this creative interaction.[4]

Some Comments on Modernist Tendency in Teilhard

With regard to the concern of modernist tendency, all extreme forms of Modernism, with accompanying exaggerated claims regarding the accomplishments of contemporary science and attempts to belittle the importance and relevance of religion will have to be shunned. At the same time, it is very important to realize that modern science is a gift of God, just as religion is a gift of God, and so there is need for Catholicism to learn from the findings of science with befitting openness, care and caution. Here also the spirit and substance of Vatican II and the proclamations of the Popes in recent times are very important. Of special significance is the Letter of Pope John Paul II to late Fr. George Coyne, SJ, the then Director of the Vatican Observatory in 1988.[5] Some of the writings and observations of Pope Benedict XVI can be of help in ensuring that no uncritical assent is given to the data and findings of modern science.

Some Comments on Relativism

Coming to the mater of relativism, it is important to avoid all forms of irresponsible relativism.Perhaps the worry of the critics may be that since Teilhard subscribes to a universe which is evolutionary in nature, change becomes a fundamental principle, thereby banishing the possibility of any abiding or unchanging principles. My understanding in this context is that evolution does not involve any wholesale change. Unlike in the case of revolution where a total break with the past may be involved, in evolution the change is not discontinuous. There is a core that does not change. In the case of evolution of religion, the core beliefs remain, but its understanding, interpretation, application, etc., may change. Controversy can come with regard to which are the items that go into this core of beliefs. This will have to be decided by the appropriate authority in the appropriate way.

Teilhard and Pantheism

Pantheism is another objectionable point raised by critics. Pantheism basically means identifying the material universe with God. Often many people mistake pantheism for panentheism, which means that God is in everything, although God transcends everything. Some Teilhard scholars point out that in him sometimes one can see elements of panentheism. Some of the passages from his *Hymn of the Universe,* for instance, are given as illustrative example. But to call Teilhard a pantheist, is very unjust and incorrect. Also it is important to note that Teilhard was not just a writer of pure philosophical or scientific treatises, where often one expects a literal understanding. Teilhard was very much a poet and a mystic, and his writings often were both mystical and poetic, and to read and understand them literally misses the point. Often he uses metaphorical language and he has to be understood as such and his passages need to be interpreted in their appropriate context. In any case, my knowledge of Teilhard, both as an exemplary Jesuit and a serious scholar, convinces me that he can never be considered a pantheist.

Differences of Worldviews and the Problem of Incommensurability

It seems to me that one of the most important points that is often overlooked while understanding, interpreting and critiquing Teilhard is the dynamic worldview he subscribes to. His biographers point out that right from the beginning of his philosophical training as a Jesuit, he was very much dissatisfied with the traditional Aristotelian philosophy, be it in the form of Thomisticor scholastic philosophy, neo-Thomistic philosophy or some other form. The principal reason was that they all assumed a static worldview, wherein the universe was looked upon as a gigantic container with fixed boundaries, fixed laws, fixed principles, immutable species, fixed patterns of behaviour, etc. In such a world change was a sign of weakness, and any being that underwent change was considered inferior. Naturally in such a world the concept of evolution would be highly problematic, even unacceptable. Understandably, in such a worldview contemporary science dominated by ideas of evolution, on-going change and progress could find no welcome home. Teilhard was firmly convinced that our universe was an evolving world, and evolution was a fundamental feature of our universe and all beings in it. His was a dynamic worldview. The difference between the static and dynamic worldviews is not just theoretical and insignificant, rather it is very real and highly significant. This often leads to the situation of incommensurability or communication breakdown, as Thomas Kuhn has argued in his *Structure of Scientific Revolutions*.In any serious discussion involving the traditional system and the Teilhardian system this point has to be taken into account. It may not be giving rise of total communication breakdown, but can lead to much misunderstanding and misinterpretation. It seems to me that the traditional Thomistic system is more than two thousand years old since it has its firm roots in Aristotle, and so deeply entrenched. On the other hand, the dynamic, evolutionary system is comparatively young – in many religious circles it is very much in its infancy. Also much more efforts will have to be made to develop a well-thought out metaphysics and epistemology of the dynamic worldview. When that happens, there is a good chance that much of the misunderstanding or even un-understanding will be cleared up.

Some Positive Aspects of the Teilhardian View

Does Better Justice to Contemporary Scientific Findings

According to many scholars, modern science is the most important achievement of humans, and it has been tremendously successful. We have seen that many of the presuppositions of the Aristotelian system and those based on it like Thomism, Neo-Thomism, etc., have been challenged and shown to be untenable by modern science. The dynamic, evolutionary system, on the other hand, is quite at home with modern science and its new findings. As far as I can see, there is no way that Thomism in any meaningful way can face the challenges of modern science. It can certainly point out the shortcomings of modern science, and thus demand modern science to refrain from making undue claims. Aristotelianism, Thomism, etc., were developed mostly in prescientific days with limited data and knowledge. Some of its intuitions and insights are very valuable, and should be preserved. But there is serious question whether it can be considered a viable philosophy and worldview in the world of modern science. We know that tremendous changes have taken place with regard to human understanding, ideas, behaviour-pattern, value system, criteria, etc., over the last two thousand years. Philosophy, especially those related directly to humans, will have to make appropriate changes if it is to be of relevance to contemporary men and women. There is good reason to believe that the Teilhardian system, or some system along this line of thought, can do better justice to this human situation. No doubt, there are areas of concern in this new system. But, hopefully, they will be responded to as more and more scholars with better skills and data engage in this field.

Also it is important to note that in an evolving system one talks of only better systems and answers, not final or perfect answers. The possibility of perfect answers in the future is not denied, but the emphasis is on better, more productive and fruitful solutions.

Better Agreement with the Original Hebrew Insights

When it comes to the human person and human soul, modern scientific view shows better affinity with the original Hebrew tradition. Some scripture scholars point out that the Hebrew tradition had a unified view, according to which the human was "flesh animated by God's breath (ruah)." It believed that humans enjoyed fellowship with God in life. This implied that even death was not the end of life, since even death couldnot annul the fellowship with God. With regard to life after death the Hebrew tradition talked of "*shades (rephaim)*, which were a sort of pale replica of human as a living creature."[6]This point also endorses a holistic, unified view since at death no separation into parts is implied.[7]

Conclusion

It is ironic that, although we humans have been able to solve rather successfully many problems concerning the material universe around us, the issue of the identity and nature of humans still remains, in many ways, elusive. History tells us that each generation has delved deeply into this mystery to shed valuable light on it. Thanks to these ongoing efforts, we are getting better and better ideas on who humans are and where they are heading to. Aristotelian-Thomistic attempt was part of this search in ancient and medieval times. Neo-Thomism, Transcendental-Thomism, etc., were more recent human attempts along this line. They all have their points and have made their contribution to unravel this complex mystery. Teilhard's attempt is to be seen as a part of this incessant quest of humans. One might say that this type of view is bound to lead humans into relativism. Irresponsible relativism is foolhardy and cannot be approved. On the other hand, recent studies and reflection by many serious scholars reveal that responsible relativism is unavoidable in our constantly evolving and progressing world. It is for each one of us to continue this search and contribute our own little mite towards it.

Endnotes

[1] Scientism believes that today science is in a position to solve all serious problems.

[2] Teilhard de Chardin, *The Future of Man* (London: Collins, St. James' Place, 1964), p. 309.

[3] See Arthur Vermeersch, "Modernism," in *The Catholic Encyclopaedia*, Vol. 10 (New York: Robert Appleton Company, 1913).

[4] I am well aware that, in some ways, religious fundamentalism is on the rise. At the same time, I also see that more than ever men and women of goodwill are expressing their disapproval of such fundamentalistic groups and activities.

[5] See Robert Russell, William Stoeger, SJ, and George Coyne, SJ, eds., *Physics, Philosophy and Theology: A Common Quest for Understanding* (Vatican City State: Vatican Observatory Publications, 1988).

[6] See George Eldon Ladd, "Greek Versus the Hebrew View of Man" in his *The Pattern of New Testament Truth*, p.11.

[7] This point is discussed in detail in this volume by Thomas Karimundackal, SJ. See his "Human Soul – Mortal or Immortal? A Biblical Perspective."

Chapter 2

The Soul
Entangled Wave of Potentiality

Heidi Russell

Abstract

Using theologian Karl Rahner's understanding of the human soul as the capacity for the infinite, the concept of particle wave complementarity in quantum physics gives us an analogy for thinking about the soul. The soul is our wave of potential which is collapsed in our embodiment, the particle equivalent of that complementarity. As quantum physics has further taught us, however, entangled particles do not operate as individuals. They operate as a system. While a particle that is measured has definitive properties, we know that those particles do not have properties apart from the whole. Thus analogically, we can talk of the infinite potential we call soul as being limited by the inherent relationality of our existence. We are not individuals apart from a larger system to which we belong. This paper will explore these aspects of a quantum anthropology of the human soul.

So much rhetoric around each human soul being created individually by God has to do with the concern of making humanity singular among creation. First, if God is part of the ongoing creation, the choices of God creating each soul uniquely and individually, and the soul being an evolving or emergent property of that creation need not be mutually exclusive. God can create in and through evolution and emergence. Second, when we begin to see our embodied souls/ensouled bodies as part of an interconnected system, and perhaps as part of creation's ability to observe and reflect on itself, the perceived threat of a "natural" explanation for the soul lessens. In this model, God creates a universe that becomes conscious, and thus able to respond to God's offer of self-communication, i.e., grace. In such a model, some form of soul as creation's capacity for God is part of the plan for creation as a whole. If creation is for the sake of God's self-communication, then we can think of creation as a whole system that is created for relationship with God. The soul is a function within that system that enables the system in and through human persons to respond to God's self-communication. Are humans the only way the system becomes conscious and capable of response? We do not know, but there could be other ways in the vastness of the cosmos through which the system responds to God that are not yet known or cannot be known by us, but those other potentialities need not threaten our unique, individual relationship with God. Biblical narratives are full of stories of God choosing that which is insignificant and small. We can be chosen by God and still be cosmically insignificant. We are not chosen by God because we are significant; we are significant because we are chosen by God.

Key Words: Karl Rahner, wave-particle complementarity, quantum entanglement, relationality, emergence, self-communication

Introduction

Practically speaking, many Christians think of a soul as some*thing* that is in our body that leaves our body when we die and goes to this *place* called heaven, or for the not so fortunate, hell. In Catholicism, we also have this bus stop place called purgatory people have to wait at to catch the bus to heaven. How long they have to wait depends on how good or bad they have been and how many people they have left on earth praying for them.

Right from the start, we can see that while people carry a disembodied notion of the soul, they nonetheless retain a spatial and temporal concept of the soul along with a spatial and temporal understanding of what happens to us after death. That tendency is not surprising, because our brains really cannot conceive of a reality that does not include space and time. We experience reality in terms of space and time and so when we try to talk about what is "after" death – you see, "after" already implies time, we talk about where we "go" space, who we will "see," etc.

Quantum physics can actually help us start to break down our normal assumptions and presuppositions about what is called the soul. It is also true that we struggle a little bit, or even a lot, to talk about quantum physics as well, to put it into words, because it also defies our experiential concepts of time and space.

I want to start by talking a bit about how I am going to define the soul and how that definition is different from how it might typically be imaged. Then I want to talk about two concepts in physics – particle wave complementarity and entanglement. These two concepts in physics can give us new images for how we understand the soul and what it means to be ensouled bodies or embodied souls. Finally, I want to touch on how we might move away from an either or paradigm of the creation of the soul, that it must be created directly and uniquely by God or evolve from nature.

Nancey Murphy tells a story of how she likes to poll her audience about their beliefs on the soul. She gives them the following four options:

The question is which of the following comes closest to your view of human nature?

a.   Humans are composed of three parts, a body, soul, and spirit. This is called trichotomism.

b.   Humans are composed of two parts. This is called dualism, and there are two versions here, abody and a soul or a body and a mind.

c.   Humans are composed of one "part": a physical body. This can be called either materialism or physicalism.

d.   I don't understand why you're asking.[1]

Murphy sets up a sort of trick question here, where her answer is d and could also be stated as none of the above. She argues for a nonreductive physicalism. My own answer, and I believe hers as well, is actually not listed as an option - humans are composed of one part, a body/soul. She uses the term "spirited bodies."[2] Following biblical scholar James Dunn, Murphy points out: "The biblical authors were not interested in cataloguing the metaphysical parts of a human being—body, soul, spirit, mind. Their interest was in relationships. The words that later Christians have translated with Greek philosophical terms and then understood as referring to parts of the self originally were used to designate aspects of human life. For example, spirit refers not to an immaterial something but to our capacity to be in relationship with God, to be moved by God's Spirit."[3]

The question Murphy asks her audience highlights the same problem physicists have when they ask:Is an electron a particle or a wave? The answer is yes. It would be as if she were asking, is an electron composed of two parts, a particle and a wave, or is it just one part, a particle. She excludes the option of complementarity - the human person as body/spirit. Murphy also raises an important point about terminology – there is no consensus on what any of these terms mean, so we have to define them. I am going to use spirit and soul interchangeably. I agree with Murphy that spirit and mind have a lot of overlap, so that the debate over the relationship between body and spirit is often similar or the same as the debate between body and mind, with the difference that spirit has religious overtones that mind does not have.[4] Daniel Siegel defines the mind as "is an embodied and relational process that regulates the flow of energy and information within the brain and between brains."[5] Spirit could also be seen as both embodied and relational, regulating the flow of energy and information and experience of God/the infinite within the brain, between brains, and in relationship to God. One of the key aspects of Siegel's definition of mind is that it does not exist in isolation, but rather is interrelational.

I would like to suggest that we can think of the person as body/spirit in the way that an electron can be particle/wave.[6] If we ask a body question, we get a body answer, e.g., can we locate personal identity in the brain? If we ask a spirit question, we get a spirit answer, e.g., does my personal identity continue after death?

To flesh out this analogy, we need to go back to the science and explain what exactly we mean by particle/wave complementarity. This concept was demonstrated in the dual slit experiment. If you were to shoot pellets at a barrier with a slit in it, the markings on the wall behind the barrier would show the pellets hitting in a line where the slit was in the barrier. Put two slits in the barrier and you get two lines at the wall. Now, if you send water waves through one slit, the water will likewise hit the wall behind strongest where the slit was, with diminishing intensity on either side. However, if you put two slits in the barrier and send a wave of water at the barrier, the resulting two waves will interfere with each other – doubling in intensity where the peaks or troughs of one wave meet the peaks or troughs of another, cancelling out where the peak of one wave meets the trough of another. The pattern of alternating bands left on the wall is called an interference pattern. In short, when scientists did this experiment with electrons with two slits in the barrier, the electrons left an interference pattern on the wall, even when shot out one at a time. So is the electron a wave? Well, when the scientists set up an instrument to measure which hole the electrons went through when they were shot at the barrier, the pattern that appeared on the wall was one of two bands, same as the pellets. John Gribbin explains:

When we try to look at the spread-out electron wave, it collapses into a definite particle, but when we are not looking it keeps its options open. In terms of Born's probablilies, the electron is being forced by our measurement to choose one course of action out of an array of possibilities. There is a certain probability that it could go through one hole, and an equivalent probability that it may go through the other; probability interference produces the diffraction pattern at our detector. When we detect the electron, though, it can only be in one place, and that changes the probability pattern for its future behavior—for that electron, it is now certain which hole it went through. But unless someone looks, nature herself does not know which hole the electron is going through.[7]

When the scientists asked a wave question, they get a wave answer. When they ask a particle question, they get a particle answer. Another way of saying this point is that we cannot simultaneously measure the location or position and the momentum of a particle. When we are not directly observing the particle, all we get is a wave of probability. The electron could actually be anywhere in the universe, but the most extreme possibilities will cancel each other out, and the most likely possibilities will reinforce one another. So there can be a greater likelihood of the electron being in certain places, but any location is possible. Once we measure the particle, there is no wave of probability. We know exactly where the particle is located. Gribbin concludes, "The idea of wave and particle being complementary facets of the electron's complex personality is called complementarity."[8]

What does all of this have to do with body/spirit? Well, as scientists for a long time considered particles and waves to be two completely separate things, so did many people of faith, at least since Descartes and substance dualism, think of the body and the spirit as two separate things. I would like to suggest that complementarity gives us a great analogy for thinking about body/spirit as two complementary facets of the human person. As I already said, it is important that we define our terms in this conversation. I am going to be using the theologian Karl Rahner's understanding of embodied spirit or spirit in the world. For Rahner, spirit as an aspect of human nature is our capacity for the infinite, and thus our capacity for God.[9] Spirit is our human transcendence, the experience of being unbounded, created for something more. There is a dynamism to the human person so that we transcend or move beyond any finite thing, answer, or goal. We always want more. We want it all. As St. Augustine famously puts it, "You created us for yourself, O Lord, and our heart is restless, until it rests in you."[10] That drive and openness to the more, to the all, to the infinite is what Rahner calls spirit. We are created with this unlimited wave facet because we are created by God and for God, for the infinite mystery of Love that we name God. God is the horizon toward which we move.

However, we are not infinite. We are finite. So we experience ourselves as spirit only in and through the concrete, the embodied. Likewise, we only experience the infinite, which is to say God for Rahner, in and through the concrete, the finite, and the embodied. We enact our potentiality in time and space. Through collapsing this infinite possibility into concrete, finite choices, acts of freedom, we become individuals. As a side note, in an interesting connection to neuroscience, in a recent PBS special on the Brain with David Eagleman, Eagleman explains that the development of our brains is all about rapidly making new connections up until about the age of two when that growth halts. He then states, "The process of becoming someone is about pruning back the possibilities that are already present. You become who you are not because of what grows in your brain, but because of what is removed."[11] So in our spirit function, we actually become individuals by removing possible choices, by pruning back the possibilities of infinite spirit in and through making concrete, embodied choices.

In each moment, that wave of probability is spread out before me, but I cannot live all of my possibilities. I must make choices. In doing so, that wave of possibility collapses to the one thing that I choose. Our embodiment is our particle property. When I actualize a possibility, all other paths I could have taken collapse into the one path I do choose, but in that same moment, another wave of possibility spreads out before me. Analogously Gribbin tells us that when you collapse the wave by detecting the location of an electron: "At that moment, it is 100 percent certain where the electron is. But once you stop looking, the probability starts leaking out from that location. The probability of finding the electron in the same place that you last looked decreases, and the probability of finding it somewhere else increases as the probability wave spreads out through the universe."[12]

Being human is living in that dynamic of the possible and the actual, as we co-create the person we are. Who we are as human beings is a unity that is expressed in a plurality of moments in space and time. We cannot manifest who we are as persons in any one moment in time. Our spirit is expressed in a history and in an embodiment as we live and become who we are. For Rahner, spirit is the unlimiting of matter, and matter is the particularizing of spirit,[13] which is to say the collapsing of our potentiality into actuality. We could also say our body is our location, and our spirit is our momentum. We do not have only a single path open to us in the future, but rather all possible paths are open. From where we are, we cannot say where we will go. Once we are going, we cannot say where we will be or who we will become.

Furthermore, we do not become individuals in isolation. Just as there is no such thing as an isolated, individual particle apart from the system to which it belongs, there is no such thing as an isolated, individual human person. We are also part of a whole, part of a system. Within this system, our embodiment is the way that we are able to express who we are to others and interact with others. So in the same way a particle with definite properties that finds its properties impacted by being entangled with another particle, so too do we find our wave of potential impacted by the fact that our embodiment is contextualized and interrelational.

In our analogy, spirit as our capacity for the infinite, is our wave of infinite potential. We are open to absolutely everything. Anything is possible. However, not all possibilities are equal. We are embodied in history, in social-political contexts, in families, and in relationships, just to name a few aspects of our context. My freedom is not unlimited. My freedom is limited by your freedom and how you exercise your freedom, and vice versa.[14] We are interrelated. To return to Nancey Murphy, she uses the concept of context sensitive restraint to talk about downward causation as whole part constraint, where the history and context of the whole impacts the part.[15] The example she uses from the work of Alicia Juarrero is rolling dice, which is context free, that is to say any given roll of the dice is not impacted by any of the rolls that went before, to playing cards, which is context sensitive.[16] The probability of the cards you will be dealt changes depending on the history of the cards that have been previously played. The inifinite capacity Rahner calls spirit, because it is embodied, is constrained. That capacity is context sensitive, and so the whole system impacts our individual possibilities.

So as embodied spirits we have a wave of potentiality that manifests itself as probability. Like the particle that could be located anywhere in the universe, but has higher probabilities of being in certain locations, not all of our possibilities are equal. It is possible for me to be the next President of the United States, but not very probable. It is even less probable for me to become the next Prime Minister of India, since I am not a citizen of India. On a more personal level, my possibilities can be limited by my race, my religion, my socio-economic status, my genetics, my family of origin issues, etc.

We are interrelated. We are contextual. We are part of a system, a whole, that is bigger than simply the adding up of the parts. We are entangled.

In quantum physics, when two electrons are entangled, they operate as one system.[17] Thus you can send the particles to laboratories many miles away, hypothetically even on opposite sides of the universe, and when the spin of the electron, an aspect of the electron that is completely random and we have no way of predicting before measuring, when that spin is measured on one entangled electron, we know that the spin of the other electron will be anti-correlated. In other words, if we measure the spin of one and find it to be up, when we measure the spin of the other electron, it will be down. Thus while particles seem to be individuals possessing certain properties, in fact we know that these particles do not have properties apart from the whole.[18] Likewise, who we become as individuals actualizing our spirit potential does not exist apart from the larger system to which we belong. Who we are comes from that system, and in turn, shapes that system.

In an article in Quanta Magazine online, Frank Wilczek does a fantastic job of explaining the relationship between entanglement and complementarity using the images of square or round, red or blue cakes.[19] Starting with shape, if we have two cakes, there are four possible joint positions – two round, two square, #1 round and #2 square, #1 square and #2 round. Each possibility would have a 25% chance of occurring. Knowing the shape of one, for example, round, does not tell us anything about the shape of the other, but it does tell us something about the possible combinations. We could have two round cakes or #1 round cake and #2 square cake. We would know that we cannot have 2 square cakes nor #1 square and #2 round. Now the 2 possible combinations would each have a 50% chance of occurring. Entanglement, Wilczek goes on to explain is when knowledge about one increases our knowledge about the other, so for example, if we knew that when the #1 is round, #2 will also be round, but when #1 is square, #2 will also be square. There is now a 50/50 chance that both cakes are round or both are square, but there is a 0% chance we will have a round/square combination. Furthermore, there would be a 50/50 chance that cake #1 is square or round, but once we "measure" or "observe" it, we now know with 100% certainty the shape of cake #2, even before we "measure" or "observe" it.

Now Einstein actually believed this system was still deterministic, as if, to use Brian Green's example, I had a pair of gloves,[20] and I dropped one at my house when leaving for work. When I get to work and pull out my left glove, I know that the glove at home will be my right glove. However, quantum entanglement is trickier than that example. It is non-deterministic.

To introduce the addition of quantum complementarity to this example, Wilczek adds colors, red and blue. In a quantum world, Wilczek explains, you cannot measure shape and color at the same time. Wilczek states:

> If we measure the shape of one member of an EPR pair, we find it is equally likely to be square or circular. If we measure the color, we find it is equally likely to be red or blue. [50/50 random chance for either] The interesting effects, which EPR considered paradoxical, arise when we make measurements of both members of the pair. When we measure both members for color, or both members for shape, we find that the results always agree. Thus if we find that one is red, and later measure the color of the other, we will discover that it too is red, and so forth. On the other hand, if we measure the shape of one, and then the color of the other, there is no correlation. Thus if the first is square, the second is equally likely to be red or to be blue.[21]

A couple of things to understand about entanglement is that the results are truly random. Anthony Zeilinger uses the example of dice.[22] He suggests imagining a pair of quantum dice, where you have one and I have one, and when we roll the dice, what number appears is random, but we know that the same number will always appear on both dice. Two electrons that are entangled are part of the same system. They are interconnected. What happens to one, happens to the other. In the Christian tradition, we have an analogous idea in the Body of Christ. What happens to one, happens to the other. Your joy is my joy. Your sadness is my sadness, Paul tells us. Putting this idea together with our idea of the soul as infinite possibility, but finite probability, we see that our probabilities are shaped by the fact that we are all part of one system.

So much rhetoric around each human soul being created individually by God has to do with the concern of making humanity singular among creation. Entanglement teaches us that at the fundamental level of reality, creation is interrelated, it is one whole or one system. Thus I do not think it is helpful to talk about the human soul apart from that system. In our observable universe, we all come from the Big Bang. We are made of stardust. On this speck of dirt we call earth in the boondocks of the Milky Way, life as we know it came to be and became conscious. Scientists are still studying and divided on the question of the role or significance of human consciousness in the evolution of the cosmos. Some would suggest that the ability of the universe to become conscious, to observe itself, in and through the human being is an important part of the evolution of the cosmos. Others would see it as a statistical quirk. From a Christian standpoint, if God is part of the ongoing creation, not simply that which put everything in motion, the choices of God creating each soul uniquely and individually, and the soul being an evolving or emergent property of that creation need not be mutually exclusive. God can create in and through evolution and emergence.

This paradigm shift moves us away from separating the material world from the spiritual world. If God is the whole, there is nothing apart from God. So all of the material world is held in God and God moves and creates in the whole material world. Possibility and thus the soul emerges in this act of creation, but it is one continuous act, not separate individual acts. All of our possibilities are held in God, even our possibility of not-God, of disbelief, even our blindness to the whole of which we are a part.

Perhaps God does not have to intervene because God is not distant. Perhaps each soul is created individually by God as emergent property – soul as capacity for God. Does the soul evolve? Does God bring this relationship, which is always already present from the moment of creation to fruition in human consciousness? This view of the soul as creation's ability to respond to God is admittedly a very anthropocentric view. One might ask, is God present, self-communicating to the rest of creation? If creation and self-communication are not understood as separate, but are rather distinct gifts, then that offer of God's self-gift must be part of all that exists, not just humans.

Likewise, if the spirit is not separate from the material world, so is the material world not separate from the spiritual, and thus we can think of the resurrection of the body differently. In the old paradigm we struggle with what to do with the body after death. There is some spatial-temporal image of the body waiting around for the final resurrection when it is finally reunited with the soul that had been removed from it. First we have to recognize that what we think of as solid matter, even in this life is mostly space and energy, so some form of transformation beyond time and space is not such a hard stretch. Science itself is full of the unseen from dark matter and dark energy to string theory with its multiple extra dimensions. So we have to move away from the idea that the body is a solid object identified by how much space it takes up in our three dimensional perception. Second, the body is nothing more or less that the definitive culmination of who I became over the course of my lifetime. In death my body/spirit is my definitively actualized potential. Spirit as my capacity or potential for God is now actualized in my union with God. My body is my embeddedness in history and relationship, and thus I do not leave that behind in the resurrection, but rather that co-created person I have become is precisely that which is in union with God. Because we are always interconnected and part of a whole, my personal resurrection is bound up with the final resurrection, when God will be all in all. The person I definitively became in my death continues to impact the world and those with whom I was entangled. Their becoming is part of my own. And so the final resurrection of the dead is about the Body of Christ, the whole in its union with God.

We can talk scientifically about human consciousness and self-identity emerging from evolution, while also talking theologically about God creating each individual part of the whole uniquely. Thus our coming to be as capacity for the infinite, capacity for God was always part of the plan of creation, as was the fulfillment of that capacity in the person of Christ. Christ is the union of God and creation, creation's potential perfectly filled by God. God and nature do not compete. They are not competing causes, but rather complementary causes of the human soul.

When we begin to see our embodied souls/ensouled bodies as part of an interconnected system, and perhaps as part of creation's ability to observe and reflect on itself, the perceived threat of a "natural" explanation for the soul lessens. In this model, God creates a universe that becomes conscious, and thus able to respond to God's offer of self-communication, i.e., grace. In such a model, some form of soul as creation's capacity for God is part of the plan for creation as a whole. If creation is for the sake of God's self-communication, then we can think of creation as a whole system that is created for relationship with God. The soul is a function within that system that enables the system in and through human persons to respond to God's self-communication.

Some physicists, such as John Wheeler and Andrei Linde, would suggest that human observation is in fact necessary for the cosmos to exist at all.[23] A profile of Wheeler in Scientific American states: "Wheeler was one of the first prominent physicists seriously to propose that reality might not be a wholly physical phenomenon. In some sense, Wheeler suggested, reality grows out of the act of observation, and thus consciousness itself; it is 'participatory.'"[24] Similarly, physicist Andrei Linde argues:

> The universe and the observer exist as a pair," Linde says. "You can say that the universe is there only when there is an observer who can say, Yes, I see the universe there. These small words — it looks like it was here— for practical purposes it may not matter much, but for me as a human being, I do not know any sense in which I could claim that the universe is here in the absence of observers. We are together, the universe and us. The moment you say that the universe exists without any observers, I cannot make any sense out of that. I cannot imagine a

consistent theory of everything that ignores consciousness. A recording device cannot play the role of an observer, because who will read what is written on this recording device? In order for us to see that something happens, and say to one another that something happens, you need to have a universe, you need to have a recording device, and you need to have us. It's not enough for the information to be stored somewhere, completely inaccessible to anybody. It's necessary for somebody to look at it. You need an observer who looks at the universe. In the absence of observers, our universe is dead.[25]

So Wheeler and Linde, even if in a minority of physicists, suggest that there might be some way in which the consciousness of humanity is necessary for the existence of the universe. If we are defining the spirit function of humanity as our capacity for God, our movement toward God, and our ability to respond to God, then we may be able to say both that there is something unique about the human as embodied spirit *and* that spirit function is a function not just of the human, but of the system of creation itself, coming from creation as a whole and effecting creation as a whole. Our spirit function might evolve from creation, but because the plan of creation from the beginning was for God to create that which can be in relationship with God. Thus our spirit function and humanity itself can be thought of as being created directly by God in and through the whole act of creation and evolution.

Are humans the only way the cosmic system becomes conscious and capable of response? We do not know. There could be other ways in the vastness of the cosmos through which the system is conscious, and thus responds or is capable of responding to God, that are not yet known or cannot be known by us. An infinite universe or a multiverse or the death and birth cycle of universes need not jeopardize our understanding of humanity as created for relationship with God. If any of those other possibilities turn out to be the case, God's relationship to creation and thus humanity is not jeopardized, because God is not one cause among others. God is primary cause underlying all that exists, so God's creation can be the multiverse.

Furthermore, other potential life in our universe or in other universes of a multiverse need not threaten our unique, individual relationship with God. Biblical narratives are full of stories of God choosing that which is insignificant and small. The God of the Hebrew and Christian Scriptures tell us stories of God choosing those who protest that they are too young, too insignificant, too ill-spoken to be chosen. God works through Mary, a young, unmarried peasant girl. God is made present through Jesus, born of the smallest tribe and raised in Nazareth, a town ridiculed as insignificant. God chooses Israel, imaged as an orphan found wandering in a wasteland of howling desert– the most fragile and vulnerable person in society. What is humanity cosmically if not a people wandering in a cosmic wasteland? And yet, God chooses to be in relationship with us, to love us. We can be chosen by God and still be cosmically insignificant. We are not chosen by God because we are significant; we are significant because we are chosen by God.

Even more importantly, to be chosen by God does not mean being loved more or being more significant than others who exist. Rather to be chosen by God means that one is bound to the mission of God, to be God's presence of love and mercy in the world. Our cosmic insignificance is a good check on our human anthropocentric tendencies so often undergirded by the notion that humans are created in a way that is special or unique amongst creation.

Bibliography

"Nature's God: Nancey Murphy on Religion and Science." *The Christian Century* 122, no. 26 (2005): 20-26.

Folger, Tim. "Does the Universe Exist if We're Not Looking." *Discover* 23, no. 6 (2002): 44-48.

Greene, Brian. *The Fabric of the Cosmos: Space, Time, and the Texture of Reality.* New York: A.A. Knopf, 2004.

Gribbin, John. *In Search of Schrödinger's Cat: Quantum Physics and Reality.* New York: Bantam Books, 1984.

______. *Schrödinger's Kittens and the Search for Reality: Solving the Quantum Mysteries*. Boston: Little, Brown & Co., 1995.

Horgan, John. "Profile: Physicist John A. Wheeler, Questioning the "It from Bit"." *Scientific American* (1991): 36-37.

Kuhlmann, Meinard. "What is Real?" *Scientific American* 309, no. 2 (2013): 40.

Murphy, Nancey. "Do Humans have Souls? Perspectives from Philosophy, Science, and Religion." *Interpretation: A Journal of Bible and Theology* 67, no. 1 (2013): 30-41.

Murphy, Nancey C. *Bodies and Souls, Or Spirited Bodies?*. Cambridge, UK: Cambridge University Press, 2006.

______. "How to Keep the 'Non' in Nonreductive Physicalism." *Journal of European Baptist Studies* 9, no. 2 (2009): 5-16.

Rahner, Karl. *Foundations of Christian Faith: An Introduction to the Idea of Christianity* . Translated by William Dych. New York: Crossroad, 1978.

______. *Grace in Freedom* [Gnade als Freiheit.] . Translated by Hilda C. Graef. New York, NY: Herder and Herder, 1969a.

______. "The Unity of Spirit and Matter in the Christian Understanding of Faith." In *Theological Investigations: Concerning Vatican Council II*. Translated by Boniface Kruger and Karl-H Kruger. Vol. 6, 153-177. Baltimore: Helicon Press, 1969b.

Russell, Heidi. *Quantum Shift: Theological and Pastoral Implications of Contemporary Developments in Science*. Collegeville, Minnesota: Liturgical Press, 2015.

Saint Augustine. *Confessions* . Translated by Henry Chadwick Oxford: Oxford University Press, 1991.

Siegel, Daniel J. *The Developing Mind: How Relationships and the Brain Interact to Shape Who we Are*. 2nd ed. New York: Guilford Publications, 2012.

Wilczek, Frank. "Entanglement made Simple." https://www.quantamagazine.org/entanglement-made-simple-20160428/ (accessed January 25, 2018).

Zeilinger, Anton. "Quantum Physics: Ontology Or Epistomology?" In *The Trinity and an Entangled World: Relationality in Physical Science and Theology*, edited by John C. Polkinghorne, 32-40. Grand Rapids, MI: William B. Eerdmans, 2010.

Endnotes

[1] Nancey Murphy, "Do Humans have Souls? Perspectives from Philosophy, Science, and Religion," *Interpretation: A Journal of Bible and Theology* 67, no. 1 (2013): 30-31.

[2] Nancey C. Murphy, *Bodies and Souls, Or Spirited Bodies?* (Cambridge, UK: Cambridge University Press, 2006). From a review of her work, "Murphy holds the view that humans are composed of a "spirited body." By this she means that we are not just body, but that the spiritual quality which we possess is not a separate entity. As such she would be a physicalist, but is clear that she does not reduce the nature of the human being to "just a body"—a reductionist point of view." Miller, Wendy J. "Nancey Murphy's Bodies and souls, or spirited bodies?: a review essay." Direction 37, no. 2 (September 2008): 215-222. ATLA Religion Database with ATLASerials, EBSCOhost (accessed January 23, 2018).

[3] "Nature's God: Nancey Murphy on Religion and Science." *The Christian Century* 122, no. 26 (2005), 21.

[4] Murphy, *Bodies and Souls, Or Spirited Bodies?* 2.

[5] Daniel J. Siegel, *The Developing Mind: How Relationships and the Brain Interact to Shape Who we Are*, 2nd ed. (New York: Guilford Publications, 2012)., 24.

[6] For an expanded form of this theory, see Ch. Two, Particle Wave Complementarity in Heidi Russell, *Quantum Shift: Theological and Pastoral Implications of Contemporary Developments in Science* (Collegeville, Minnesota: Liturgical Press, 2015).

[7] John Gribbin, *In Search of Schrödinger's Cat: Quantum Physics and Reality* (New York: Bantam Books, 1984), 171.

[8] Ibid., 118.

[9] See Karl Rahner, *Foundations of Christian Faith: An Introduction to the Idea of Christianity*, trans. William Dych (New York: Crossroad, 1978).

[10] Saint Augustine, *Confessions*, trans. Henry ChadwickOxford: Oxford University Press, 1991).

[11] Eagleman, David, "What Makes Me Me?" Episode 2 *The Brain with David Eagleman* (Films Media Group, Public Broadcasting Corporation, 2016).

[12] John Gribbin, *Schrödinger's Kittens and the Search for Reality: Solving the Quantum Mysteries* (Boston: Little, Brown & Co., 1995), 12.

[13] Karl Rahner, "The Unity of Spirit and Matter in the Christian Understanding of Faith," in *Theological Investigations: Concerning Vatican Council II*, trans. Boniface Kruger and Karl-H Kruger, Vol. 6 (Baltimore: Helicon Press, 1969b), 170.

[14] See Karl Rahner, *Grace in Freedom* [Gnade als Freiheit.], trans. Hilda C. Graef (New York, NY: Herder and Herder, 1969a).

[15] Nancey C. Murphy, "How to Keep the 'Non' in Nonreductive Physicalism," *Journal of European Baptist Studies* 9, no. 2 (2009), 10-11.

[16] Ibid. Cites Alicia Juarrero, Dynamics in Action· Intentional Behavior as a Complex System (Cambridge, MA: MIT Press, 1999).

[17] See Ch. 3, Entanglement in Russell, *Quantum Shift*.

[18] Meinard Kuhlmann, "What is Real?" *Scientific American* 309, no. 2 (2013), 43.

[19] Frank Wilczek, "Entanglement made Simple," https://www.quantamagazine. org/entanglement-made-simple-20160428/ (accessed January 25, 2018).

[20] Brian Greene, *The Fabric of the Cosmos: Space, Time, and the Texture of Reality* (New York: A.A. Knopf, 2004), 502, n14.

[21] Wilczek, "Entanglement made Simple,"

[22] Anton Zeilinger, "Quantum Physics: Ontology Or Epistomology?" in *The Trinity and an Entangled World: Relationality in Physical Science and Theology*, ed. John C. Polkinghorne (Grand Rapids, MI: William B. Eerdmans, 2010), 35-6.

[23] Tim Folger, "Does the Universe Exist if We're Not Looking," *Discover* 23, no. 6 (2002): 44-48.

[24] John Horgan, "Profile: Physicist John A. Wheeler, Questioning the "It from Bit","" *Scientific American* (1991): 36-37.

[25] Folger, "Does the Universe Exist if We're Not Looking," : 44-48.

Chapter 3

The Soul of the Matter
and the Matter of the Soul:

A Scientific Perspective

Vincent Braganza

Abstract

The origins of the universe and of the soul are associated. The notion of the soul is contained in the 'Big Bang' or any other theory that claims to explain how our universe came into being, and how human beings graduated (were calibrated?) into existence. Time and eternity thus become essential elements in any elaboration that tries to grasp the nature of the soul. Furthermore, soul becomes intrinsically bound-up with matter (Doesn't the creation narrative in the Bible suggest this?). Almost every religious school of thought admits, however, that this intrinsic aspect is not inevitable for the ongoing subsistence and prevalence of either (A corpse is lifeless matter from which a living soul has departed is how we express it most often). In the light of contemporary scientific evidence such views need to be nuanced. The insights gained thus can enrich our existence!Modern science however looks at reality as dual, without duality. The valuable currency which we call life has two faces – matter and energy, in it is body-soul combine. The dissection of this reality into two distinct parts(duality) is destructive of life and does violence to it. As materiality graduates to dynamic vitality, substances display characteristics that exude the soul of the matter, features that are not superimposed, but that are immanent and so emerge essentially from the nature of the material. Hence, a question that one may seek to answer satisfactorily is "How far into the evolutionary ladder of life does the soul extend?" Is the answer perhaps self-evident in the current context of our scientific thought? May be!

In our own labs at the Xavier Research Foundation, we have been looking at ageing, intelligence and memory in the worm *C. elegans*. This organism demonstrates soul traits like memory and the ability to learn, which translates into intelligence. In fact our choice of this worm as an experimental model is based on the fact that it has the corresponding genetic variants (orthologs) of a wide set of human genes. Do these aspects of the soul also appear in the bacteria that these *C. elegans* feed on, and are they extended all the way to viruses – the boundary limit entity between life and lifelessness? And, what of stones, and all the myriads of inanimate 'subjects' of nature? Is there relevance to such a question in the light of the observations made in this study? A reading of Teilhard de Chardin corroborates the observations made above.A core dimension of a human being, associated with the soul, is happiness. Links established by neurobiology today offer us an understanding of the connectedness of brain parts and stimulatory neurotransmitters and peptides. It has established a foundational link between these body parts and the states of peace, joy and bliss that the soul component of a being enables the human to experience as happiness. Wouldn't it be right then to assume that the soul subsists in the synergy of the system, investing body-matter with the dual states (wave-energy and particle-matter) expressed in the Heisenberg Principle and the de Broglie Hypothesis? Here, however it is perhaps law, not hypothesis?

Keywords: Duality, dynamic vitality, *c. elegans*, Teilhard, synergy

Introduction

This paper on "The Soul of the Matter and Matter of the Soul" has several parts: It first connects the origins of life to the origins of the soul and to the Bible. It then looks at memory as a key aspect that reflects the presence of a soul in living beings, and proceeds to look at the boundary between life and non-life in viruses and explores the presence of the soul in them. It does this by looking for memory in viruses. It then progresses to provide laboratory evidence of memory reflected in *C. elegans,* an actual experimental system that we are working with, and claims soul for living creatures. It also looks at the specific case of ageing and Alzheimer's disease and the implications for memory and the soul. It then considers memory after death as an energy that returns to the universe and attempts to preserve its immortal character in a consistent way. With Teilhard de Chardin it proffers an idea of the soul as a dynamic entity that is constantly expressed in different ways just as biological life takes form in different species. Soul thus reaches a culmination in human beings. Developments in the neurosciences today further contribute to the connection between soul and matter in human beings and usher in an era that strengthens and corroborates our views above.

The Origin of the Soul

A TV serial that started a few years ago caught my attention because of its title: "The Big Bang Theory." The episodes are hilarious; the brand of humour remarkable. The focus is on characters who are mostly science and tech people and the thread of their relationships. The only and distinct reference to the Big Bang Theory is in the theme song of the series as it explodes repeatedly at each new episode and at every break:

Our whole universe was in a hot, dense state,

Then nearly fourteen billion years ago expansion started, wait.

The earth began to cool, the autotrophs began to drool Neanderthals developed tools.We built a wall (we built the pyramids)

Math, science, history, unraveling the mysteries. That all started with the big bang! Hey!"[1]

The Big Bang Theory is catching the attention of the common people, has it however impacted their religious dimension? It must, and where the soul is concerned its connection with the Big Bang needs to be understood so that we may comprehend its significance.

We are today in a privileged position to claim insights into the origin of the Universe. In his classic work, *The Theory of Everything: The Origin and Fate of The Universe*, Stephen W Hawking, traverses the classical physics of Newton, maps across the theory of gravity of Einstein that demonstrated that "the universe could not be static; it had to be expanding or contracting. This, in turn, implied that there must have been a time between ten and twenty billion years ago when the density of the universe was infinite. This is called the big bang. It would have been the beginning of the universe."[2] The history of the universe that is accepted today in scientific circles, is summarized in the table below.[3,4]

History of the Universe	
Time (in years)	**Associated Phenomenon**
13.5 billion	Matter and energy appear. Beginning of Physics. Atoms and molecules appear. Beginning of Chemistry.
4.5 billion	Formation of Planet Earth.
2.5 million	Evolution of the genus Homo in Africa. First stone tools.
200,000	Homo Sapiens evolve in East Africa. Cognitive Revolution.
12,000	The Agricultural Revolution. Domestication of plants and animals. Permanent settlements.

500	The Scientific Revolution. Humankind admits its ignorance and begins to acquire unprecedented power. Europeans begin to conquer America and the oceans. The entire planet becomes a single historical arena. The rise of Capitalism.
200	The Industrial Revolution. Family and community are replaced by state and market. Massive extinction of plants and animals.

It seems it all began about 14 billion years ago. With a view to giving us a working handle on the time scales involved, it may help to use the analogy employed by an eminent luminary in the field, "Carl Sagan has compressed the 15 billion years into one calendar year. If the Big Bang or birth of the universe happened on January 1st, the Milky Way was born on May 1st, the Earth formed on September 14th, and September 25th is when life originated on earth. The first human was produced at 10.30 pm on December 31st, and the whole of recorded human history occupies the last 10 seconds of the year." It seems apparent to me that we can simplify our discussion, if we identify in this analogy of the calendar year, three concentric 'cyclic unfoldings' (cu) of time that are overlapped. Separating the three will enable us to grasp "the soul of the matter and the matter of the soul," in a more organized fashion. I do not intend to enter here into any debate about 'time' and the Big Bang; my practical concern is to demonstrate through these three 'time layers' (tl) (another possible term/label for them in place of cu), that there is an ontological connection between matter and soul.

The three cus or tls of time are a) cosmological time, b) biological time, and c) homo sapiens time. Cosmological time (corresponding to the entire calendar year in the analogy of Carl Sagan) surges forward into biological time (corresponding to last 99 days of the calendar year – 25th September to 31st December) and onto homo sapiens time (corresponding to the final ten seconds of the calendar year). Biological time thus emerges from cosmological time where it moors its beginnings, as does homo sapiens time; the latter veers its way through biological time.

One could illustrate them with concentric circles of decreasing diameters as shown in the figure below. In terms of the calendar year analogy above, the circle of cosmological time would involve an area of 365 days, while the biological time circle within would entail an area of 99 days and Homo Sapiens time would be barely a dot in the center with an area of 10 seconds.

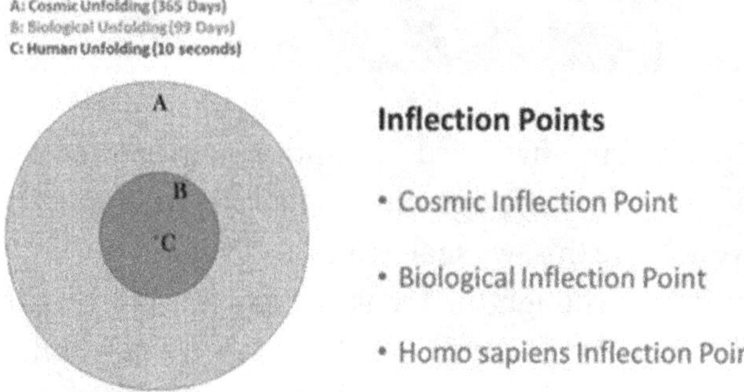

In order to prevent any distortions in our understanding, it makes sense to steer away from this static picture to a more dynamic image of a typhoon or active vortex where the mouth of the vortex has a 365 days, calendar year area. The vortex spirals, narrowing down through the 99 days area circle of biological time and is concentrated at its bottom at the homo sapiens time to an area of 10secs which covers the existence of human beings, our existence on earth. This is meant to be a dynamic image not a static one, and implies movement and energy spinning to the bottom and surging to the top continuously in equilibrium. Such an image could reflect the cosmic eternal soul.

Interestingly, Hawking has tried "to find a unified theory that will include quantum mechanics, gravity, and all the other interactions of physics. If we achieve this, we shall really understand the universe and our position in it."[5] Though the focus of his work was on the physics and cosmology of the universe, he did discuss the implications of his theories for our understanding of a personal creator and in this sense does affirm what Christian de Duve says "Life is an obligatory manifestation of matter, bound to arise whenever conditions are appropriate"[6]

An important point that I would like to highlight from this discussion so far is that our origins go back to energy. The significant inflection points are: a) the conversion of energy to matter, b) the conversion of non-living matter to living entities,and c) living entities culminating in humans. These inflection points correspond to the three time layers that I have alluded to above. This may be the appropriate moment to pose the question: when does the soul make its appearance, at what inflection point? Before we get down to answering the questions or in the process of doing so, let us see what the scriptures say.

The Bible says: If one goes to the story of creation, one can find there a reflection of the three cyclic times, and the three inflection points I have pointed out above. The relevant passages are in the Book of Genesis. The Cosmic Unfolding is reflected in the following lines at the very beginning of the book which is placed at the very beginning of the Bible."1 In the beginning God created the heavens and the earth. 2 Now the earth was formless and empty, darkness covered the surface of the watery depths, and *the Spirit of God was hovering*over the surface of the waters. 3 Then God said, "Let there be light," and there was light. 4 God saw that the light was good, and God separated the light from the darkness. 5 God called the light "day," and He called the darkness "night." Evening came, and then morning: the first day."

Biological Unfolding can be traced in a number of verses, from which we give just a couple below as a sample:"11 Then God said, "Let the earth produce vegetation: seed-bearing plants, and fruit trees on the earth bearing fruit with seed in it, according to their kinds." And it was so." 12 The earth brought forth vegetation: seed-bearing plants according to their kinds and trees bearing fruit with seed in it, according to their kinds. And God saw that it was good"

Human Unfolding: 26 Then God said, "Let Us make man in Our image, according to Our likeness. They will rule the fish of the sea, the birds of the sky, the animals, all the earth,' and the creatures that crawls on the earth." 27 So God created man in His own image; He created him in the image of God; He created them male and female.

The spirit (the soul) inheres through cosmology, biology and andrology.

Scripture scholars also point out that there are two creation stories in Genesis written in two different traditions. I will not go into the nitty-gritty of the second story. It is contained in the second chapter of the Book of Genesis verses 4 to 24. One can do a similar exercise successfully and identify the three unfolding or layers of time in this second creation story too.

One could explore the Koran and since its traditions go back to the Bible, we may logically surmise that the observations made above apply to the creation stories in the Koran as well. Explorations to find similar unfolding of time in Indian scriptures relating to Buddhism, Jainism, Hinduism and Sikhism, will bear, I believe, similar fruit. Be that as it may, all scriptures in their own unique way insinuate a boundary between the material world and the biological world and between the biological world and the world of human beings.

The point being put forward here is that the integral unity between materiality and *'spirit-ality/soul-ality* alluded to by scientists like Hawking, is reflected in the scriptures, though the scriptures and religions may not have this as the only exclusive view.

One must proceed at this point to ask where does the idea of the soul come in, in this scheme of things? If one looks for the understanding of the soul from the common person's perspective, one may say that the incorporeal essence of a living being is called the soul or psyche (Greek: "psyühē", of "psychein", "to breathe"), and may be mortal or immortal (only human beings in Judeo-Christianity). Greek philosophers, such as Socrates, Plato, and Aristotle, understood that the soul (psūchê) must have a logical faculty, the exercise of which was the most divine of human actions; the mental abilities of a living being: *reason, character,feeling, happiness, consciousness,memory, perception, thinking, etc.,* are all associated with the soul. We know too that the Catholic theologian Thomas Aquinas attributed "soul" (anima) to all organisms but argued that only human souls are immortal. Other religions (most notably Hinduism and Jainism) hold that all biological organisms have souls (atman, jiva) and a 'vital principle' (prana). *Anima mundi* is the concept of a "world soul" connecting all living organisms on planet Earth.

In this article I will focus on one of the features of the soul that is essential to its existence, namely, memory. Therefore in what follows below the relationship between memory and the existence of the soul will be pursued. Hence the working idea with which we will move forward to look at the existence of the soul will be memory. As a scientist, I consider memory a quantifiable quality of the soul, one that can be measured through experiments and experimental data.

Br. Gurruchaga and Alzheimers

In this context let me allude to a real life experience going back to my school days. In 1963 a Jesuit Brother from Spain, Br. Gurruchaga, was assigned to our hostel at St Xavier's School, Ahmedabad. He was a healthy, energetic young man who went on to work in the Gujarat missions for more than thirty years, productively. As situations changed across the globe, he opted to go back to Spain. About fifteen years ago I had the opportunity to visit Spain, and thought of him and expressed my wish to meet him. I was informed that he was in the infirmary, and had been diagnosed with Alzheimer's. I visited the infirmary and as I was entering, I saw, to my great joy, Br. coming towards me. Moved by the memories of the times we had with him during my school days, I called out his name and rushed towards him with all the enthusiasm in the world. There was a smile on his face but I could see already that it was just a physical smile, which had no connection to me. Even as I moved forward he just passed me by! He had no memory of me, in fact Alzheimer's had robbed him of all his memories and for all practical purposes he was just vegetating. Without memory I asked myself what person was present in the body that had just passed me. Certainly no Br. Guruchagga personality existed! Had his soul which is intertwined with memory left him as Alzheimer's took over? What does this tell us about the nexus between the human body and the human soul?

Our Experiments with *Caenorhabditis elegans* (*C. elegans*)

In our own labs, we are looking at ageing and Alzheimer's disease, since both are related to memory loss. Our goal is to find plant extracts that can prevent memory loss/restore memory capacity. We need a fast through-put model for this: In our studies we take herbal plant extracts with claims in this area and validate them and also study the mechanism and molecular basis of ageing and memory. Non-vertebrate models because of a number of advantages (beyond the scope of this paper) are widely used.

The particular organism chosen for this project is *C. elegans*. It is a nematode with a *simple neural system* compared to higher organisms. Nonetheless, it has been a model system to study neuronal development and neuron mediated behaviours.[7]*C. elegans* is an ideal model to study ageing. Moreover it is chosen as a whole organism model, and hence can also provide links for the mechanism of action for plant-based medicines to promote healthy ageing and as a prophylaxis to prevent neurodegenerative diseases like Alzheimer's[8]. *C. elegans* is a soil-dwelling nematode 1mm as seen in the figure below.

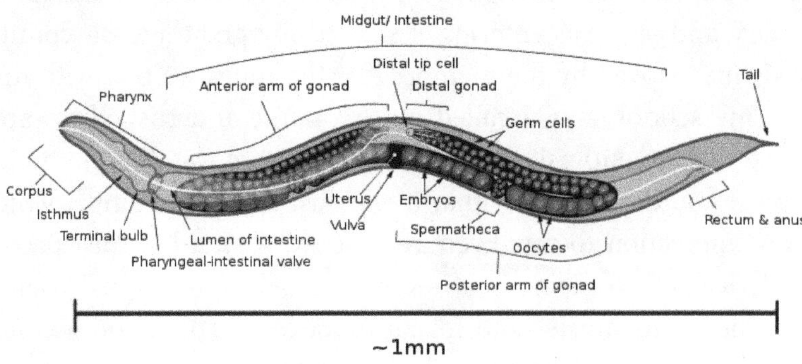

Though it is a complex multicellular organism with a reproductive system and a nervous system, it is easy to raise in petri plates like a microorganism. *C. elegans* as a model of ageing has advantages as it has a very small life cycle of 2-3 weeks and does not have inbreeding effects on lifespan. For ageing research *C. elegans* is a preferred organism as lifespan in *C. elegans* is straightforward, it does not have any effect on parental lifespan.

Memory can be classified as implicit memory, which includes the formation of skills, habits, and explicit memory is the one which allows one to recall an event or episode or facts. Associative memory is an implicit memory which associates multiple types of information and results in the formation of habit or behaviour pattern. Organisms use this form of memory to build an association between food and odour, environmental threat and temperature, availability of food and salt concentration and so on. The decline in associative memory with ageing was observed in a wide variety of organisms including *C. elegans*, Aplysia, Drosophilci melcinogaster, Honeybee, snails, rodents and humans.[9]

In our labs we have done experiments using *C. elegans*, demonstrating the three types of associative memory. One of these, called Chemotaxis, is studied via building the association of food with odour and tracking movement of the organism towards odour-producing agents like butanone or benzaldehyde as shown in the figure below.

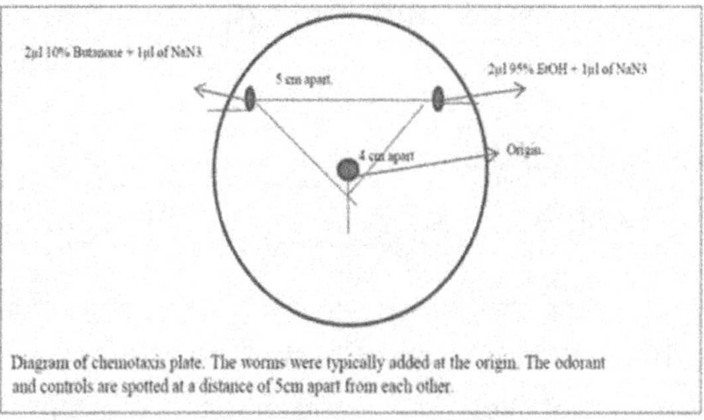

Diagram of chemotaxis plate. The worms were typically added at the origin. The odorant and controls are spotted at a distance of 5cm apart from each other.

A sample set of results shown below in the histogram and the table, shows that *C. elegans*, possesses associative memory which is susceptible to positive outcomes when treated with extracts of the plant *B. Monnieri*.

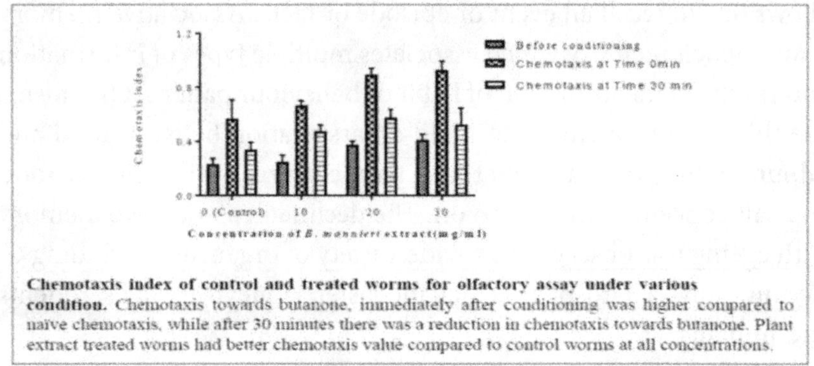

Chemotaxis index of control and treated worms for olfactory assay under various condition. Chemotaxis towards butanone, immediately after conditioning was higher compared to naïve chemotaxis, while after 30 minutes there was a reduction in chemotaxis towards butanone. Plant extract treated worms had better chemotaxis value compared to control worms at all concentrations.

Chemotaxis index of control and treated worms at various time points.			
	Before Conditioning	**At time t=0 minute**	**At time t=30 minute**
Control	0.23	0.57	0.34
B. *monnieri* 10mg/ml	0.25	0.66	0.48
B. *monnieri* 20mg/ml	0.37	0.89	0.57
B. *monnieri* 30mg/ml	0.41	0.93	0.53

In presenting this material from our laboratory experiments here, we have demonstrated that even as one goes back through the evolutionary ladder, instances of memory in organisms occur. If one goes all the way to the interface between life and non-life, one encounters viruses at the boundary. Since they can replicate and have genetic material they can be considered as part of the living world. Do viruses have memory one can ask, with the idea of then making a claim of a virus soul.

Today we can think of viruses as having immunological memory. The well known HIV for instance poses problems for developing a successful vaccine because it mutates to avoid destruction by drugs as they are developed. The virus 'remembers' its enemies and takes preventive protective action one could claim, personifying the virus!

Since memory pervades the entire living world, the soul whose culmination is claimed in human beings (in whom the culmination of memory also takes place), could be perceived as evolving from the virus onwards, that is from the earliest form of life. The non-life material world is devoid of memory. When memory arrives, matter becomes living and memory is expressed not as material but as non-material energy. The material world as it emanated via the Big Bang was the result of the conversion of energy. From the perspective then of the energy inherent in the nonliving and the living world the soul is intimately tied up with all of reality. There is an ontological connection between the Big Bang and the soul.

The New Science of the Brain

Advances in neuroscience today have made inroads into the brain, which is the seat of memory. When one speaks of happiness as a reflection of the soul, one automatically involves memory. Three levels of happiness are generally listed: pleasure, joy and bliss(*tamasik, rajasik and satvik in Indian terms*).All of us fall into one of these groups... those who are spiritually awake (satvik), those who are asleep (tamsik) and those who are somewhere in the middle (rajsik). One's own personal definition of happiness depends on which of these groups one belongs to. From the scientific point of view, where neurochemistry has progressed, we have knowledge of the molecules related to these states, as indicated in the tables below:

Chemicals of Joy

	NORMAL	DEFICIENCY
OXYTOCIN	Good social recognition, calm and relaxed mood, ego faculty	Become negative, depressed, socially withdrawn, anxious

VASOPRESSIN	Good social Recognition, Prompt-responsive, attentive to stressful situations	Socially withdrawn, feel overwhelmed in stressful situations

Chemicals of Bliss

Blissful Chemicals		
	NORMAL	DEFICIENT
ENDORPHINS	You are full of cozy feelings of comfort, pleasure, and euphoria.	You may be crying during commercials and overly sensitive to hurt.
GABA	You are relaxed and stress-free.	You will be wired, stressed, and overwhelmed.

Today we have also identified the genes associated with these molecules, for instance Vesicular Mono Amine Transporter (VMAT) produces the sensations of mystic experiences, including the presence of God and spirituality as a state of mind, and its gene is located on chromosome 10q25. Monoamine oxidase A (MAOA) is located on the X chromosome, and low-expression is associated with higher self-reported happiness in women.

Teilhard de Chardin and the Soul

In support of the discussion on the soul and the observations made above, I would like to point out that the great mystic-scientist and paleontologist P. Teilhard de Chardin also seems to have had a view of the soul that expanded into the entire universe and cosmos:

> Without the slightest doubt there is something through which material and spiritual energy hold together and are complementary. In the last analysis, somehow or other, there must be a single energy operating in the world. And the first idea that occurs to us is that the 'soul' must be

as it were the focal point of transformation at which, from all the points of nature, the forces of bodies converge, to become interiorized and sublimated in beauty and truth.[10]

He is known to have observed that "God is not remote from us. He is at the point of my pen, my (pick) shovel, my paintbrush, my (sewing) needle, my heart and thoughts."[11] He has further observed, "We see not only thought as participating in evolution as an anomaly or as an epiphenomenon; but evolution as so reducible to and identifiable with a progress towards thought that the movement of our souls expresses and measures the very stages of progress of evolution itself. Man discovers that he is nothing else than evolution become conscious of itself."[12]

His observation: "We are not human beings having a spiritual experience. We are spiritual beings having a human experience," has been paraphrased thus: "Our bodies are temporary. We are souls. We are immortal; we are eternal. We never die; we merely transform to a heightened state of consciousness, no longer needing a physical body. We are always loved. We are never alone, and we can never be harmed, not at this level.[13]

Teilhard's faith in the survival of the spirit may come across as questioning the special or direct creation of the human soul by God, and has been singled out as one of the weakest links in Teilhard's attempt to synthesize Christianity and evolution – one of the two major concerns expressed by Pope Pius XII in the 1950 encyclical *Humani generis*, even though neither Teilhard nor Henri de Lubac, whose work had also been under suspicion, were named explicitly in the document. Teilhard's own masterwork, *Le Phénomène Humain*, was never officially approved despite repeated revisions. And today, even after several later papal commendations of his visionary efforts to reconcile religion and science, the situation apparently remains the same.

But that should not stop us from continuing to explore and reconcile the two. This article is an attempt to continue a dialogue by a professional scientist who is making an effort to also qualify as a professional theologian. Could this lead

It's expanding ever outward but one day
It will cause the stars to go the other way
Collapsing ever inward, we won't be here, it won't be hurt
Our best and brightest figure that it'll make an even bigger bang!

Australopithecus would really have been sick of us
Debating how we're here, they're catching deer (we're catching viruses)
Religion or astronomy (Descartes or Deuteronomy)
It all started with the big bang!

Music and mythology, Einstein and astrology
It all started with the big bang!
It all started with the big bang!

Endnotes

[1] The rest of the verses in the theme song are also relevant. To access, do google.com: the big bang theory lyrics.

[2] Stephen Hawking, *The Theory of Everything: The Origin and Fate of The Universe* (Mumbai: Jaico Publishing House, 2006), p. vii

[3] Lancy Lobo: from a slide in power point presentation at Seminar on Higher Education, 2017, St. Xavier's college, Ahmedabad.

[4] The table gives a historical perspective on the evolution of the cosmos that some may be more comfortable with.

[5] Hawking Stephen, p. viii

[6] Abraham Jacob, *Essays in Neurotheology: The Completeness Theory and Progress Theory* (Delhi: Indian Society For The Promotion of Knowledge, 2006), p. 6

[7] Sydney Brenner, "The Genetics of *Caenorhabditis elegan*," *Genetics* 77 (1974 - 1): 71-94

[8] Dong et al, "Neutraceutical Interventions for Promoting Healthy Aging in Invertebrate Models," Oxidative Medicine and Cellular Longevity, 2012.

[9] Amano and Maruyama,"Aversive Olfactory Learning and Associative Long-Term Memory in Caenorhabditis elegans,"Learningand Memory 18 (2011-10): 65465

¹⁰ https://www.google.co.in/search?q=teilhard+de+chardin+quotes&dcr=0&source=lnms&tbm=isch&sa=X&ved= 0ahUKEwiRyqi0wf3aAhUE5o8KHQ2VCu4Q_AUICigB#imgrc= uCN81EQ8U83SBM:

¹¹ Ibid

¹² Ibid

¹³ Ibid

Chapter 4

Developments in Neuroscience and Their Impact on Spirituality: A Critical Perspective

Roy J. J. Pereira

Abstract

In the media or in current scientific or non-scientific literature we are constantly being bombarded with information about the discovery of certain parts of the brain that are linked to spiritual or religious activities. Depending on which side of the debate the author is,conclusions are then drawn for the existence of spiritual or religious experiences, and further on for the existence or not of God or a Higher Power. Are these conclusions justified? Does the science upon which they are based truly serve as a foundation for making such claims? The discipline of 'Neurotheology' under which the dialogue between the brain and spiritual experiences is subsumed is still in its infancy and can grow up when methodologies used are well laid out, the terms used are operationalized and the underlying assumptions are spelled out. It is necessary to avoid the pitfalls of phrenology if this discipline is to emerge from its adolescence. This paper first attempts to clarify a number of terms, to put forward recent developments in

Neuroscience before listing some of the popular researches done in recent times which attempted to claim the discovery of God or the source of a God experience. The attempt to reduce spirituality to neurons in the brain or to an evolutionary need for survival is then critiqued. Can science really be an adjudicating body for some of the phenomena that we are discussing? Finally, a few suggestions to build a more robust Neurotheology are offered.

Keywords: Neurotheology, Neurology, Phrenology, God Helmet, God Module, God Gene.

Introduction – Neurology

It is helpful to begin with clarifying some terms. "Neurological sciences" is the umbrella term that covers both the discipline of neurology and the discipline of neuroscience. Neurology is the branch of medicine or biology that deals with the anatomy, functions and organic disorders of nerves and the nervous systems. The field of neurology comes under the faculty of medicine in a medical college. Neurology has been in existence for a long time in the medical field. The key focus in this specialized field of medicine is disorders and diseases of the nervous system ranging from Alzheimer's to infection and personality disorders. Neurology also deals with accidents caused to the brain either from a fall or crash where the skull could be broken and the diagnosis and treatment of the nervous system.

Towards the end of the twentieth century the development of machines like PET (Positron Emission Tomography) and fMRI (functional Magnetic Resonance Imaging) allowed one to look into a healthy brain without needing any invasive cuts into the skull. Thus, these machines allowed scientists and doctors to go beyond the study of diseased or accident-damaged brains to healthy brains and thus the discipline of neuroscience began emerging into its own, separate from Neurology. As neuroscience did not entail a medical degree, it slowly detached itself from medical schools and emerged into its own in academic universities and research institutions. It is important to understand the difference between Neurology and Neuroscience because many people tend to confuse one for the other or conflate the two.

Neuroscience

Neuroscience is the scientific study of the nervous system. The scope of neuroscience has broadened to include different approaches used to study the molecular, cellular, developmental, structural, functional, evolutionary, computational, and medical aspects of the nervous system.[1]The developments in neuroscience are proceeding along multiple tracks. One area of research concerns the localizing of various cognitive and affective functions in specific regions or distributed systems of the brain. With the development of Computed Tomography, more commonly known as a CT or CATscans it has become possible to study correlations between structural abnormalities and the behavior of people. Further, MRI scans now provide quite detailed pictures of the brain, more easily revealing locations of brain damage. PET scans allow research correlating localized brain activity with the performance of specialized cognitive tasks.

We have further offshoots from here. Cognitive Science which branched off from psychology deals with the study of cognition and thought processes. Cognitive Neuroscience involves the biological underpinnings of cognition. Computational Neuroscience deals with the brain as an information processor. As one can guess there is a lot of overlap in these various fields. In short, if one is studying the biology behind the brain, then it would be within the realm of neuroscience whereas if one is fascinated by how the human mind works, it would fall in the area of cognitive science.[2]

Three Nervous Systems

Having clarified some terminology about the various disciplines, let us offer a brief overview of the three nervous systems, of which the brain is a part of the first. The first is the Central Nervous System

(CNS) which is made up of three parts, the brain, spinal cord and retina. The brain consists of the medulla, pons, cerebellum, midbrain, thalamus, hypothalamus, basal ganglia and the cerebral cortex. The spinal cord reaches down upto the tail bone and is segmented. The retina is not just a feeder to the nervous system but part of the CNS itself. The second nervous system is the peripheral nervous system (PNS) which is basically the interface between the CNS and the environment. It consists of the autonomic (visceral) nervous system which innervates smooth muscle and glands and the somatic nervous system (dorsal root ganglion, cranial nuclei). These together constitute the total motor output of the PNS. The third nervous system is the enteric nervous system which, in the language of the lay person, is simply the gut. One must surely remember the times when one felt 'nervous.' This feeling in the mind is translated into the human body, more specifically the gut, as the feeling of 'butterflies in the stomach.' There are other times when intense anxiety and worry can produce a stomach upset. This is explained because the enteric nervous system is a part of the nervous system and therefore adverse thoughts influence the nervous system.

Brain

The brain is divided into four lobes – the frontal lobe, right in front above the forehead; behind it the parietal lobe; running along the sides above the ears is the temporal lobe and at the back of the skull is the occipital lobe where the visual system is located. Below this is the cerebellum. The pons and medulla oblongata are at the base from which the spinal cord then begins. The different parts of the brain are responsible for different functions. Even though there has been much success with regard to localization of functions, it is a fallacy to think that only one part is responsible for that particular function. Multiple parts of the brain are pulled in for a task at a given time. We shall revisit this point later.

Spiritual activities

'Spiritual nature' is an intricate term that embraces both philosophy and theology. For the sake of the topic and the connection with neuroscience I would like to focus on spiritual activities and explore how these activities link up with the brain, if they do. Spiritual activities include vocal prayer, singing hymns, psalms and bhajans or attending a community prayer service whether it be a *satsang*, Holy Mass or *aarti puja*. Then one can move towards one's internal space through reading a Holy Book and reflecting on it, contemplation and meditation. Meditation is again broadly divided into two types; concentrative and awareness-based meditation.[3] Some others would define as spiritual activities what were early called works of mercy like feeding the hungry, looking after the sick and dying and visiting the elderly and those in prison. But this could be done by anyone and so we shall leave these out for the sake of this paper and not because they are not important spiritual activities.

Besides the above – what one could call spiritual activities accessible to every human being– there are the 'out-of-this-world' spiritual experiences like trances, visions, ecstatic moments and those times when one feels united with oneself and the world. These have been investigated by many. Confer Saver and Rabin, "The Neural Substrates of Religious Experience."[4] The spiritual activities I described earlier, the more ordinary ones, have not been so much the focus of investigations. Brugger has done some work in this area.[5,6] An explanation has been offered by Norman and Jeeves, "Perhaps there is an assumption that the mundane activities are subserved by the same brain systems that would be active when we read or think about nonholy writings or participate in nonreligious social activities. The 'extra-ordinary' activities, on the other hand, might be supposed to involve unique brain circuits or at least some unique combination of circuits. Such a distinction would need to be justified, and to date no justification has been put forth."[7]

They go on to further state that such distinctions have led to debates about whether spiritual activity should be regarded as a way of perceiving, a way of experiencing, or a way of behaving. Azari and her colleagues hold from their studies that religious experience, more specifically the recitation of religious texts, rather than being an immediate affective event, is a cognitive event involving the reflexive evaluation of thought.[8] However, Norman and Jeeves feel that most researchers seem to define spirituality or religiosity in affective terms or according to our hermeneutics of the world.[9]

Brain activities

In the previous section we tried to pin down what could be considered 'spiritual activities' which as we saw involved a range of activities. It may be easier to determine what we mean by 'brain activities.' Norman and Jeeves have this to say, "Once we decide on the level we wish to examine (e.g., neuro-chemical, single-cell recording, patterns of blood flow), we would then choose an established procedure for making measurements. Of course, there is always the possibility that nonstandard or less commonly used procedures could be used (e.g., Persinger's transcranial stimulation procedure). This might raise questions about just what is being measured or manipulated."[10]

Let us look into how these brain activities are measured and what machines are used. Thanks to the invention of some high imaging instruments in the last few decades we can study the brain in detail. We have instruments like the Magnetic Resonance Imaging (MRI) and the real time functional Magnetic Resonance Imaging (fMRI) which gives information regarding the part of the brain functioning during a particular task. When we are seeing a certain area of the brain light up on the screen it merely means that there is an electrical and chemical activation taking place in the brain. There is also the Positron Emission Topography (PET) which is a specialized radiology procedure used to examine various body tissues to identify certain conditions. PET may also be used to follow the progress of the treatment of certain conditions in the fields of neurology, oncology, and cardiology; applications in other fields are currently being studied.[11]

Neurotheology

Bringing together the above spiritual activities and brain activities puts us in the domain of neurotheology. Neurotheology also known as spiritual neuroscience is the multidisciplinary field of scholarship that seeks to understand the relationship between the human brain and religion or more specifically between the mind and theology.[12]It includes the fields of neuroscience, cognitive science, biology, psychology, anthropology, philosophy, theology, religious studies and religious experience and practice. "Each of these fields may contribute to neurotheology and conversely, neurotheology may ultimately contribute in return to each of these fields. Ultimately, neurotheology must be considered as a multidisciplinary study that requires substantial integration of divergent fields, particularly neuroscience and religious phenomena."[13]Scholars in the field strive to explain the neurological ground for spiritual experiences such as "the perception that time, fear or self-consciousness have dissolved, spiritual awe, oneness with the universe."[14]

Neurotheology also known as neuroscience of religion,seeks to explain religious experience and behavior in terms of neuroscience. The field looks at correlations of neural phenomena with subjective experiences of spirituality and proposes hypotheses to explain these phenomena. Secular humanists or atheists would hold that there is a neurological or evolutionary basis for subjective experiences that would be generally categorized as spiritual or religious.

God Helmet

So, let us see what work has been done in this area of brain activities and spiritual activities. We consider the ones that have become more popular in contemporary understanding. The first we shall consider is the God Helmet, though it was not actually called that by its creators. As the helmet became popular it was first called the Koren helmet and then the God helmet. A God helmet is a magnetic cap / helmet that is worn on the head of the subject and which stimulates the temporal lobe which has for long been associated with religious-type experiences, especially the amygdala and hippocampus. This was invented by neuroscientist Stanley Koren based on the measurements given by neuroscientist Michael Persinger. They published the results in 1990[15] and then in 1993,[16] among a host of other publications. Can a God experience be stimulated by a God helmet? Through the means of the "God" helmet Dr. Michael Persinger intended to try and stimulate certain neuronal pathways and allow the subject to "feel" a God experience. The helmet uses a network of low-intensity magnetic signals or a field-to-field interaction onto the brain causing mild disruption that allows for a 'sensed presence' or what from a believer's perspective may be called a religious experience. Persinger conducted this God Helmet test on over 2000 participants. Nearly eighty percent of the subjects admitted that the mild disruption that the helmet caused resulted in their experiencing of a 'sensed presence' which was described as 'religious or spiritual' by both believers and non-believers alike. "The experience of using the helmet highlights the brain's central role to what is recognized as a deep spiritual embodiment, normally associated with activities such as prayer, fasting, or meditation. Sessions are held in the quiet of an acoustic chamber, or totally silent room with electromagnetic insulation."[17]

Such 'sensed presence' can be placed under the broad category of mystical experience. It should be noted that mystical experience has been associated with epilepsy from earlier times. *The Idiot* by Dostoyevsky describes a detailed account of this which is based on the author's own experience. Epilepsy has now been found to be caused by temporal lobe dysfunction.

God Spot

This research led to the media claiming that the 'God spot' in the brain had been located. This led many secular humanists and atheists to jump to the conclusion that all religious experiences are but a product of the brain. Isabel Clarke has drawn our attention to the title of Persinger's earlier theoretical study, "Religious and Mystical Experiences as Artifacts of Temporal Lobe Function."[18]This has revealed his own reductionist stance by presenting religious experiences as brain artifacts. Clarke adds, "However, his general line of argument is consistent with the conclusion that the interpretation of such experiences – whether they are taken as an encounter with god or some other supernatural being, or merely as a somewhat uncanny episode – depended on the participants' prior religious and philosophical context."[19]

God Module

Dr. V. S. Ramachandran and his team of neurologists at U.C. San Diego reported at the annual conference of the Society of Neuroscience in 1997 that they had found the "God Module" a portion of the brain that was very active during intense religious experiences. This data arose from a study of epilepsy patients and the section of the brain was the temporal lobes.[20] Dr. Ramachandran's team performed experiments on three patients suffering from a type of temporal lobe epilepsy. In such patients, seizures were quite often accompanied by intense mystical or religious experiences. Sometimes mystical experiences followed in between seizures. Ramachandran's team found that there was an increase in activity in that area of the brain with a sort of increased involuntary response to religious symbols and words.

In that same year neurologists Sava and Rabin published their findings on epilepsy patients. The cause of their epilepsy was a result of a neuronal malfunction in the limbic region of the brain which caused a minor electrical disturbance in an otherwise normal brain. From this they put forward the argument that the limbic system of the brain – a system that is located in the area close to the temporal lobes and channelizes emotions – is responsible for the religious, spiritual and mystical experience (RSMEs) that occur. They further claimed that RSME is also a kind of brain disorder, a divine madness that triggers a kind of "God Module." Many religious leaders belong to the type 'temporal lobe personality' and they would exhibit symptoms of Temporal-lobe Epilepsy (TLE).[21] Beauregard and O'Leary challenge this claim. Mystical experiences are indicators of an altered state of consciousness that allows the mystic to become cognizant of cosmic realities that would not otherwise have come into consciousness during ordinary, everyday awareness. To compare TLE to intense religious mystical experiences is a big jump. Further,a correlation cannot really be established between such religious experiences and epilepsy. To then make the claim that honoured religious personalities are 'temporal lobe personalities' is too simplistic.[22]

God Part

The next naturalistic explanation came through the publication of Mathew Alper's *The God Part of the Brain* which was first published in 1996 and then again in 2001.[23]His premise in his own words is as follows:

> Essentially, what I am suggesting is that humans are genetically predisposed to believe in some form of a spiritual reality as we create religions with their myths and rituals through which to bolster these beliefs. This is why every human culture has maintained a belief in everything from a host of superstitions, the paranormal, the supernatural and all forms of mysticism.
>
> If what I'm suggesting is true, it would imply that God-along with all things spiritual is not something that exists "out there," beyond and independent of us, but rather as the product of an inherited instinct, the manifestation of an evolutionary adaptation that exists within the human brain. And why would our species have evolved such a seemingly abstract cognitive trait? I suggest that we evolved such an adaptation in order to help our species to cope with the otherwise debilitating anxiety that came with our unique awareness of inevitable death. Here lies the origin of humankind's spiritual function, an evolutionary adaptation – a

coping mechanism – that compels our species to believe that though our physical bodies will one day perish, our "spirits" or "souls" will persist for all eternity.[24]

Mathew Alper has gathered data from neurobiology and evolutionary psychology and has put forward the argument that humans are innately hardwired for perception of a spiritual reality and to believe in forces that transcend our human limitations in this physical realm. This is how he puts it in an interview, "What I mean by this is that the human species possesses a mechanism, an evolutionary adaptation in our brain – a religious/spiritual function – which compels us to perceive and believe that there exists a transcendental / supernatural quality in the universe. But differences of opinion exist as to whether the neural basis of religious experience involves a relatively localized or a network of interconnected areas."[25]

Response to God Helmet / God Spot / God Module/ God Part

In the initial attempts to try and find out which part of the brain is responsible for our connection with God the focus was on the higher than average reports of visions from those who had epileptic fits. This was the reason the temporal lobe was pinned down as the portion for being in contact with God. Persinger's main point was that the temporal lobe transients are an important factor in explaining religious experiences. However as pointed out by Norman and Jeeves "the purported microseizures are however sometimes too weak to detect. Perhaps technological advances will allow for measurement of these transients. However, until that happens, they appear to be a convenient fiction that fills in gaps in the theory."[26]

The replication of the God helmet experiment (published in 2004) by the Swedish group led by Dr. Pehr Granqvist with the hardware and software obtained from Dr. Persinger did not give the expected results.[27] The criticism from this group was that the result of Persinger was due to suggestibility. Persinger responded, after examining their findings,that the experiment had not been set up in the right manner.

They had run the signals, using magnetic fields too fast and not long enough. A more recent experiment refuted Dr. PehrGranqvist showing that the effects from the God Helmet are not due to suggestion or suggestibility in the participants. This experiment by Tinoco and Ortiz of Brazil simply proved that the effects of the God Helmet are real without seeking to answer a host of other questions that Persinger's experiment has raised. The experiment did not try to give the participants visions of God. They were instead subjected to the same kind of magnetic stimulation and then analyzed the language used to describe their experience.[28] This same experimental method was used by Persinger in his 1993 experiment and Tinoco and Ortiz were able to replicate the effect in 2014.

As one can see above, there can be an ongoing back and forth discussion about the God Helmet experiment. But success or failure does not have a bearing on the position we are taking.The argument I am making against the God Helmet / God Part / God module is that the temporal lobe (or any other part of the brain or networks within the brain) that lights up during a scan (or shows activity when a person is made to perform some spiritual activity)is thatarea of the brain that helps the person to experience the spiritual activity. Just because the helmet can create a similar experience to that of a "God experience" it does not negate the "God experience" that believers have had down the centuries without the use of any helmet.

I find it perfectly acceptable that God would use his own creation, the human brain to be a channel for him to communicate. From a faith perspective a believer would have no problems in accepting that God would use his or her own creation, i.e., the very brain that God has created to make Godself known to God's creation. The summary answer to the God helmet, the God spot and the God part is "The brain is the locus of God experience not the cause of God experience."[29]

The Bishop of Oxford Richard Harries expresses the same sentiment but puts it differently, "It would not be surprising if God had created us with a physical facility for belief."[30] A more detailed explanation follows.

> It should not surprise us that our brains show specific activity during religious experiences. Christians do not (or should not) believe that our relationship to God occurs entirely within immaterial soul, of which our bodies are mere vessels. Our whole being – soul and body, mind and brain – should respond to God. Nor do our brains have a singular "God Module," as the site of all religious activity. Our relationship to God is personal and complex, not limited to just one kind of experience. No doubt many parts of our brain participate in many kinds of religious experiences. The temporal lobe, for example, is known to be important for intense emotional experiences. We should expect it to participate in intense religious experiences. It is certainly intriguing that a particular sub-region is rather specialized, at least in these patients, for religious imagery.[31]

God Gene

While the God Helmet, God Spot, God Module were all discovered within the field of neuroscience, the God gene comes to us from genetics. The origin of the 'God Gene' which has now become popular in the media and literature begins with Dean Hamer, molecular geneticist at the US National Cancer Institute. His argument is that experiences of a spiritual nature and religion are universal attributes.

> Hamer measures spirituality on a scale of 'self-transcendence,' or the ability to see beyond oneself, a concept first introduced by psychologist Robert Cloninger. He draws a sharp distinction between spirituality, which is a personality trait that some of us have to a greater or lesser extent than others, and religion as a belief in a particular god, which is culturally transmitted expression of spirituality. It might be that some of that variation in spirituality is explained by genetics, although spirituality is probably a complex trait influenced by many genes as well as the environment. If there are genetic influences, ever-more-sophisticated techniques in molecular genetics should be able to tease them out. These genetic factors may have been favored during human evolution because spirituality has some positive effect on the individual's ability to reproduce.[32]

The gene referred to is SLC18A2, also called VMAT2 (vesicular monoamine transporter 2). A variation in VMAT2 where cytosine rather than an adenine is at the position 33050 of this gene was determined to be at a higher level in the subjects tested for self-transcendence. Thus, his conclusion that VMAT2 is the God gene. For this study Hamer used twins. He studied nine genes that were responsible for the release of brain chemicals called monoamines which include dopamine, adrenaline and serotonin, among others. These chemicals regulate mood and motivation.[33]

A second study dealing with identical twins this time threw up the findings that children do not learn spirituality from some culture or society. This conclusion came about because even though the environmental and cultural surroundings were same for both the fraternal twins and the identical twins there were dissimilarities with regards to the extent that self-transcendence was correlated. Hence the conclusion that self-transcendence is an inherited trait.[34]

Response to God Gene

In their critique, Mario Beauregard and Denyse O'Learyagree that Hamer's intention is not to negate any religious doctrine or belief but rather to account for the variation in cytosine and adenine which determines lower or higher experiences in human beings. Consequently, their findings only encompass the mere variation taking place in any experience of certain intensity. The reason for this is that even in the expression of a minor human trait, there is an interplay of hundreds or thousands of genes.[35] Hence the conclusion to the 'God gene' is a big jump. Further replication has been problematic. When we consider the siblings and twin studies the counter argument can be made that despite being in the same home environment how each of the twins' experiences life is not the same. "Perhaps one sister merely encounters a certain inspirational teacher or well-loved book that the other does not. Non-shared experiences like these heap constancy upon contingency as each girl develops. In the end, the two sisters may essentially grow up in divergent emotional environments – and as a result make very different choices about the role of spirituality in their lives" points out Barbara J. King, an anthropologist.[36]

Critique of the Localization Argument of God Part/ God Spot

As can be seen in the statement of Alper with which I concluded his section, there was already growing criticism about the localization of human experience to one 'part' or one 'spot' in the brain or one 'gene' in general and of course consequently to the 'God' part of 'God' spot.

Let me dwell on this point a little more by speaking of phrenology and some similarities between it and neurotheology, the relation between neuroscience and spirituality and religion defined earlier. This would allow us to learn from the past and not repeat the same mistakes. 'Phren' comes from the Greek word *'phren'* meaning 'mind.' Thus, phrenology is study of the mind or as defined by Oxford, "the detailed study of the shape and size of the cranium as a supposed indication of character and mental abilities." In the nineteenth century there was a main tenet that mental functions were the result of a discrete number of faculties. Now each of these would correspond to a different part of the surface of the brain.

> The task was to relate the contemporary picture of a 'psychology of faculties' with current knowledge of the structure of the brain. In this endeavor, it was the leading anatomists of the time who gave the impetus to research.[37] In his 1835 treatise on the functions of the brain, Franz Gall took as one of his starting points, the contemporary 'psychology of faculties.'He argued that the whole cerebral cortex is an aggregate of individual organs, each of which is the substrate of a particular mental faculty.[38] It was left to the German physician Johann Spurzheim, a collaborator with Gall in his neuroanatomical research, to popularize the term phrenology.[39]

In phrenology, analysis of the relative size of individual organs and their relation to behavior was the norm. If a person was helpful and kind, it was assumed that she had a large organ of altruism. But this simplistic one-to-one relationship did not hold in many cases. We can thus learn from phrenology when it comes to establishing a correlation between the temporal lobe and spiritual experience and thus making claims that now the "God spot" or "God part" has been found. This is a far too simplistic explanation of a more complex phenomena. Further,although not so well-known, phrenology also put forward explanations in terms of connections or networks. When one made a judgment that rested on combinations of interacting organs it became complicated. It could be invoked but it was rarely explicated. Norman and Jeeves thus point out a similar trajectory occurring in neurotheology. Explanations of religious or spiritual behavior based only on "temporal lobe activity" are today considered naïve. Models that come in later on by d'Aquili and Newberg recognized the need to expand the number of brain areas involved.[40] Beauregard also reported multiple areas of the brains of Carmelite nuns that showed notable activity.[41]Thus, they summarize:

> It would be neat and simple if there was a single "God spot" in the brain or perhaps abnormal activity in the temporal lobes and underlying limbic structures. However, it appears that religious / spiritual behavior must be understood in terms of emotion, perception, self-consciousness, memory, and many other functions. The relationship between brain activity and religious / spiritual behavior may be diffuse and context-dependent, too much so, in fact, to build a neurotheology.[42]

Taking off from the learnings of phrenology that were applicable to neurotheology we can propose as Azari has done that religious experience may be a cognitive process, mediated by a pre-established neural circuit, involving dorsolateral prefrontal, dorsomedial frontal and medial parietal cortex.[43] Using Proudfoot,[44]Azari goes on to explain that because religious attributions are made in anomalous or ambiguous situations, when a person does not know what to expect or what to do, yet actively and persistently seeks a solution, an assiduous, internally generated 'readiness' emerges, which subsequently serves to re-activate the religious schema in the presence of salient religious cues. This 'readiness' is probably mediated by the dorsomedial frontal cortex, leading to the commonly reported felt immediacy of religious experience. The experience, however, becomes religious when the subject has consciously identified it as consistent with the subject's own religious schema... This cognitive process most probably involves the dorsolateral prefrontal and medial parietal cortex.[45]

Further Studies in the Field of Neurotheology

The studies we are going to look at now moved away from the understanding of a single God spot or God part that could explain religious or spiritual experience. They pointed out to a network of different parts of the brain. Further, the studies discussed above (with regard to the relationship between brain activities and spiritual activities)belong to a body of scientific research which tried to pin down to neurology or genetics the biologically driven religious tendency toward frequent prayer / a strongly felt presence of the divine. The following studies were more focused on finding neural correlates of religious experience without necessarily pointing to a reductive understanding of such experiences like the earlier studies did.

Andrew Newburg

A study by Andrew Newburg on Franciscan nuns in prayer revealed activity in the superior parietal lobe, that part of the brain that is responsible for our sense of orientation. The activity decreases during prayer. The insights from this study are developed in *The Mystical Mind*; religious experience or more specifically mystical experiences are better comprehended as the result of the integrated functioning of specific processing units in the brain.[46] "The generation of such experiences is neither the result of malfunctioning in these systems nor is it a primary function of these systems, working together, to generate religious experiences." Norman and Jeeves unpack this statement further:[47]

> In certain respects, d'Aquili and Newberg's model is an updated and more detailed version of the one put forward by Michael Gazzaniga in his 1985 book, *The Social Brain*.[48] D'Aquili and Newberg propose an explanation of mystical experiences with a model based on the two divisions of the autonomic nervous system (one, ergotropic or arousing; the other,

quiescent), portions of the limbic system (namely, the hippocampus and amygdala), and tertiary association areas of the neocortex which function as primary cognitive operators (holistic, reductionist, causal,abstractive, binary, quantitative, and emotional value operators). In addition to these components is added the process of deafferentation whereby incoming information to one component of the system is inhibited. When this happens that portion of the system functions on its own according to its own internal logic.[49]

Mario Beauregard

In the study done by neuroscientist Mario Beauregard of the University of Montreal, Canada, fifteen nuns belonging to the religious congregation known as Cloistered Carmelites, whose age range was between 23 to 64, were the subjects of a brain scan. They were asked to relive the most intense mystical experience they ever had as members of their religious congregation. The sisters were not asked to try and actually achieve a state of spiritual union with God during the experiment because, as the nuns put it, "God cannot be summoned at will."As neuroscientist Mario Beauregard puts it, "The main goal of the study was to identify the neural correlates of a mystical experience. This does not diminish the meaning and value of such an experience,and neither does it confirm or disconfirm the existence of God."[50]

Furthermore Beauregard and his investigators found evidence to support the point that we made earlier in this paper and at the start that there is not a single organ or part of the brain that can be fixed for a given task or experience. Multiple areas are pulled in for a given task. They discovered, as had others before them,that there is noticeable activity in the temporal lobe. However, there was significant activity in the inferior parietal lobule, caudate nucleus, left brain stem, visual cortex, left anterior cingulate cortex, right medial prefrontal cortex, left insula, right superior parietal lobule, right medial orbitofrontal cortex, and right middle temporal cortex. Thus, there is no 'God spot' or any single section of the brain where one can localize a task fully.

Multiple brain regions and systems mediate mystical experiences. Religious and / or mystical experiences (RSMEs) are mediated by brain regions that subserve perception, cognition, emotion, body representation and self-consciousness.[51]

Beauregard along with writer Denise O'Leary summarizes their arguments in their book, *The Spiritual Brain: A Neuroscientist's Case for the Existence of the Soul.*

> The nonmaterialist approach to the human mind is a rich and vital tradition that accounts for the evidence much better than the currently stalled materialist one. Second, nonmaterialist approaches to the mind result in practical benefits and treatments, as well as promising approaches to phenomena that materialist accounts cannot even address. Lastly ... our book shows that when spiritual experiences transform lives, the most reasonable explanation and the one that best accounts for all the evidence,is that people who have such experiences have actually contacted a reality outside themselves,a reality that has brought them closer to the real nature of the universe.[52]

In the earlier part of this paper I presented the research of neuroscientists who from their research tried to localize RSMEs to one spot or part of the brain and then make claims that they had found that part of the brain that made us believe in God or allowed us to have God experiences. From this they defended their reductionistic model of the human person boiling all experiences or behavior to activation of neurotransmitters in the brain or to the demands of evolution. Then I also presented the work of two teams of scientists who also studied spiritual experiences and their neural correlates in the brain but did not opt for reductionism of the human or the spiritual dimension of the human. Norman and Jeeves rightly ask the question, "Where does it leave us" and offer a very nuanced answer.

> Investigations of the relationship between brain functioning and religious and spiritual experiences and behavior emphasize neural systems and networks rather than centers, as did phrenology. Those networks are more circumscribed for some investigators than for others. Some take a materialist position, some a nonmaterialist one, and others are

noncommittal. We found the same diversity of opinions in phrenology. In the last section, we turn to several issues and problems at the time of phrenology and ask what bearing they might have for neurotheology.[53]

Future pathways – Cautions and Concerns

It is important to continue to welcome efforts made at understanding how our spirituality is embodied and yet how it transcends this embodiment. We need to also be conscious of the role played by our shared beliefs about God, the Transcendent, our Higher power. Caution is required in conceptualizing and operationalizing of terms and rigorous hypothesis testing.

Most serious academicians understand that there will be difficulties in how 'theology' in neurotheology will be conceptualized. One cannot just point to religious activities or spirituality. The special cases of visions or mystical experiences remain special and are different from the day-to-day spiritual activities. There also are conceptual difficulties with regard to the 'neuro' part of neurotheology. Imaging techniques have helped us a great deal about gaining knowledge of the brain but when moving from anatomy to cognition especially with regard to complex mechanisms there is still a long way to go.[54] The advancement of the field of neurotheology depends on meticulous observances of the parameters involved and willingness to critique every step of the way and spelling out the underlying methodologies and technologies.[55]

The second area of concern pointed by Norman and Jeeves is related to the first.

> Phrenology quickly became divorced from any serious attempts to ground its findings in rigorous hypothesis testing. New adherents to the discipline tacked their own observations onto previous systems with little or no regard for empirical verification. While current neurotheological investigations are based on empirical research, most currently have an observational and descriptive tone. Advances will accrue when carefully crafted hypotheses, capable of being disconfirmed, are put to the test.[56]

A third issue faced by neurotheology is how one determines the subjective state of the subject. This is an issue not only for neurotheology but also for the more general context of cognition and the field of cognitive neuroscience.[57] As Sayadmansour points out, having a subject solve a mathematical task is great but how does one know that the mind of the person was on that task continuously or whether there were times when the mind was distracted. All of us are aware of how often our mind wanders off to something else even in the midst of performing a mental task. One might be able to determine if the subject did the test correctly or incorrectly, but that in and of itself cannot determine why he or she was right or wrong. Thus, subjectivity is an issue in neurotheology.[58] Sayyadmansour explains:

> When considering spiritual states, the ability to measure such states empirically while not disturbing such states is almost impossible. Hence, it is important to ascertain as much as possible what the person thinks they are experiencing. Neurotheology research can help better refine subjective measurements. Spiritual and religious states are perhaps the best described of all states and thus, can be an important starting point for advancing research in the measurement of subjective states.[59]

A fourth area of research and one that I am currently working on is the area of neuroscience, health and spirituality. Some of my work has been in the area of stress and how bodies are broken.[60] Also, in the area of meditation and its effect on the human body.[61] An increasing number of studies point to the relation of positivity on health as well as the effect of negative emotions on health and wellbeing.[62] Some outcomes would be a decrease in feelings of depression and anxiety, an enhanced immune system, and a reduction in the mortality rate of those who profess to have a religious orientation. On the opposite side, it has been found that persons who have conflicted views on religion or God sometimes experience increasing stress, anxiety and health issues especially in times of uncertainty and pandemics.[63]

A fifth area of research especially in the field of cognitive neuroscience is to deepen our understanding of the thinking process of humans and the interaction with eco systems around them. "In particular, this relates to our perception and response to the external reality that the brain continuously presents to our deep consciousness,"[64]argues Sayyadmansour to whom we shall also turn to for a well-expressed concluding line, "Neurotheology is in the unique position to be able to explore epistemological questions that arise from neuroscience and theology. Thus, integrating religious and scientific perspectives might provide the foundation upon which scholars from a variety of disciplines can address some of the greatest questions facing humanity."[65]

Conclusion

In this paper, I have attempted to spell out the terms or phrases which comprise of neurotheology: neurological sciences, neurology, neuroscience, spiritual activities and brain activities. We have tried to list what could come under spiritual activities and how these can be located in the brain through neural correlates. We did this through a number of research projects some of which were attempting to reduce all spiritual activities to either a neurological basis or as a bye-product of evolution. There were other research endeavours which did not make far-reaching claims but were more interested in mapping out neural correlates of spiritual activities with the acceptance or rather the logical necessity of God acting through the physicality of the human without the need of comprising on the possibility of transcendence. Finally, we offered some future pathways for the further development of neurotheology as well as some concerns that would have to be borne in mind.

In summary, the finding of neural correlates of spiritual activity cannot act as an argument against the existence of God or to argue against a claim of transcendence just by the fact that the neural correlates are located in the brain. Neither, can we reduce spirituality to an evolutionary trait for survival. What this does point towards is the emerging view that the human person as body/mind/soul/spirit is one entity. Further, a lot of the faculties that were put on the 'soul' can be located in the brain. Does that mean there is no separate thing as the soul? While we would have to probably give up the concept of soul as separate, we need not jump to the conclusion that the death of a human being means a complete end. It does not mean that there is no after-life. For a believer all this is true. But these are from a faith perspective. Science cannot adjudicate on these matters. Science is successful because it has boundary conditions and lays out clearly which parameters are being measured or tested. And the result that one gets is within these boundary conditions. But there is so much more beyond the boundary conditions that science places on itself. Science itself will say that there exists phenomenon beyond that which science can measure or explain. In the ultimate analysis, recent developments in neuroscience have helped us to get a better understanding of the human body with its brain and the spiritual dimension of the human. It has also helped us to shoot down outrageous claims which were going beyond the science.

Endnotes

[1] Imedpub.com/neurological-science-journal/

[2] Gregory Caremans, "Neuroscience or Cognitive science?"https://brainacademy.com/blog/18223/neuroscience-or-cognitive-science.

[3] Roy J. J. Pereira, "Meditation and Beyond: Phenomena Beyond Materialism" online http://www.metanexus.net/conference2009/abstract/Default.aspx?id=10835

[4] J. L. Saver and J. Rabin, "The Neural Substrates ofReligious Experience," *The Journal of Neuropsychiatry and Clinical Neurosciences* 9 (1997): 498–510.

[5] P. Brugger et al., "Functional Hemispheric Asymmetry and Belief in ESP: Towards a Neuropsychology of Belief," *Perceptual and Motor Skills* 77 (1993), 1299–308.

[6] P. Brugger et al., "Meaningful Patterns in Visual Noise: Effects of Lateral Stimulation and the Observer's Belief in ESP," *Psychopathology* 26 (1993), 261–5.

[7] Wayne D. Norman and Malcolm A. Jeeves, "Neurotheology: Avoiding a Reinvented Phrenology,"*Perspectives on Science and Christian Faith,* 62,(4), (2010),244.

[8] P. Azari et al., "Neural Correlates of Religious Experience," *European Journal of Neuroscience* 13 (2001), 1649–52. See also N. P. Azari, "Neuroimaging Studies of Religious Experience: A Critical Review," *Where God and Science Meet,* ed. McNamara, pp. 33–54.

[9] Norman and Jeeves, "Neurotheology: Avoiding a Reinvented Phrenology," *Perspectives on Science and Christian Faith,* 62 (4), December 2010,245.

[10] Norman and Jeeves, "Neurotheology: Avoiding a Reinvented Phrenology," 244.

[11] http://www.hopkinsmedicine.org/healthlibrary/test_procedures/neurological/positron_emission_tomography_pet_scan_92,P07654/

[12] A. Sayadmansour, "Neurotheology: The relationship between brain and religion," *Iran J Neurol* 2014; 13(1), 52.

[13] A. Sayadmansour, "Neurotheology: The relationship between brain and religion," 52.

[14] R. Burton, "Neurotheology," *On Being Certain: Believing You are Right Even When You're Not,* Ed. R. Burton (New York, NY: St. Martin's Press: 2009).

[15] L. Ruttan, M.A. Persinger, & S. Koren, "Enhancement of temporal lobe-related experiences during brief exposures to milligauss intensity extremely low frequency magnetic fields,"*Journal of Bioelectricity,* 1990, 9(1), 33-54.

[16] P. Richards, M.A. Persinger, &S. A. Koren, "Modification of activation and evaluation properties of narratives by weak complex magnetic field patterns that simulate limbic burst firing,"*International Journal of Neuroscience,*71 (1993), 71-85.

[17] Lisa Trank, "God on the Brain; The God Helmet and How We Experience the Divine" https:// www.gaia.com/article/god-on-the-brain-the-god-helmet-and-how-we-experience-the-divine (August 23, 2019 with a minor correction on November 19, 2019).

[18] Michael A. Persinger, 'Religious and Mystical Experiences as Artifacts of Temporal Lobe Function: A General Hypothesis', *Perceptual and Motor Skills,* 57/3.2 (1983), 1255–1262.

[19] Isabel Clarke, "Beyond the God Spot: Transcendence and the Brain," www.isabelclarke.org/general/psychandspi_2_4232886832.pdf

[20] V. Ramachandrana, W. Hirstein, K. Narmel, E. Tecoma, and V. Iraqui, "The Neural Basis of Religious Experience" (paper presented at the annual conference of The Society of Neuroscience, New Orleans, LA, October25-30, 1997), 23.

[21] J.L. Saver, J. Rabin, "The neural substrates of religious experience," *J. Neuropsychiatr.Clin.Neurosci.*, 9 (1997),498-510. View Record in ScopusGoogle Scholar

[22] Mario Beauregard and Denyse O'Leary, *The Spiritual Brain: A Neuroscientist's Case for the Existence of the Soul*(New York: HarperOne, 2007), 68-69.

[23] Mathew Alper, *The God Part of the Brain: A Scientific Interpretation of Human Spirituality and God* (New York: Rogue, 2001).

[24] Mathew Alper's "The Premise" of *The "God" Part of the Brain: A Scientific Interpretation of Human Spirituality and God*www.godpart.com

[25] F. Tremblay, an interview with Mathew Alper, posted on July 1, 2003, www.suite.101.com/article.cfm/rational_spirituality/10114/1

[26] Norman and Jeeves, "Neurotheology: Avoiding a Reinvented Phrenology," 244.

[27] PehrGranqvist et al., "Sensed presence and mystical experiences are predicted by suggestibility, not by the application of transcranial weak complex magnetic fields," *Neuroscience Letters,*2005, 379 (1), 1-6 (https://doi.org/10.1016/j.neulet.2004.10.057).

[28] Carlos A. Tinoco & Joao P. L. Ortiz, "Magnetic Stimulation of the Temporal Cortex: A Partial 'God Helmet' Replication Study," *Journal of Consciousness Exploration & Research*5(3) (2014),234-257.

[29] Roy J. J. Pereira, "Has Science and Technology Eliminated God or Proved the Existence of God? A Look into the Findings from Neuroscience,*Science-Religion Dialogue and Its Contemporary Significance* (Bengaluru: ATC Publishers, 2018), pp. 195-207.

[30] Steve Connor, "'God Spot' is Found in Brain," *LA Times,* October 29, 1997, http://cas,bellarmine.edu/tietjen/images/new_page_2.htm

[31] *Perspectives: A Journal of Reformed Thought* 14, (2) (1999), 17, 23 (author unknown).

[32] M. Goldman, The God Gene: How Faith is Hardwired into Our Genes. *Nat Genet* 36, 1241 (2004). https://doi.org/10.1038/ng1204-1241.

[33] See, Dean Hamer, *The God Gene: How Faith is Hardwired into our Genes,* (New York: Anchor, 2005).

[34] Beauregard &O'Leary, *The Spiritual Brain,*20.

[35] Beauregard & O'Leary, *The Spiritual Brain*, 20.

[36] Barbara J. King, "Spiritually Explained? Reflections on Dean Hamer's The God Gene," *Bookslut,* June 2005.

[37] For example, in 1664 the English anatomist Thomas Willis proposed that imagination was located in the corpus callosum while sensation

and movement were situated in the corpus striatum (Thomas Willis, "Cerebrianatome:cuiaccessitnervorumdescriptio et usus," Thomas Willis: *The Anatomy of the Brain and Nerves*, ed. J. Martyn and J. Allestry, Tercentenary ed., 1664–1964 (Montreal: McGill University Press, 1965). A historical survey of brain anatomy and function can be found in Stanley Finger, *Origins of Neuroscience: A History of Explorations into Brain Function*, (Oxford: Oxford University Press), pp. 1994, 18–31.

[38] Gall accepted the labeling of the faculties from contemporary psychological teachings. Thus, relatively simple functions (as they then thought) such as vision, auditory memory, or orientation in space, were assigned to separate areas of the cortex. In addition, he localized such traits as "an instinct for the continuation of the race," a "love of parents," "sociability," "courage," "ambition," etc. There was immediate opposition to some of Gall's ideas of localization of function. The view that the brain is an aggregate of separate organs was rejected by some physiologists who supported an alternative localization theory. Previous to Gall, Albrecht von Haller (1708–1777), for example, while accepting that the brain is a single organ, had argued that it is composed of parts of equal importance. Half a century later, Pierre Flourens, in 1824 (Marie Jean Pierre Flourens, Recherchesexpérimentalessur les propriétéset les fonctions du systémenerveux, dans les animauxvertébrés, 1st ed. [Paris: J. B. Balliére, 1824]. See also Marie Jean Pierre Flourens, Recherchesexpérimentalessur les propriétéset les fonctions du systèmenerveux, dans les animauxvertébrés, 2d ed. [Paris: J. B. Ballière, 1842]) based his alternative views on the results of his physiological experiments on animals. He noted that when isolated areas of the cerebral hemispheres of birds were destroyed, the behavior of the birds was nevertheless largely preserved and that there was approximately the same degree of recovery, whichever part of the cerebral hemispheres was destroyed.

[39] Norman and Jeeves, "Neurotheology: Avoiding a Reinvented Phrenology," 236.

[40] Andrew Newberg, Eugene D'Aquili& Vince Rause, *Why God Won't Go Awy: Brain Science and Biology of Belief*(New York, NY: Random House, 2002).

[41] Mario Beauregard &Vincent Paquette, "Neural Correlates of a mystical experience in Carmelite Nuns," *Neuroscience Letters,* 405 (3): 186-90.

[42] Norman and Jeeves, "Neurotheology: Avoiding a Reinvented Phrenology," 245.

[43] Nina P. Azari et al., "Neural correlates of religious experience," *European Journal of Religious Experience,* 13,8, (2001), 1649-1652.

[44] W. Proudfoot, *Religious Experience*(Berkeley: University of California Press, 1985).Google Scholar

[45] A. Partiot, J. Grafman, N. Sadato, J. Wachs, & M. Hallett, "Brain activation during the generation of non emotional and emotional plans," *Neuroreport*, 6, (1995) 1269–1272.Crossref CAS Web of Science®Google Scholar

[46] Eugene G. d'Aquili and Andrew B. Newberg, *The Mystical Mind: Probing the Biology of Religious Experience* (Minneapolis, MN: Fortress Press, 1999).

[47] Norman and Jeeves, "Neurotheology: Avoiding a Reinvented Phrenology," 242.

[48] Michael Gazzaniga, *The Social Brain: Discovering the Networks of the* Mind (New York: Basic Books, 1985). Writing about the "inevitability of religious beliefs," Gazzaniga proposed systems of the brain that are built to interpret events around us, and systems that provide the capacity for magical thinking. In some not-so-obvious manner, unexplained happenings are processed through these systems and the result is religious belief.

[49] For additional comments on neurotheology by d'Aquili and Newberg, see "The Neuropsychological Basis of Religions, or Why God Won't Go Away," *Zygon* 33 (2) (1998),187–201; "The Neuropsychology of Aesthetic, Spiritual, and Mystical States," *Zygon* 35 (1) (2000), 39–51; "The Creative Brain/the Creative Mind," *Zygon* 35 (1) (2000), 53–68; Newberg, "Putting the Mystical Mind Together," *Zygon* 36 (3) (2001), 501–7; Newberg and Bruce Y. Lee, "The Neuroscientific Study of Religious and Spiritual Phenomena: or Why God Doesn't Use Biostatistics," *Zygon* 40 (2) (2005), 469–89; Newberg, "Religious and Spiritual Practices: A Neurochemical Perspective," *Where God and Science Meet*, ed. McNamara, 15–1.

[50] Ker Than, "No 'God Spot' in the Human Brain," in www.livescience.com/7116-god-spot-human-brain.html August 29, 2006.

[51] Beauregard & O'Leary, *The Spiritual Brain*, 272.

[52] Beauregard & O'Leary, *The Spiritual Brain*, xvi.

[53] Norman and Jeeves, "Neurotheology: Avoiding a Reinvented Phrenology," 243.

[54] For differing views on the ability of brain imaging techniques to elucidate cognitive functioning, see M. Brett, I. S.Johnsrude and A. M. Owen, "The Problem of Functional Localization in the Human Brain," *Nature Reviews: Neuroscience* 3 (2002): 243–9; David Dobbs, "Fact or Phrenology?"*Scientific American Mind* 16, (1) (2005): 24–31; David I. Donaldson, "Parsing Brain Activity with fMRI and Mixed Designs: What Kind of State Is Neuroimaging In?" Trends inNeuroscience 27 (8), (2004): 442–4; Karl Friston, "Beyond Phrenology: What Can Neuroimaging Tell Us about Distributed Circuitry?" *Annual Review of Neuroscience* 25 (2002):221–50; John-Dylan Haynes and Geraint Rees, "Decoding Mental States from Brain Activity in Humans," *Nature Reviews: Neuroscience* 7 (2006): 523–34; D. J. Heeger andD. Ress, "What Does fMRI Tell Us about Neuronal Activity?" *Nature Reviews: Neuroscience* 3 (2002): 142–51; S. M.Kosslyn,

"If Neuroimaging Is the Answer, What Is the Question?" *Philosophical Transactions of the Royal Society of London*B 354 (1999): 1283–94; N. K. Logothetis and B. A. Wandell,"Interpreting the BOLD Signal," *Annual Review of Physiology*66 (2004): 753–69; C. B. Nemeroff, C. D. Kilts, and G. S. Burns,"Functional Brain Imaging: Twenty-First Century Phrenology or Psychobiological Advance for the Millennium?"*American Journal of Psychiatry* 156, no. 5 (1999): 671–3; R. A. Poldrack and A. D. Wagner, "What Can Neuroimaging Tell Us about the Mind? Insights from the Prefrontal Cortex,"*Current Directions in Psychological Science* 13, (5) (2004):177–81; and William R. Uttal, The New Phrenology: The Limitsof Localizing Cognitive Processes in the Brain (Cambridge, MA:MIT Press, 2001).

[55] Norman and Jeeves, "Neurotheology: Avoiding a Reinvented Phrenology," 246.

[56] Norman and Jeeves, "Neurotheology: Avoiding a Reinvented Phrenology," 246.

[57] M. K. Sim, W. F. Tsoi, "The effects of centrally acting drugs on the EEG correlates of meditation," *Biofeedback Self Regul*17(3):215–20 (1992). [PubMed] [Google Scholar]

[58] Francis Crick, *Astonishing Hypothesis: The Scientific Search for the Soul* (New York, NY: Scribner, 1995), 53. [Google Scholar]

[59] A. Sayadmansour, "Neurotheology: The relationship between brain and religion."*Iran J Neurol* 2014; 13(1): 52-5

[60] Roy J. J. Pereira, "Broken Bodies, Broken Minds – A Medical Critique," Paper presented at the University of Guelph, Canada (due for publication).

[61] Roy J. J. Pereira, "Meditation and Beyond: Phenomena Beyond Materialism" online http://www.metanexus.net/conference2009/abstract/Default.aspx?id=10835

[62] R. Carter, *Exploring Consciousness* (Berkeley, CA: University of California Press), 2004. 44–7. [Google Scholar]

[63] M. King, P. Speck, A. Thomas, "The effect of spiritual beliefs on outcome from illness," *SocSci Med.* 1999;48(9):1291–9. [PubMed] [Google Scholar]

[64] L. Miller, "Chaos as the Universal Solvent" [Online] [cited 2013]; Available from: URL: http://asklepia.tripod.com/Chaosophy/chaosophy3.html

[65] A. Sayadmansour, "Neurotheology: The relationship between brain and religion," 55.

Chapter 5

Neurosciences – Religion Dialogue
Towards a New Domain of Neuro -Theology

František Mikeš and Geraldine Edith Mikes

Abstract

This paper introduces the reader to the new emerging field of Nuerotheology – reflective study of the linkage between the brain/mind and religion/theology. More specifically it studies the nexus between neural correlates of the brain and religious/spiritual systems of beliefs, experiences and practices. It points out, on the one hand, the importance of this field and, on the other hand, the unpreparedness of present and future leaders of the Church to understand and appreciate the challenges recent developments in the neurological sciences pose to traditional religions. Special emphasis is placed on the pioneering and ground-breaking empirical studies conducted by Eugene d'Aquili and Andrew Newberg. In addition to presenting some important introductory ideas about neurotheology and the related problematics, it gives a rather up-to-date highlights of the current literature on the matter. It discusses briefly the phenomenon of psychedelic substances and neurotransmitters and how the operations of these can produce behaviour patterns that are usually associated with the human soul. Specifically it discusses the actions of serotonin, psilocybin mushrooms, psilocybin, etc., all capable of producing the feeling of wellbeing in humans. At the same time, it emphasizes the fundamental metaphysical point that similarity of effects does not lead to sameness of cause. These phenomena and related experimental studies may point to correlation, not to causal relation.

Keywords: Neurotheology, Eugene d'Aquili, Andrew Newberg, psychedelic subtances, neurotransmitters, serotonin

Introduction

The first scientific summary of our understanding of "neurology and religion" was presented by psychologist William James in his Gifford lectures 1901-1902 and published under the title *The Varieties of Religious Experience.*[1] His book remains a treasured classic on the psychology of religious belief and human spiritual experiences.

The term "neurotheology" was first used in a scholarly journal by James Ashbrook in 1984 in an article "Neurotheology: The Working Brain and the Work of Theology."[2,3] He uses this term to show how theology could understand *the relationship between the Brain and God via the Mind.* "Because the mind is the significance of the brain and God is the significance of the mind, the concept of 'mind' bridges how the brain works and traditional patterns of belief."[4] Mind, as an emergent of the brain, is a medium for God as a significant entity.

Eugene d'Aquili and Andrew Newberg also began their work in neurotheology with an emphasis on 'mind' as described in their book *The Mystical Mind.*[5] Later Newberg initiated his scientific studies of the brain using neuroimaging techniques to study how prayer and meditation can affect different parts of the brain. Thus began his emphasis on brain neuro-science, rather than Ashbrook's mind-psychology, in relationship to "meta' experiences, which he defines as neurotheology.

After d'Aquili's early death in 1998 at age 58, neuroscientist Newberg continued their work with an emphasis on brain-theology.

The basics of neurotheology, as defined by Newberg, are presented in his major book *Principles of Neurotheology*[6] which includes precise neurological data.

Since then neurotheology[7] has developed with a focus on neuroscientific studies of religious/spiritual practices and experiences, and has drawn some scholars to this field. To date there is only a relatively small group of scientists involved in it because of the demand to be schooled in both branches – neurosciences, spirituality, religion or theology.[8]We believe that neurotheology is probably today the most needed branch on its own merit in the area of the Science-Religion Dialogue.

Our article will present a number of studies emphasizing the link between the brain and spiritual experiences. It will include the following: 1) A more detailed discussion of the goals of neurotheology as defined by Newberg, 2) Some current research using neuroimaging of meditating subjects, 3) Effects of psychedelic substances on neurotransmitter receptors, and the intensity of spiritual experiences versus receptor densities, 4) Transcendental experiences by sudden epileptic events in persons usually not epileptic, 5) additional significant publications related to neurotheology.

What is Neurotheology?

Newberg begins his book *Principles of Neurotheology* with this definition: "Neurotheology is a unique field of scholarship and investigation that seeks to understand the relationship specifically between the brain and theology, and more broadly between the mind and religion."[9] The reciprocity should be a two way conduit between science and religion resulting in a "megatheology."[10] Based on such a definition, this is the major advantage of neurotheology and its challenge to scholars in every religious system. Just as Evolutionary Christianity could be considered as a "new phylum" with a trajectory on a convergent vector leading to the Omega Point which is God, a similar journey could be expected in any religion which adopts evolution into its system and starts to develop its specific neurotheology.

Newberg is even suggesting that neurotheology might be able to prove God's existence. That idea is very likable but an infinite God will always remain a challenge for finite human beings to be creative and do science, in order to discover "how He is doing it." We may have better and better approximations toward his creativity, but belief in God will ultimately remain a matter of faith.

We may state that the basic approach of neurotheology is to detect and describe the *nexus of neural correlates of the brain and religious/ spiritual systems of beliefs, experiences and practices.* This means to try to understand the bridge between brain and faith, reason and mysticism, using empirical as well as subjective data. One would like to determine how and why human biology has always kept certain convictions about the existence of the Transcendent, the Divine or a spiritual realm.

Basic Goals of Neurotheology[11]
Newberg gives 3 principal goals for neurotheology:

1. Neurotheology should be a careful scientific study of contemplative practices to provide a better understanding of human consciousness and lead to a new era of advancement for the earth and its inhabitants.

2. Neurotheology should provide a better understanding of the human mind and brain, and lead to a better understanding of religion.

3. Neurotheology should encourage a global improvement in human health by providing data on positive brain and health changes resulting from spiritual practices.

Some Expected Positive Outcomes of Neurotheology[12]

1. To improve our understanding of the human mind and brain.

2. To improve our understanding of religion and theology.

3. To improve the human condition in the context of health and wellbeing.

4. To improve the human condition in the context of religion and spirituality.

Neurotheology Seminar in Our Seminary and Some Findings

As part of the course on Science-Religion Dialogue, at our university we introduced a seminar on Neuro-theology, as an attempt to include a neuroscientist and specialist in Fourier Magnetic Resonance Imaging (fMRI), Prof. Petr Hluštík, M.D. From the overall impression or response of the 13 seminarians, we concluded the following: 1) Seminarians today are not prepared for such a diversified presentation because they are still following a traditional set of theological curricula set in an old paradigm where evolutionary Christianity is not yet taught. Pierre Teilhard de Chardin's works are still on the Index at the Vatican. Pope Francis has not yet acted on a petition to waive the "monitum," warning, about his work from 1962.[13] 2) To remedy such a state, the course on Science-Religion Dialogue should be moved from optional to compulsory for seminarians.

It is also worth mentioning that among young students 16 to 29 years old, the Czech Republic has the highest number of atheists (91%)[14] in the European Union of 28 states. In addition, the negligence of dialogue between science and religion in some traditionally Christian countries has already paid a heavy price. In 9 countries with liberal democracies, and a high standard of living and education, statistical analysis shows that religion is on a trajectory to extinction. The Czech Republic is one of them.[15]

Neuroimaging Experimental Study by Newberg and d´Aquili

In some of their early work, Newberg and d'Aquili studied Tibetan monks in deep meditation and Franciscan sisters at prayer, using Single Photon Emission Computed Tomography (SPECT).[16] The meditators were imaged during a resting state, considered to be baseline wakefulness, and imaged again at their peak of meditation. The two images were compared to determine what areas had increased or decreased activity.

Increased blood flow was detected in the frontal lobes of the brain, and lowered blood flow in the parietal lobes. Part of the parietal lobes is known to be responsible for the orientation of objects in three-dimensional space. If it is denied input during deep meditation, it creates a sense of pure space, and may obliterate the distinction between self and the other.

Newberg has also conducted studies to help individuals who are experiencing memory problems. He took one group of older individuals, scanned their brains, and then taught them a mantra-based type of meditation. They were asked to practice that meditation for 12 minutes a day for eight weeks. At the end of the eight weeks, they came back for another scan, and Newberg found some dramatic differences. "We found some very significant and profound changes in their brain, particularly in the areas of the brain that help us to focus our mind and to focus our attention," he said. Many of the participants related that they were thinking more clearly and were better able to remember things after eight weeks of meditation. "They had improvements of about 10 or 15 percent," Newberg said. "This is only after eight weeks at 12 minutes a day, so you can imagine what happens in people who are deeply religious and spiritual and are doing these practices for hours a day for years and years."[17]Newberg emphasizes that while neurotheology won't provide definitive findings about things like the existence of God, it will provide a deeper understanding of what it means for a person to be religious.

Additional data from Newberg's work was published in his 2018 book *Neurotheology: How Science Can Enlighten Us about Spirituality*. It contains some of his more recent studies with other imaging techniques like PET (Positron Emission Tomography).

Neurotransmitters and Psychedelic Agents – Relationship to Neurotheology

The neurotransmitters which transmit signals between neurons should not be neglected in our discussion of brain events related to neurotheology. One very illustrative example is the neurotransmitter Serotonin which affects mood, cognition and memory processing. Higher amounts of Serotonin are associated with well-being and happiness, while lower concentrations can lead to depression. On the other hand, psychedelic chemicals like Psilocybin and LSD can affect the Serotonergic System leading to atypical experiences and perceptions. Research results on the interaction of these chemicals with Serotonin Receptors are significant, and are shown here.

Research Study 1. Eating "magic mushrooms" containing Psilocybin can initiate spiritual experiences like those experienced by shamans and might have been the *Soma* mentioned in Rigveda texts.[18] The table below shows structures of the neurotransmitter Serotonin, the psychedelic substance Psilocybin, and hallucinogen Psilocin. *In vivo*, Psilocybin is quickly converted to Psilocin which is the actual hallucinogen which binds with the Serotonin receptor.

	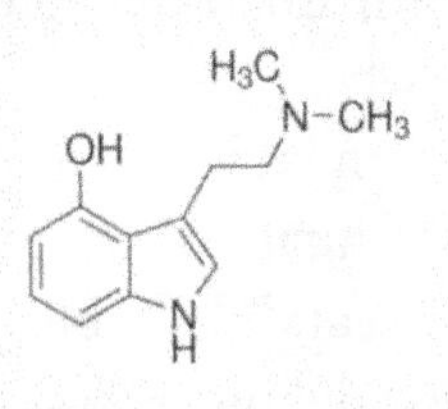	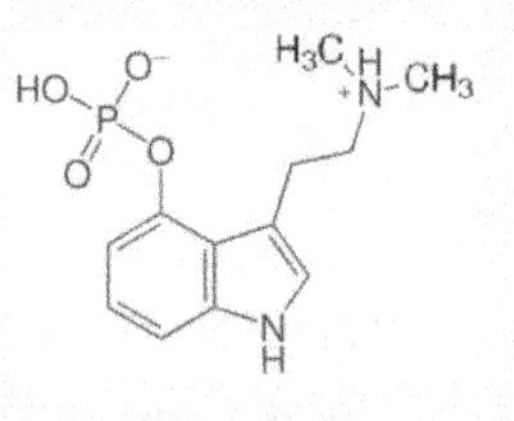
Serotonin (neurotransmitter)	**Psilocin** (hallucinogen)	**Psilocybin** (Psilocin prodrug)

To better understand how Psilocybin produces its effects on the Serotonergic System of the brain, Carhart-Harris et al. conducted a study using fMRI to determine the "Neural Correlates of the Psychedelic State" produced by Psilocybin.[19] Two groups of 15 healthy volunteers were intravenously infused with Placebo and Psilocybin, and changes in cerebral blood flow (CBF) and venous oxygenation measured. Significant changes in consciousness were seen after Psilocybin infusion, but only decreases in cerebral blood flow and blood oxygen levels. "These [decreases] were maximal in hub regions, such as the thalamus," a brain structure involved in regulation of consciousness, sleep, and alertness. "The magnitude of the decrease predicted the intensity of the subjective effects."[20] The results are remarkable since it is commonly assumed that psychedelics work by increasing neural activity while the opposite was seen in this study. This implies that the subjective effects of Psilocybin are caused by "decreased activity and connectivity in the brain's key connector hubs, enabling a state of unconstrained cognition."[21]

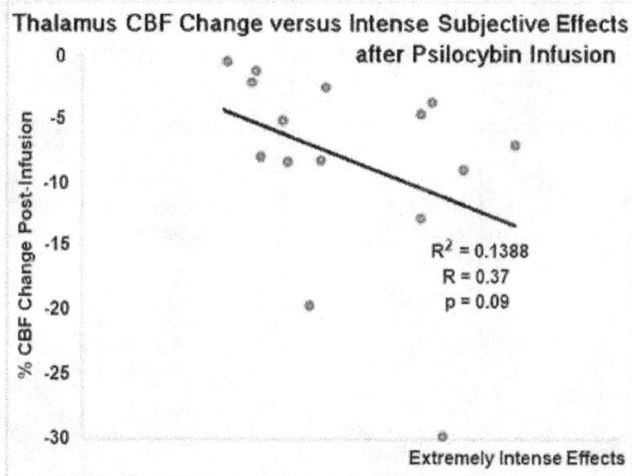

The figure above shows the intensity of psychic effects reported by subjects versus change in Cerebral Blood Flow (CBF) in the Thalamus after Psilocybin infusion. Each data point is an average of postinfusion recordings at 5 and 12 minutes from 15 subjects. A correlation is seen between greater decreases in CBF and increased psychic effects.

Research Study 2. *LSD* (Lysergic acid diethylamide) is the second psychedelic chemical of interest, based on its interaction with Serotonin receptors. Scientists have wondered how the effects of LSD could last up to a day or longer when its half-life in blood is only a half to one hour, and later is undetectable in blood while some effects continue.

An explanation for these effects is provided in a new study published in the *Cell* journal[22,23] using crystallographic studies. Researchers crystallized a complex of LSD with the Serotonin 5-HT$_{2B}$ Receptor,[24,25] and representations of the complex were obtained from X-ray data like the picture shown on the right in the table below. (LSD is partly visible, outlined in black.) It was observed that LSD became "trapped" in a pocket in the upper part of the receptor. This is partly due to LSD's diethylamide group (the upper left part of its structure shown in the middle picture below) which fits tightly in a configuration that constrains LSD. In this conformation LSD "cannot exchange readily with alternate conformational states." In addition the receptor's protein structure folds over it, forming a "lid." Notice the U-shaped loop above LSD in the representation. It was concluded that these restrictions lead to LSD's long residence time and slow kinetics.[26]

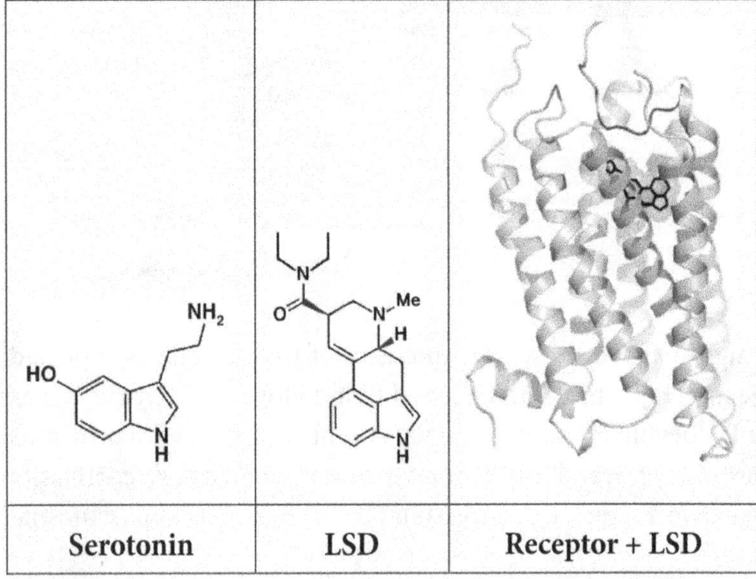

Serotonin	LSD	Receptor + LSD

Knowledge from this study with LSD should be applicable to designing new drugs which interact with Serotonin Receptors. The objective would be to formulate drugs that get trapped in neurotransmitter receptors but don't cause hallucinogenic or other adverse effects.

Research Study 3. One additional very revealing neuroimaging study was of normal subjects without a psychedelic chemical. The study showed a correlation between spiritual "sensitivity" and the density of serotonin receptors (DSR) in the human brain. Borg et al.[27] measured DSR with position emission tomography (PET) in three areas of the brain (brain stem raphe nuclei, hippocampus, and the neocortex) in 15 normal male subjects and compared the results with the subjects' self-reporting personality traits. From 10 personality traits there was a correlation of DSR with only 2 traits: 1) self-transcendence and 2) spiritual acceptance versus material rationalism. Interestingly, an inverse relationship is seen between DSR and these spiritual traits – the lower the Serotonin receptor density, the greater the spiritual traits. This correlates with the psychedelic chemicals' results mentioned previously where the psychedelics bind to the receptors, diminishing their effective density. Thus, lower effective densities of serotonin receptors, naturally or after taking psychedelics, may lead to greater spiritual experiences.

But in summarizing these neuro-biology/chemistry studies, we may still agree with Roy Pereira that the brain being the *locus* of a religious experience *does not imply* that the brain is the *cause* of a religious experience.[28]

Epilepsy and Neurotheology – How Personalities Change

A detailed and concise research paper by Saver and Rabin, "The Neural Substrates of Religious Experience,"[29] demonstrates how epilepsy can change a person's personality. The authors begin with a statement that all human experience is brain based, including religious experience, scientific approaches and reasoning, deduction in mathematics, artistic creation, and moral judgment. But from this knowledge nothing should be given lesser or higher significance, i.e., whether religious experiences point to an external reality or not. "The external reality of religious percepts is neither confirmed nor disconfirmed by establishing brain correlates of religious experience."[30] However, it has been argued that showing the existence of a neural substrate which sustains religious experiences can reinforce a belief that it is evidence for a higher power that has equipped humans with a capacity to experience the divine. Humankind has long been recognizing a direct link between epilepsy and the divine. Ancient Greeks even considered epilepsy as a sacred disease.

The authors outline some distinctive neural substrates of religious experiences and how they may alter the brain. One of the experiences involves the brain disorder epilepsy.[31] Cases are presented of selected personalities who had *ictal*[32] events, which are mainly epileptic episodes. The epileptics' experiences are compared with the religious experiences of normal individuals.

In studies using electroencephalography (EEG), the recording during a seizure is said to be *ictal* when it refers to a physiologic state or event such as a seizure, stroke, or headache. Ictal events may become the subject of some type of religious, e.g. , cosmogonical, explanation. "Seizures are paroxysmal, unexpected – sudden intrusion of unanticipated and often extraordinary experience into the ordinary daily flow of consciousness."[33]

From the available data, the authors conclude that "the hippocampus and especially the amygdala are likely the critical generators of a feeling of unreality about self or external reality."[34] After a detailed search, they compiled a table where "a substantial number of founders of major religions, prophets, and leading religious figures have been documented as having or been suggested to have epilepsy."[35] They prepared a table[36] containing 15 such personalities with five descriptors for each person. A simplified table of 7 of those religious or other historical personalities is given below.

TABLE 1

Person	Spell Description	Possible Epilepsy	Diagnosis	Religious Aspects
St. Paul (7-65)	Conversion on road to Damascus, bright light, falling to ground, hearing Jesus, 3 days blind	+	Complex partial seizure (CPS)	Apostle of the Church ecstatic aura
Muhammad (570-632)	Visual and auditory hallucinations, falling, profuse sweating	+	Complex partial seizures	Islamic prophet
St. Joan of Arc (1412-1431)	Hearing voices, great light	+	Ecstatic partial seizure	Catholic saint
St. Teresa of Avila (1515-1582)	Visions, chronic headaches, tongue biting, Loss of Consciousness	++	Complex partial seizure, hysteria	Catholic saint
Dostoievsky (1921-1981)	Seizure with frothing at mouth, a fall, sense of bliss	+++	Complex partial seizure, hysteria	Russian novelist

Vincent Van Gogh (1853-1890)	Sense of vertigo, delirium	+	Complex partial seizure	Renowned painter
St. Terese of Lisieux (1873-1897)	Visual hallucinations, wounded by shaft of fire	++	Complex partial seizure	Catholic saint, Doctor of Church

In a second table,[37] partly duplicated below, Saver & Rabin summarized some characteristics that distinguish mystical and psychotic states. Many epileptic effects may be characterized as mystical.

TABLE 2

Feature	Mystical State	Psychotic State
Hallucinations	Often visual*; typically elderly*, wise counselors	Predominantly auditory; often accusatory
Vocabulary	Religiously imbued word choice, generally harmonious connotations*: God*, Christ, soul, peace, spirit	Frequent themes of illness and deviance
Personal role	Individual as self-negating vessel for higher power*	Personal grandiosity and omnipotence
Affect	Ecstatic*, joyful*	Indifferent or terrified
Duration of state	Transient, usually hours*, resolves completely*	May persist for months or years and leave residual delusions, reduced social function

Withdrawal	Facultative: eventual return to share experience of psychotic state with others***	Obligatory: progressive isolation
Disordered speech output	Glossolalia (speaking in tongues): output language is unknown and incomprehensible to speaker; fluency retained	Thought disorder: output may contain neologisms and bizarre associations, but is predominantly in known language; thought blocking may occur
Cultural compatibility	Beliefs are recognized as valid by others in the person's culture* or subculture	Beliefs are rejected by others in the patient's culture or subculture

* Stars in the Mystical State column mark some characteristics of former Czech atheist Prof. Miloslav Král during or following two epileptic events that changed him to a believing scientist/Christian. (See next section.)

Epilepsy and Personality Change – A Contemporary Example

It's worth demonstrating here a case where only two epileptic events (each lasting a few hours), spaced 9 years apart, by an academic in his 60th and 69th years (1990, 1999), can reverse a man's personality. Visions during these events lead to a 180 degree turn, a restructuring, from his atheistic system to a theistic evolutionary one with a dictum that God certainly exists. That was also the title of the book *God Demonstrably Exists*[38] by Czech Assoc. Prof. Miloslav Král (1931-2017).

Under the totalitarian regime of former Czechoslovakia (today Czech Republic), Král had been one of the best known knowledgeable atheists, teaching cybernetics and the theory of science with a privilege to access all forbidden literature. Then in 1968 during the occupation of Czechoslovakia by the former Soviet Union, his privilege ended due to his support of the Prague Spring to change the dictatorship into "socialism with a human face." Only after the Velvet Revolution in November 1989, when the communist dictatorship was removed, Král was taken back to the Academy of Sciences and could again teach, still as an atheist.

It was then after retirement and his second epileptic event at age 69 that he had a total change of view from being an atheist to a believer in God. He is calling this event by various names, e.g., a *spontaneous entry into unconsciousness*, where he met divinity, God, and received "knowledge" about himself and the universe. He was given forgiveness and "a mission" to spread such grace to his family and other people. His atheistic system became reformatted to a theistic one. In the period from 1999 to 2015, he published 7 books where he suitably combined natural sciences, cybernetics, and Jungian psychology. His message was to inform readers that God's existence is necessary and science is the domain proving it. To illustrate his firm diction and pleasant personality, one may watch online a brief video (2:18 min) of his message in Czech, and read an English translation below it. Summaries of his books in English are available on the same website.[39]

Neurotheology from a Theological Perspective – Some Additional Publications

In this connection we should mention the proceedings of a conference on the theme *Neuroscience and the Person – Scientific Perspectives on Divine Action* as a significant resource. The conference was organized in 1999 by the Vatican Observatory in Castel Gandolfo, Rome, in cooperation with the CTNS (Center for the Natural Sciences and Theology) in Berkeley, CA. The proceedings are published in a hefty volume of almost 500 pages, including 21 research papers by 18 scholars.[40] The contributions explore the creative interaction among the cognitive neurosciences, philosophy, and theology. The content presents neuroscientific research done in the last decades of the 20th century related to scripture/biblical and theological accounts of human nature. Participants tried to bridge neurosciences and philosophy, neurosciences and Christian anthropology, questioning whether theism is fundamental to human nature.

A second selected reference is a chapter dedicated to neurosciences in relation to theology in a book by Ian G. Barbour, *Nature, Human Nature, and God*.[41] What is unique in this chapter is Barbour's bold reminder to all believing scientists and theologians working in the domain of dialogue between science and theology that one of their tasks is to encourage reformulation of certain doctrines which contradict scientific knowledge (e.g.,doctrines of creation, human nature). In this spirit, he proposed a *Theology of Nature*[42] formulated as a critical reflection within a tradition, based on historical revelation and religious experience, in which theological beliefs concerning nature are re-defined in light of contemporary science.[43]

Concluding Remarks

If one still questions "Why Neurotheology?" we might reply with a quote from the introduction to *The Mystical Mind* : "It may be absolutely necessary to employ the study of the mind and brain in order to understand fully the relationship between human beings and God. This being the case, it seems that the concept of neurotheology may be crucial to our understanding of the theologies of religions in general and essential to our understanding of any possible metatheology."[44]

Newberg states that "a metatheology can be understood as an attempt to evaluate the overall principles underlying any and all religious or ultimate belief systems and their theologies."[45]His research with d'Aquili is an attempt "to allow the scientific and spiritual perspectives of reality to enhance, rather than diminish, each other" with a confirmation that "this approach can be accessible to those of virtually any religious tradition as well as of those of science."[46] He expresses his optimism and vision, saying: "It is our profound hope that this approach will provide a framework for people of virtually every perspective to feel secure about their beliefs and about science so that we can enter into a constructive dialogue about the neurological interface between science and religion."[47]He adds that "it is at this interface that we think we have the best chance of integrating science and religion."[48] Based on this, we may consider the neurotheology developed to date as a *scaffolding structure*, expecting that each religious tradition will fill in and develop its own proper neurotheology/metatheology. As an example, one could mention a paper by an Islamic scholar Alireza Sayadmansour. He sees in neurotheology "many potentially rich areas to consider in the context of Islam."[49] The recent participation of dozens of Iranian scholars at the "International Congress on Science and/or Religion: a 21st Century Debate" at the new Sigmund Freud University in Vienna in August 2015, was encouraging.

Neurotheology and the Need for a New Model of God

In neurotheology we need to distinguish between two types of theology – the traditional and emergentist one. The former is looking backwards postulating God as the cause of all things, the latter postulates Him as the goal toward which all things are leading. The latter allows for emergence. The laws which science studies are not deterministic but stochastic or probabilistic. Although regularities still exist, the outcomes are not determined in advance. More complex states emerge in the course of evolution because God has inserted or set in motion a process of ongoing creativity.[50] We may agree with Gordon D. Kaufman that God is Creativity.[51] Homo sapiens is then a new emergence, or mode of action of divine transcendence with body, *mind* and will. The rules of emergence are then features of God's immanence. And we have emerged and become created co-creators.[52]

Some Possible Areas of Neurotheology to Be Developed

We suggest some future areas of interest for neurotheology, if it is to function as a scaffold.

1. One open space in the phenomenon of neurotheology seems to be an absence of reference to Pierre Teilhard de Chardin's *Law of Complexity–Consciousness*[53] in relationship to the brain, mind and transcendence (an emergent property of God's immanence), including his concept of the *noosphere*.

2. Another open area is chemical, in neuropsycho-pharmacology, i.e., an area of research for discovery of new drugs which may modulate our behavior and perhaps intelligence. Neurotheology could be a decisive voice to utilize novel drugs *properly*.

3. A further area is to extend the endo-neural domain of our brain into the exo-neural domain. The fast development of nanotechnologies, artificial intelligence, robotics, prosthetic devices, internet, and other media fields is already beginning to provide more and more extrasomatic parts for our brain, leading to transhumanism and cyborgs. Thus neurotheology will open gates to many other scientists, and become the *integrated domain* which Barbour presented as the most ambitious 4th type in his four-fold typology of science-religion relationship.[54,55] Every religion then could develop its own transhumanism, in our case a Christian one, as discussed by Ilia Delio.[56] Her challenge to transhumanism - *to remain "informed by love"* - may also be addressed to neurotheology.[57]

Endnotes

[1] See William James, *The Varieties of Religious Experience: A Study in Human Nature* (London: Collins, Fontana Library, 6th Impression, 1974). Downloadable at: https://csrs.nd.edu/assets/59930/williams_1902.pdf [accessed May 7, 2018].

[2] James B. Ashbrook, "Neurotheology: The Working Brain and the Work of Theology," *Zygon* 19/3 (1984) 331-350. [Ashbrook 1925-~2000, exact date of his death not found.]

[3] The term might have been taken from author Aldous Huxley who coined this term in his utopian novel *Island* (London: Chatto & Windus, 1962) 139.

[4] Ashbrook, p. 331.

[5] See Eugene d'Aquili, Andrew B. Newberg, *The Mystical Mind* (Minneapolis, MN: Fortress Press, 1999).

[6] See Andrew B. Newberg, *Principles of Neurotheology* (Burlington, VT, USA: Ashgate Publishing Co., 2010). (Newberg is Director of Research at the Myrna Brind Center for Integrative Medicine at Thomas Jefferson University Hospital in Philadelphia, and Assoc. Prof. in the Dept. of Radiology and Psychiatry at the University of Pennsylvania, where he also teaches in the Dept. of Religious Studies.)

[7] Neurotheology is a neologism that describes the scientific study of the neural correlates of religious or spiritual beliefs, experiences and practices. Other researchers prefer to use terms like "spiritual neuroscience" or "neuroscience of religion."

[8] Theology, in contradistinction to religion or spirituality, is concerned with analysis of a given religious doctrine or belief system.

[9] Newberg, p. 1.

[10] Newberg, p. 66. (Megatheology = Theology acceptable to all religions, e.g. based on two universal elements: religion and human brain.)

[11] Newberg, pp. 18-19.

[12] Newberg, p. 18.

[13] Heidi Schlumpf, "Time to Rehabilitate Teilhard de Chardin?" *National Catholic Reporter*, Jan 26-Feb 8, 2018. https://www.ncronline.org/news/people/time-rehabilitate-teilhard-de-chardin [accessed April 12, 2018]

[14] Harriet Sherwood, "'Christianity as Default is Gone': the Rise of a Non-Christian Europe," *The Guardian*, March 21, 2018. https://www.theguardian.com/world/2018/mar/21/christianity-non-christian-europe-young-people-survey-religion?CMP=twt_gu [accessed April 28, 2018]

[15] Daniel M. Abrams, Haley A. Yaple and Richard Wiener, "Dynamics of Social Group Competition: Modeling of the Decline of Religious Affiliation," *Physical Review Letters* 107 (2011) 088701-1 to 088701-4. The other countries are: Australia, Austria, Canada, Finland, Ireland, the Nederlands, New Zealand and Switzerland.

[16] Andrew B. Newberg et al., "The Measurement of Regional Cerebral Blood Flow during the Complex Cognitive Task of Meditation: a Preliminary SPECT Study," *Psychiatry Res*, 106/2 (2001) 113-122. https://repository.upenn.edu/cgi/viewcontent.cgi?article=1024&context=neuroethics_pubs [accessed May 7, 2018]

[17] http://www.wbur.org/npr/132078267/neurotheology-where-religion-and-science-collide [accessed May 7, 2018]

[18] R. Gordon Wasson, *Soma: Divine Mushroom of Immortality* (New York: Harcourt Brace Jovanovich, 1968).

[19] Robin L. Carhart-Harris et al., "Neural Correlates of the Psychedelic State as Determined by fMRI Studies with Psilocybin," *PNAS* 109 (2012) 2138-2143. http://www.pnas.org/content/109/6/2138?etoc="%3B [accessed May 10, 2018]

[20] Ibid., p. 2138

[21] Ibid.

[22] Daniel Wacker et al., "Crystal Structure of an LSD-Bound Human Serotonin Receptor," *Cell* 168 (2017) 377–389. https://www.cell.com/cell/fulltext/S0092-8674(16)31749-4 [accessed May 10, 2018]

[23] Claire Maldarelli, "LSD Literally gets Stuck inside your Brain," *Popular Science*, January 26, 2017. https://www.popsci.com/lsd-gets-stuck-in-brains-receptors-serotonin [accessed May 10, 2018]

[24] 5-HT = 5-Hydroxy-tryptamine = Serotonin.

[25] The serotonin $5\text{-HT}_{2B}\text{R}$ receptor is a protein with 481 amino acids imbedded in neuron membranes in the brain. Like other receptors, this protein receptor is organized into 7 alpha helix transmembrane domains, where each helix has a right-handed spiral conformation. In this study with LSD, the serotonin receptor was an "engineered construct", separate from a neuron membrane, prepared by DNA synthesis.

[26] Wacker, p. 386.

[27] Jacqueline Borg et al., "The Serotonin System and Spiritual Experiences," *American Journal of Psychiatry* 160/11 (2003) 1965-1969.

[28] Roy J. Pereira, "Has Science and Technology Eliminated God or Proved the Existence of God? A Look into the Findings from Neuroscience," in *Science-Religion Dialogue and Its Contemporary Significance*, Binoy Pichalakkattu, ed. (Bengaluru: ATC Publishers, 2018).

[29] Jeffrey L. Saver, M.D. and John Rabin, M.D., "The Neural Substrates of Religious Experience," *Journal of Neuropsychiatry* 9/3 (1997) 498-510.

[30] Saver and Rabin, p. 498.

[31] Epilepsy is a neurological disorder in which neurocells are "disturbed" and that causes a seizure. During that episode the person passes through abnormal behavior, including various symptoms and feelings, sometimes loss of consciousness, cramps, loss of vision, etc.

[32] *Ictal* from the Latin *ictus*, meaning a blow or a stroke.

[33] Saver and Rabin, p. 500.

[34] Ibid.

[35] Ibid.

[36] Saver and Rabin, pp. 501-502.

[37] Saver and Rabin, p. 503.

[38] See Miloslav Král, *God Demonstrably Exists – Why I am not an Atheist, a New Adventure about Spirituality of the Cosmos* (in Czech: Buh dokazatelne existuje…), (Zlin-Priluky: Karpoz CZ, spol. s.r.o., 2013) 296 pp.

[39] Miloslav Král, videorecording and book summaries: http://www.vedaavira.cz/english/index.aspx?p=4 (Note: Adobe Flashplayer is needed to watch the video.) [accessed May 10, 2018]

[40] See R.J. Russell, N. Murphy, T.C. Meyerling, M.A. Arbib (eds.), *Neuroscience and the Person – Scientific Perspectives on Divine Action* (Rome: Vatican Observatory and Berkeley: Center for Theology and the Natural Sciences, 2002).

[41] See Ian G. Barbour, *Nature, Human Nature, and God* (Minneapolis: Fortress Press, 2002). Especially Part 3 on Evolution (pp. 39-70) and Part 4 on Neuroscience (pp. 71-100).

[42] In contradistinction to Natural Theology where the existence of God can be inferred, or is supported, by evidence of design in nature, of which science has made us more aware.

[43] Ian G. Barbour, *Religion and Science: Historical and Contemporary Issues* (New York: Harper Collins, rev. ed., 1997) 360.

[44] D'Aquili and Newberg, p. 16.

[45] Newberg, *Principles of Neurotheology*, p. 64.

[46] Andrew Newberg, "Putting the Mystical Mind Together," *Zygon* 36/3 (2001) 506.

[47] Ibid.

[48] Ibid.

[49] Alireza Sayadmansour, "Neurotheology: The relationship between Brain and Religion," *Iran J. Neurol.* 13/1 (2014) 52-55.

[50] Philip Clayton, "Emerging God: Theology for a Complex Universe", *Christian Century*, Jan 13, 2004.https://www.christiancentury.org/article/2004-01/emerging-god[accessed May 22,2018]

[51] See Gordon D. Kaufman, *In the Beginning… Creativity*(Minneapolis, MN: Fortress Press, 2004).

[52] Philip Hefner, *The Human Factor: Evolution, Culture and Religion* (Minneapolis, MN: Fortress Press, 1993) 35-39.

[53] See Pierre Teilhard de Chardin, *The Phenomenon of Man* (New York: Harper & Row, 1975) 60-61, 301. (Teilhard was a major founding figure in the science-religion domain, as a theologian, mystic, and paleontologist–geologist.)

[54] See Ian Barbour, *Religion in an Age of Science* (New York: HarperCollins, 1990) 3-30.

[55] Felix Maria Davídek (1921-1988), founder of a clandestine theological faculty in Czechoslovakia, said already in 1965 during its opening seminar that one of the major tasks 'here and now' in Christianity is the need for "integration of natural sciences and theology."

[56] Ilia Delio, *Making All Things New: Catholicity, Cosmology, Consciousness* (Maryknoll, N.Y.: Orbis Books, 2015) 101-107.

[57] Jason Mast, "Ilia Warns Against Tranhumanism Not Informed by Love, Spiritual Guidance," *Chautauquan Daily*, August 15, 2016. http://chqdaily. com/2016/08/sr-ilia-delio-warns-against-transhumanism-not-informed-by-love-spiritual-guidance/ [accessed May 10, 2018]

Chapter 6

Does the Brain Make God?
A Philosophical Analysis

Chacko Nadakavely

Abstract

This paper is a critical examination of the different neuro-scientific approaches to religious experience. It intends to unravel the complex relationship between spiritual experience and the bio-chemical activities of the brain. Unlike the sociological and psychological analysis of mystical experience, it has a number of observable neural correlates. Therefore, it is argued in this paper that religious experience is biologically observable and scientifically real. The naturalistic approaches to the philosophy of mind claim that the vast micro-system of interconnected brain cells executes all the human mental features like sensing, thinking, and experiencing, etc. The religious experience is no exception and hence it results from the pure physical states and process in the brain. However, the sheer materialistic explanation of human cognitive phenomena encounters serious troubles in explaining the unique human mental features in cognition, semantics, intentionality, qualia, etc. Therefore, the paper argues that the neural correlates of religious experience revealed by the praiseworthy success of contemporary neuroscience needs to extend beyond the world of the material to the mental and to the spiritual as well.

Keywords: Neurochemicals, qualia, God-Spot, God-Gene, God-Module, physicalism.

Introduction

Neuroscience and Religion is one of the emerging disciplines in philosophy of mind that intends to unravel the complex relationship between religious experience and the brain. The studies in neuroscience reveal that the spiritual mystical experiences are not mere"wishful thinking" or "opium" to cop up with the harsh existential realities of the brute natural or unjust social structures. Rather they are associated with a number of observable neurological events. In other words,religious experience is biologically observable and scientifically real. Many experiments conducted in this field show that the contemplative practices strengthen a specific neurological circuit that generates peacefulness, social awareness, and compassion for others. It means that there are neural correlates of religious experience.[1] As a result, many contemporary neurobiologists, like Henry Newberg, claim that "if God does indeed exist, the only place He can manifest His existence would be in the tangled neural pathways and physiological structures of the brain."[2]

In this article I critically examine the different *neuro-scientific* approaches to the *religious experience.* The naturalistic approach claims that the vast micro-system of interconnected brain cells executes all the human mental features like sensing, thinking, and experiencing, etc. The religious experience is of no exception and hence it is pure physical states and process in the brain. This materialistic reduction of mystical experiences is best expressed in the words of Daniel Dennett, "There is only one sort of stuff, namely matter – the physical stuff of physics, chemistry, and physiology – and the mind is somehow nothing but a physical phenomenon."[3]However in a purely materialistic explanation human cognitive phenomena encounter serious trouble in explaining mental phenomena, like semantics, intentionality and the first person experience of human cognition which is very central to religious experience. "Neurology cannot explain how such a thing can happen – how a nonmaterial mind can rise from mere biological functions; how the flesh and blood machinery of the brain can suddenly become aware," says Andrew Newberg.[4] Therefore the neural correlates of religious experience revealed by the praiseworthy success of contemporary neuroscience needs to extend beyond the world of the material to the mental and spiritual as well.

The Biology of (Religious) Experience

The new scientific studies show the neural correlates of all cognitive experiences of the brain. Most of the human brain is located in the cerebral cortex, where all high-order cognitive functions occur. The neo-cortex, the most recently evolved region of the cortex provides the unique human and decisive phenomena of art, myth, language and culture.[5] The cerebral cortex is divided into the left and right hemispheres, and each hemisphere is further divided into four large structures known as lobes. *The temporal lobe*, located along the sides of the head is associated with language and conceptual thinking. *The Parietal lobe* which is beneath the crown of the skull is home to sensory perception, visual-spatial tasks and body orientation. *The frontal lobe*, situated directly behind the forehead, is associated with attention and initiating muscle activity.[6] The limbic lobe is responsible for the regulation of emotions, memory and some aspects of movements[7]. The key parts of the limbic system are (1) *hypothalamus*, a sort of central thermostat that regulates the body functions like blood pressure and breathing, (2) *amygdala*, located behind the hypothalamus, mediates the emotions related to safety and (3) *hippocampus*, located inside the temporal lobe, is involved in the memory and spatial navigation.[8] Studies have indicated that the limbic system is integral to the religious and spiritual experiences.

The basic functional unit of brain is called neuron. When they are arranged into intricately woven chains they form the neural pathways (nerve system) that carry sensory impulses to the brain. Sensory data in the form of the electrochemical energy, gathered by countless sensors in the senses, enters into the brain thorough the neural pathways. Inside the brain, this sensory information is processed in the appropriate lob that finally produces a meaningful and useful experience in mind. Hence, the highly complex cortical structures together with sensory input and neural pathways (nerves system) give human mind its cognitive content.[9]

Mind, Mystical Experience and Neurology

With the explosive growth in neuroscience in the last fifty years, today many believe that all vital functions of the human mind, including religious phenomenon, as neurobiological happenings. In the following pages we shall discuss some of such naturalistic explanations of religious experience.

Matthew Alper and the "God Part" of the Brain

Matthew Alper is a history teacher and screenwriter from New York City and had done his research with the aim of solving the problem of God scientifically.[10] In his book, *The God Part of the Brain* he gathered research data from neurobiology and evolutionary psychology and argued that we are innately hardwired to perceive a spiritual reality and to believe in forces that transcend the limitations of our physical realm. The term hardwired according to him means that God is not "out there," as an independent true reality, but rather "a product" of human evolutionary adaptation within our brain.[11] According to Alper, the shared characteristics of individuals in a species are genetically inherited. Religious belief is so pervasive that it also must be a genetically inherited instinct.[12] What caused the emergence of this instinct is the anxiety of death and human desire for survival. "As generations of … proto-humans passed, those whose cerebral constitutions most effectively dealt with the anxiety resulting from their awareness of death were most apt to survive." This process continued until a cognitive function emerged that altered the way the humans perceived reality by adding a "spiritual" component to their perspectives. Just as the human brain had evolved linguistic, musical, and mathematical intelligence, we apparently evolved a spiritual intelligence ("a kind of prayer-responsive mechanisms in the brain") as well.[13] Finally Alper believes that one day scientists will discover this "God Part" in which "we will have knowledge of precisely which genes are responsible or those parts of the brain that give rise to religiosity and spiritual consciousness."[14]

The above-mentioned argument of Alper's neurobiological reduction of religious experience has several scientific and philosophical flaws. First of all, there is no real scientific proof for the necessary correlation between certain widely seen cultural behavior and genetic inheritance. The most celebrated cultural practices that many communities had before a few centuries are not even there now. We do not even know the cultural suppositions of our forefathers. Therefore we cannot really say that religious phenomenon is genetically inherited .Alper's another assumption that religious belief is born out of human awareness of death and anxiety also lacks evidence. It is a sheer naturalistic view of religious belief that all serious believers of all religions will object. Finally, to look for a "God Gene" in the brain is simply misguiding. What we can *actually* inherit is the capacity for abstract ideas. However, the search for the specific inherited mechanism or process of such experience is misleading as we cannot specifically locate particular space as responsible for those experiences.[15] Hence, Alper's naturalistic reduction of religious experience appears to be non-scientific as his assumption does not pass the crucial testability criteria.

Dean Hamer and the "God-Gene"

Dean Hamer is the chief of gene structure at US National Cancer Institute. He claims that he has indeed found God in our brain and specifically in our genes. It means that he has identified a specific gene that codes for the production of neurotransmitters that administer our moods.[16] This would imply that "most profound feelings of spirituality is nothing "more than an occasional shot of intoxicating brain chemicals governed by our DNA."[17] In Hamer's own words, "we're a bunch of chemical reactions running around in a bag" and religious experience is simply a firing of a strange gene. With the help of Temperament and Character Inventory (TCI) personality test administered to 1000 volunteers, Hamer demonstrated our ability to have "the self-transcendence" or spiritual experience. According to Hamer, "the self-transcendence" is an adaptive trait that we inherit, and helps survival and fertility. It has the ability to see everything in its totality and to adjust to the situation.

Dean Hamer explained his theory with the help of twin studies. According to the first study conducted in the volunteers, he concluded that the phenomenon of self-transcendence is nothing but a chemical reaction. For this, he studied nine genes that promote the production of brain chemicals called monoamines. It includes dopamine, adrenaline, serotonin, etc. These chemicals are responsible for the regulation of moods and motivation. A variation in a gene called "VMAT2[18] (vesicular monoamine transporter) was higher in the case of those volunteers who tested for self-transcendence. From this he concluded that "VMAT 2 is the "God- Gene responsible for "self-transcendence.[19] The second study was conducted on identical twins. According to his findings, the children do not learn spirituality from somebody or from some culture or society. Even though all the influences are shared equally by the identical and fraternal twins who are raised together, they show dissimilarities in the extent to which they correlate self-transcendence.[20] Hence self-transcendence is an inherited trait caused by VMAT 2, the "God Gene."

The theory of Hamer is not aimed at disqualifying any religious doctrine or traditional beliefs but rather it accounts for the variation in cytosine and adenine which determines lower or higher experiences in human being. Hence his findings are limited to the mere variation that can take place in any experience of certain intensity because even in the exhibition of a minor human trait, there is interplay of hundreds or thousands of genes.[21] From this it is improper to conclude that VMAT2 is a "God Gene" responsible for religious experience. Moreover Hamer's assumption of the "God Gene" lacks scientific evidence. There are difficulties in reproducing such findings. As science writer Carl Zimmer criticizes VMAT2 assumption and says it can be better titled as, "A Gene That Accounts for Less Than One Percent of the Variance Found in Scores on Psychological Questionnaires Designed to Measure a Factor Called Self-Transcendence, Which can Signify Everything from Belonging to the Green Party to Believing in ESP, According to One Unpublished Unreplicated Study."[22] Thus, Hamer's theory died a death of minimal evidence. The siblings and twin studies are also less convincing. Even though siblings are identical and share the same house, they need not have the same *life experience*. As anthropologist Barbara J. King says, "Perhaps one sister merely encounters a certain inspirational teacher or well-loved book that the other does not. Non-shared experiences like these heap constancy upon contingency as each girl develops. In the end, the two sisters may essentially grow up in divergent emotional environments – and as a result make very different choices about the role of spirituality in their lives."[23]

Saver and Rabin's God Module

Neurologists Jeffery Saver and John Rabin claimed that the limbic system of the brain – a system that lies within reach of the temporal lobes and functions as a medium for emotions – plays a pivotal role in the religious or mystical experiences (RSME).[24] Epilepsy is caused by the neural disorder in the limbic region of the brain. It is a brief disturbance in the normal brain functions. Mystical experiences indicate a "pursuit of an altered state of consciousness that enables the mystic to become aware of cosmic realities that cannot be grasped during normal states of consciousness." From this, Saver and Rabin also argue that RSME is so also a sort of brain disorder. It is a *divine madness* that triggers a kind of "God Module." In their view great religious leaders are "Temporal-lobe personality" and showed the symptoms of Temporal-lobe Epilepsy (TLE).[25]

I think the comparison between TLE and RSMEs is shallow and unwarranted. First of all, TLE is not a meaningful interpretation of intense religious mystical experience. Secondly, there is no sufficient correlation between epilepsy and religious experience. Can one show all RSMEs are TLE? For instance, St. Paul who had the experience of a vision on the road to Damascus was interpreted as an epileptic. The materialists consider his experience as heat prostration, aggravated by a sense of guilt over his persecution. However, there is no historical data to support this claim. Or to call the great religious leaders like Gandhi as "temporal lobe personality" is too naïve.[26]In short, Saver and Rabin's necessary association between TLE and RSME are scientifically and logically faulty. As Devinsky noted, "the genesis of intense religious experiences associated with neurological disorders remains poorly defined."[27]

A Critical Analysis of the Neurology and Religious Experience
The above neurological interpretation of religious experience is in principle reductionist. They all claim that religious experience can be reduced to neuro-biological activities of the brain. This neural reduction is based on the modern neuro-scientific studies of the brain. For instance, neuroscientists like, Drs. D'Aquili and Newberg have specifically studied the brain activation during mystical experiences. The experiments conducted by Newberg on Tibetan Buddhist monks and Franciscan nuns with the help of SPECT scan unraveled scientific insights into the mysterious working of the human brain during mystical experience. They showed the exact location and the specific brain process during spiritual and mystical experience. In the Tibetan monks there was an increased activity in the frontal lobe where the focusing of attention takes place. At the same time, the amygdale, the neural seat of anxiety and fear, became inactive. The monks were in a calm, serene and unstressed state.[28] They found broadly the similar neurological results in the Franciscan nuns also.[29]

It is true that today neurology can tell us the neural bases of religious experience to a greater extent. But this neural correlation of religious experiences and the identification of their locations do not mean that those experiences can be reduced to workings of those parts of the brain.[30] In other words, neural correlation of religious experience does not mean neural causation, because every human brain assembles its perceptions of God in uniquely different ways, giving different understanding, values and meaning to God. Each mystical experience is person-specific. This person-specificity of religious experience is the backbone of the diversity of religious experience. It indicates a vital intuition that religious experience cannot be reduced to mere bio-neural activities of the brain. Even Newberg himself acknowledges this when he says, "It has always been our hope that our work will advance the exploration of the intersection of science and religion in a way that allows each perspective to enhance, rather than diminish, the other."[31]

Moreover, neurology is in grave difficulty to explain human religious experience in mere materialistic terms. Even the defenders of physicalism would agree that there is an 'inner' intensive aspect to our experience like, 'being loved by God, 'being forgiven by God, etc. This inner qualitative nature of that mystical experience revealed in introspection cannot be explained by or reduced to mere bio-chemical reaction in the limbic system of the brain. For instance, 'my feeling of being fervently loved by God' is not merely a matter of stimulation of the corresponding temporal lobe neuro-cells causing the feeling of a physical transcendence. Hence religious experience has an intrinsic inner qualitative character, which cannot be explained by mere materialistic theories of brain.

Finally human acts, including religious experience are not mere neurological activities. They have intentional and moral dimensions. For instance, my deep mystical experience is often not caused by my genetically inherited trait, or by my evolutionary adaptations but by my passionate desire for an intense spiritual union with the Ultimate Reality. Similarly my biological drive to satisfy my sexual desires can be pacified and refined by my religious and moral convictions (normative facts). Neurologist ontology cannot satisfactorily answer the intentional and moral dimensions of human behaviour. The explanatory power of materialism is hence limited with regard to this point. If phenomena like intentionality and moral consciousness cannot be adequately explained by mere reference to neuro-chemical entities of the brain alone, then there is good reason to assume that the human mind stuff consists of more than just material entities.

Conclusion

Religious experience is an important facet of what it is to be human. Neuroscience has helped us to realize the various correlations between spiritual experience and the limbic neural structures of the brain. It might enable us to better understand the nature of these experiences and how the brain interprets and incorporates such experiences into belief systems. The neurologist reductive approach not only aims to show the neural correlates of spiritual experience but wants to eliminate spirituality entirely by arguing that these experiences are entirely caused by the neurological apparatus of the brain. But as I have argued above, it is totally an unjustified leap from correlation to causation. I firmly believe that we need the physical to appreciate the spiritual without imposing limits on the spiritual. And this paper is not an attempt to disprove the neurological aspect of religious experience, but to show that there is more to human existence than sheer material existence.

General Conclusion

The research indicates that our only way of comprehending God, asking questions about God, and experiencing God is through the brain. But whether or not, God exists "out there" is something that neuroscience cannot answer. The evidences compel us to believe that if God does indeed exist, the only place He can manifest His existence would be in the tangled neural pathways and physiological structures of brain. Religious and spiritual experiences are typically highly complex, involving emotions, thoughts, sensations, and behaviors. These experiences seem far too rich and diverse to derive solely from one part of the brain. It is much more likely that many parts of the brain are involved. The temporal lobes are clearly important in religious and spiritual experiences. The amygdala and hippocampus have been shown to be particularly involved in the experience of visions, profound experiences, memory, and meditation. The main reason God won't go away is because our brains won't allow God to leave. Our brains are set up in such a way that God and religion become among the most powerful tools for helping the brain do its thing: self-maintenance and self-transcendence. Unless there is a fundamental change in how our brain works, God will be around for a very long time. [32]

There are unwarranted generalizations on matters of philosophy and theology which various thinkers have made either in support of a materialist or non- materialist perspective. The neural correlates of religious experience explain that these days science has taken many steps in deciphering the mystery, thereby revealing that the reaches of contemporary science extend beyond the world of the material to the mental and spiritual as well. As human beings science and religion are two integral aspects of our civilization. Our study shows that there is no reason for religion to tremble at the new scientific discoveries and interpretation.

Endnotes

[1] Cf. Augustine Pamplany, "Neural correlates of Religious Experience," in Academic Sessions at Marymatha Major Seminary on October 31, 2016 (Thrissur, India: Marymatha Major Seminary Notes), 2.

[2] Andrew B. Newberg and Bruce Y. Lee," The Neuroscientific Study of Religious and Spiritual Phenomenon: or Why God Doesn't Use Biostatistics", *Zygon* 40, no. 2(2005): 84.

[3] Daniel Dennett, *Consciousness Explained*(Boston: Back Bay Books, 1991), p. 33.

[4] Andrew Newberg, Eugene D'Aquili, and Vince Rause, *Why God Won't Go Away: Brain Science and Biology of Belief*(New York: Ballantine Books, 2002), p. 32. Hereafter referred to as *Why God Won't Go Away.*

[5] See, *Why God Won't Go Away*, 18-23.

[6] Cf. Carol Rausch Albright, "ZYGON's 1996 Expedition into Neuroscience and Religion,"in*Zygon* 31, no.4(1996), 77.

[7] Gomathi Gopinath, *The Brain a Precious Possession*(New Delhi: National Book Trust, India, 1995), p. 6 (Hereafter we use, Gomathi, *The Brain*).

[8] Cf. Mario and Denyse, *Spiritual Brain*, 62-63.

[9] Cf. Andrew B. Newberg and Bruce Y. Lee," The Neuroscientific Study of Religious and Spiritual Phenomenon, 84.

[10] Cf.*Matthew Alper, The "God Part of the Brain* (Naperville, Illinois:Sourcebooks, Inc. 20206), p.8. (Hereafter we use Alper, *The God Part of the Brain*).

[11] Cf. Mario Beauregard, Denyse O'Leary,*The Spiritual Brain: A Neuroscientist's Case for the Existence of the Soul* (New York: Harper, 2007), p.44.

[12] See, Alper, *The God Part of the Brain*, 56

[13] Cf. idem, p.123.

[14] Idem, p.134.

[15] See, Mario and Denyse, *Spiritual Brain*, 45.

[16] Cf. Idem, p.48.

[17] As quoted by Jeffry Kluger, Jeff Chu, Broward Liston and the rest in "Is God in Our Genes?" in *Time*, October 25, 2004. Hereafter referred to as "Is God in Our Genes?"

[18] Cytosine rather than adenine is present at the position 33050 of this gene.

[19] "Is God in Our Genes?".

[20] Cf. Mario and Denyse, *Spiritual Brain*, p.52.

[21] Cf. idem, p.49.

[22] Carl Zimmer, "Faith-Boosting Genes: A Search for Genetics Basis of Spirituality," in *Scientific American* (September 27, 2004), 77.

[23] Barbara J. King, "Spirituality Explained? Reflections on Dean Hamer's The God Gene," *Bookslut*, June 2005.

[24] Cf. Mario and Denyse, *Spiritual Brain*, p.60.

[25] See, Jeffrey L. Saver and John Rabin, "The Neural Substrates of Religious Experience," in *Journal of Neuropsychiatry and Clinical Neuroscience* 9 (1997), 498-510.

[26] Cf. Mario and Denyse, *Spiritual Brain*, pp.68-69.

[27] Devinsky, "Religious Experiences and Epilepsy," in *Epilepsy & Behavior* 4, (2003), 76-77.

[28] Cf. Newberg, D'Aquili and Vince, *Why God Won't Go Away*, p.7.

[29] Cf. idem, p. 8.

[30] Cf. p,9.

[31] Newberg, D'Aquili and Vince, *Why God Won't Go Away*, pp.173-74.

[32] http://www.andrewnewberg.com/research/

Chapter 7

Neurology and Soul:
Exploring the Story of
Spiritual Dimension of Human Existence

Kuruvilla Pandikattu

Abstract

Basing ourselves on the Centre of Gravity in physics and phenomenology, we try to explore the nature and possibilities of the human soul, understood as the self, as the centre of our narrative self, and soul as the centre of our spiritual self. For this we base ourselves on Paul Ricoeur. Then we deal briefly with the nature of the soul, especially from the Thomistic and transcendental perspectives. Then we explore the neurological implications of such a view, assuming that brain is central to our physical, psychological, intellectual and spiritual self. We also dwell on the immortality of the soul and on the transcending (self-actualization) function of it in human lives.

Key Words: Narrative self, spiritual self, Paul Ricoeur, immortality, self-actualization

Introduction

What is soul and how can we understand and explain it neurologically? Can the neurological research throw more light on the spiritual aspect of human beings? How can we deepen our spiritual life and enhance our understanding of soul?Taking clues from these questions, we first explore some insights on God and spirituality from neurological sciences. After having studied "God part" and "God module" from neurology, we investigate "God gene" from biological sciences. Then we take up the understanding of identity and self from philosophical or phenomenological perspectives. We explore the power of story and the possibilities of narratives in fostering our own self-understanding, following mainly the vision of the French Philosopher Paul Ricoeur. In the concluding part, we draw from both these sections and talk of the soul as the centre of our spiritual experiences. Here we focus the experience of a practicing Indian-American neurosurgeon, who died at the young age of 38 in 2015. He shows to us that it is in experiencing mercy and compassion, that we experience God. In other words, we can see the soul as the emplotment (or focal point) of the narrative stories of "hope, fear, love, hate, beauty, envy, honor, weakness, striving, suffering, virtue."

Neurological God

With the explosive growth in neuroscience in the last fifty years, today many believe that all vital functions of the human mind, including religious phenomena are purely neurobiological happenings. In the following pages, we shall discuss some such naturalistic explanations of religious experience.[1]

Matthew Alper and the "God Part" of Brain

Matthew Alper is a history professor and screenwriter from New York City. He did his research with the aim of solving the problem of God scientifically. In his book, *The God Part of the Brain,*[2] based on research data gathered from neurobiology and evolutionary psychology he argued that we are innately hardwired to perceive a spiritual reality and to believe in forces that transcend the limitations of our physical realm. The term hardwired, according to him, means that God is not "out there," as an independent true reality, but rather "a product" of human evolutionary adaptation within our brain.[3] According to Alper, the common shared behaviours of individuals in a species are genetically inherited. Religious belief is so pervasive that it must also be a genetically inherited instinct.[4] What caused the emergence of this instinct is the anxiety of death and human desire for survival. "As generations of … proto-humans passed, those whose cerebral constitutions most effectively dealt with the anxiety resulting from their awareness of death were most apt to survive."[5] This process continued until a cognitive function emerged that altered the way the proto-humans perceived reality by adding a "spiritual" component to their perspectives. Just as the human brain had evolved linguistic, musical, and mathematical intelligence, we apparently evolved a spiritual intelligence ("a kind of prayer-responsive mechanism in the brain") as well.[6] Finally, Alper believes that one day scientists will discover this "God Part" in which "we will have knowledge of precisely which genes are responsible or those parts of the brain that give rise to religiosity and spiritual consciousness."[7]

The above-mentioned argument of Alper's neurobiological reduction of religious experience has several scientific and philosophical flaws. First of all, there is no real scientific proof for the necessary correlation between certain widely seen cultural behaviour and genetic inheritance. The most celebrated cultural practices that many communities had before a few centuries are not even seen now. We do not even know the cultural suppositions of our forefathers. Therefore, we cannot really say that religious phenomena are genetically inherited. Alper's another assumption that religious belief is born out of human awareness of death and anxiety also lacks evidence. This sheer naturalistic view of religious belief will not find acceptance by the genuine believers in any religion. Finally, to look for a "God Gene" in the brain is simply misguiding. What we can *actually* inherit is the capacity for abstract ideas. However, the search for the specific inherited mechanism or process of such experience is misleading as we cannot specifically locate particular space as responsible for those experiences.[8]Hence, Alper's naturalistic reduction of religious experience appears to be non-scientific as his assumption does not pass the crucial testability criteria.

Saver and Rabin's "God Module"

Neurologists Jeffery Saver and John Rabin claimed that the limbic system of the brain – a system that lies within the reach of the temporal lobes and functions as a medium for emotions – plays a pivotal role in the religious, spiritual and mystical experiences (RSME).[9] Epilepsy is caused by the neural disorder in the limbic region of the brain. It is a brief disturbance in the normal brain functions. Mystical experiences indicate the pursuit of an altered state of consciousness that enables the mystic to become aware of cosmic realities that cannot be grasped during normal states of consciousness.[10] From this, Saver and Rabin also argue that RSME is also a sort of brain disorder. It is a *divine madness* that triggers a kind of "God Module." In their view great religious leaders are "Temporal-lobe personality" and showed the symptoms of Temporal-lobe Epilepsy (TLE).[11]

I think the comparison between TLE and RSMEs is shallow and unwarranted. First of all, TLE is not a meaningful interpretation of intense religious mystical experience. Secondly, there is no sufficient correlation between epilepsy and religious experience. Can one show all RSMEs are TLE? For instance, St. Paul who had "an intense experience of the Risen Lord" on Damascus road was interpreted as epilepsy. The materialists consider his experience as heat prostration, aggravated by sense of guilt over his persecution. However, there are no historical data to support this claim. Or to call the great religious leaders like Gandhi as "temporal lobe personality" is too naïve.[12]In short, Saver and Rabin's necessary association between TLE and RSME is scientifically and logically faulty. As Devinsky noted, "the genesis of intense religious experiences associated with neurological disorders remains poorly defined."[13]

A Critical Analysis of Neurology and Religious Experience

The above neurological interpretations of religious experience are, in principle, reductionistic. They all claim that religious experience can be reduced to the neuro-biological activities of the brain. This neural reduction is based on the modern neuro-scientific studies of brain. For instance, neuroscientists like, Drs. D'Aquili and Newberg have specifically studied the brain activation during mystical experiences. Newberg and D'Aquili conducted experiments in Tibetan Buddhist monks and Franciscan nuns with the help of SPECT scan. It has shed scientific insights into the mysterious working of human brain during mystical experience. They showed the exact location and the specific brain process during spiritual and mystical experience. In the Tibetan monks there was an increased activity in the frontal lobe where the focusing of attention takes place. At the same time, the amygdale, the neural seat of anxiety and fear, became inactive. The monks were in a calm, serene and unstressed state.[14] They found broadly the similar neurological results in the Franciscan nuns also.[15]

Dean Hamer and "God Gene"

Dean Hamer is the Chief of Gene Structure at US National Cancer Institute. He claims that he has indeed found God in our brain and specifically in our genes.[16] It means that he has identified a specific gene that codes for the production of neurotransmitters that administer our moods.[17] This would imply that the most profound feelings of spirituality are nothing "more than an occasional shot of intoxicating brain chemicals governed by our DNA."[18] In Hamer's own words, "we're a bunch of chemical reactions running around in a bag" and religious experience is simply a firing of a strange gene. With the help of Temperament and Character Inventory(TCI) personality test administered to 1000 volunteers, Hamer demonstrated our ability to have "the self-transcendence" or spiritual experience. According to

Hamer, "the self-transcendence" is an adaptive trait that we inherit for the sake of survival and fertility. It has the ability to see everything in its totality and to adjust with the complex life situation.

Dean Hamer explained his theory with the help of two studies. According to the first study conducted on the volunteers, he concluded that the phenomenon of self-transcendence is nothing but chemical reaction. For this, he studied nine genes that promote the production of brain chemicals called as monoamines. It included dopamine, adrenaline and serotoxin, etc. These chemicals were responsible for the regulation of moods and motivation. A variation in a gene called "VMAT2[19] (vesicular monoamine transporter) was higher in the case of those volunteers who tested for self-transcendence. From this he concluded that "VMAT 2 is the "God Gene responsible for self-transcendence."[20] The second study was conducted in the identical twins. According to his findings, the children do not learn spirituality from somebody or from some culture or society. Even though all the influences are shared equally by the identical and fraternal twins, they show dissimilarities in the measure with which they exhibit self-transcendence.[21] Hence self-transcendence is an inherited trait caused by VMAT 2, the "God Gene".

The theory of Hamer is not aimed at disqualifying any religious doctrine or traditional beliefs but rather it accounts for the variation in cytosine and adenine which determines lower or higher experiences in human being. Hence, his findings are limited to the mere variation that can take place in any experience of certain intensity because even in the exhibition of a minor human trait, there is an interplay of hundreds or thousands of genes.[22] Therefore, it is improper to conclude that VMAT2 is the "God Gene" responsible for religious experience. Moreover, Hamer's assumption of "God Gene" lacks scientific evidence. There are difficulties in reproducing such findings. As science writer Carl Zimmer criticizes Hamer's VMAT2 assumption and says it can be better titled as, "A Gene That Accounts for Less Than One Percent of the Variance Found in Scores on Psychological Questionnaires

Designed to Measure a Factor Called Self-Transcendence, Which can Signify Everything from Belonging to the Green Party to Believing in ESP, According to One Unpublished Unreplicated Study."[23] Thus, Hamer's theory died a death of minimal evidence. The siblings and twin studies are also less convincing. Even though siblings are identical and share the same house, they need not have the same *life experience*. As anthropologist Barbara J. King says, "Perhaps one sister merely encounters a certain inspirational teacher or well-loved book that the other does not. Non-shared experiences like these heap contingency upon contingency as each girl develops. In the end, the two sisters may essentially grow up in divergent emotional environments – and as a result make very different choices about the role of spirituality in their lives."[24]

Narrative Self

French philosopher Paul Ricoeur (1913-2005) developed an account of narrative and narrative identity that has been highly influential. A philosopher keenly engaged with hermeneutical, phenomenological, psychoanalytic and existential traditions, his ideas continue to resonate in a wide range of contexts, including anywhere where narrative and narrative versions of psychology are theorized.[25]

Ricoeur and Emplotment

Ricoeur argued against essentialist versions of the human subject, such as that of the rational, isolated Cartesian cogito, but also against postmodern versions of a radically de-centred non-subject – determined by discourse (Foucault), or language (Derrida).Instead, Ricoeur argues for a version of the human subject in which personal identity is not fully stable or self-transparent, but is also not incoherent or self-alienated. The human subject, since the "linguistic turn" in philosophy, has been understood to have access to itself (and the world) only as mediated by language. For Ricoeur, this self-relationship is essentially one of active interpretation, rather than fully autonomous self-authoring. This hermeneutical phenomenological human subject emerges, for Ricoeur, essentially through narrative. "Narrative" means more than simply a story here; narrative refers to the way that humans experience time, in terms of the way we understand our future potentialities, as well as the way we mentally organize our sense of the past.

More specifically, the past, for Ricoeur, demands narrativisation. Humans tend to carry out "emplotment" – as we draw together disparate past events into a meaningful whole, by establishing causal and meaningful connections between them. These attributions of causation, where other human subjects are involved, necessarily entail implications of moral responsibility, and so the narrative self is ineluctably established in a moral universe. For Ricoeur this retrospective figuration of events into a meaningful unity occurs from the end-point of the story (the present moment, for the individual). In this way, earlier events and their meanings are fitted into a pattern which is only seen by the later perspective. Ricoeur acknowledges that this narrative logic can lead to specious attributions of causality and purpose (teleological thinking), although this is not a necessary outcome of narrative emplotment.[26]

The future, too, exists in terms of an "inchoate narrativity" – it is always grasped as a set of potential narratives in which we might take part. Just as, for Martin Heidegger, our understanding, or *verstehen*, intuitively discloses the world to us, in terms of a future-orientated sense of the plurality of potentialities for action that lie before us, for Ricoeur this pre-understanding is always given through a "semantics of action," that is, an always meaning-rich sense of possible choices, actions and their consequences, as they might integrate into our broader structures of meaning.[27]

Interesting tensions exist between Ricoeur's version of the human subject and that of fellow French philosopher (and psychoanalyst) Jacques Lacan. Ricoeur very usefully describes how narratives, or even a single narrative identity, can readily exist in the Imaginary, the mode in which identifications – such as those formed with one's parents or one's own image in the mirror – are made, which accrete to form the ego.[28]

Despite this potential for the individual to identify with a narrative, such as a hero or princess story, and thus partially constitute a sense of self that is illusory, Ricoeur holds on to the sense that the subject can, however, meaningfully incorporate existing narratives into their own, through interpretation and emplotment, and through this activity open up new – and real – potentialities for the subject's being in the world.[29]

The Capable Self

Like Ricoeur, Daniel Dennett also speaks on the Narrative Self. Joan McCarthy gives us a careful study of the narrative account of the selfhood of Ricoeur and Dennett.[30] She presents narrative approaches to the self as an alternative to traditional discussions about the self, which have tended to see it as either a substantial entity, existing separately to any particular experience that it has, or as an illusion, a mere linguistic convention. McCarthy chooses to focus on these two philosophers because they both present a narrative view of the self, yet have vastly different influences and backgrounds. McCarthy's own view, that the self can be thought of as a "culturally mediated narrative unity of action,"[31] is closer to Ricoeur's, affirms, Mary Jean Walker, research scholar at Macquarie University, Australia, reviewing this book.

McCarthy explains the idea of narrative as a way of making things intelligible that is distinct from causal or scientific explanation. It allows a teleological kind of explanation that can get at the meaning or significance of events. She also discusses here the need for an alternative to dualist or reductionist views of the self, which she believes the narrative approach can give.

McCarthy explains Dennett's view of the self as a centre of narrative gravity. This is explained through two analogies: centres of gravity, and fictional characters. Like centres of gravity, selves are "theorist's fictions" or abstract objects. They are not 'real' in the sense that material objects are real, but they have a useful role in explanation and prediction. Like fictional characters, selves are defined by the stories told about them.

Moving further into Ricoeur's view, McCarthy focuses on what she calls the "capable self": an agent that can act, recount and impute. She explains his views on how one's identity arises from the process of making sense of action in narrative terms.

Doing justice to hermeneutic insights about interpretation, though, makes it difficult for narrative accounts to say that some narratives, such as self-deceived narratives, are in error. These moves leave us however with a narrative self that is a result of arduous self-examination. This issue is discussed further in chapter seven, as the main problem for Ricoeur's account. It leads to an "essentialist drama,"[32] where the notion of identity becomes infused with notions of autonomy. This self seems more a normative ideal than a boundary condition for persistence.

McCarthy concludes that though both narrative accounts face some problems, Ricoeur's view is broader. The work until this point has looked at these two narrative accounts primarily in epistemological and ontological terms; here McCarthy argues that narrative accounts of selfhood are the best ones we have in terms of methods for ethics, and suggests that this may be the most important aspect of any account of the self.

Idem and Ipse: The Soul and Self

The idea that our life is a story is by no means new. Thus, the great bard Shakespeare said that life "is a tale told by an idiot, full of sound and fury, signifying nothing." (*Macbeth*) However, it took philosophers some time to discover the philosophical import of this view of life. It was actually a German philosopher called Wilhelm Schapp who first gave this age-old idea a philosophical twist.[33] He maintained that we live our lives in a host of stories, which have connection with the stories of other people in various ways; so actually, our selves are nothing but cross-sections of stories. Our identities are created by a vast web of stories, as is our relationship with reality. We understand and identify things by placing them in the stories we tell about them: just like selves, things do not really exist outside of stories. We are caught in this narrative web because we cannot exist outside of it. There is a world-wide web of stories: the world is that web.[34]

Schapp's main book was published fifty years ago, and was ignored by the philosophical community of the day. But in recent years, ideas resembling those of Schapp's have become increasingly influential, writes *Stefán Snaevarr an Icelandic writer and a professor of philosophy at Lillehammer University College, Norway.*

Ricoeur thinks that our actions have a narrative dimension. We fuse the temporal units of our actions together in the same way as in a story. But in contrast to the German philosopher, Schapp, French philosopher Paul Ricoeur emphasises the difference between life and stories. Our lives are not narratives, strictly speaking. Stories are told, lives are lived. But narratives still play a decisive part in our lives.

In the first place, an examined life is a life that must be examined through stories. We relate to ourselves by relating stories! Secondly, narratives play an important role in the creation and sustaining of our identities. Narratives do that by mediating between two basic aspects of our identities. On the one hand, we can talk about our identity as *idem*, or *sameness*, or on the other hand as *ipse*, or *selfhood*. *Idem* is the simple identity of a person as a thing in time and space. *Ipse* is the being of self, i.e., the being of someone who can relate to himself and has a history which he or she can consciously reflect upon. *Idem* provides us with answer to the question 'What am I?' *ipse* the answer to the question 'Who am I?'[35]

Idem can be divided in two sub-types of identities. One is numerical identity: my body is exactly what it is and not another body. The other type is a qualitative identity of the kind we refer to when we say that two ladies have the same dress on. The dresses are identical in the sense of being exchangeable; they have exactly the same qualities. Seemingly, the *idem* is partly the identity of the body, such that I can be said to have the same body I had as a new-born baby, even though I had not developed a self, an *ipse*, at that time. Similarly, a person who has lost his/her self due to Alzheimer's disease might be considered the same as before in the *idem* sense of the word, even though he or she in some sense has lost his or her personhood.[36]

Ipse (selfhood), is on the one hand the type of identity we can have as characters, not least as characters in stories. On the other hand, the identity of selfhood is the identity of the one who keeps his/her promises, for example. This latter part of the self is the voluntary side of it. We can choose whether or not to keep promises. Furthermore, we *create* parts of our selves by keeping or not keeping promises. By such acts we create our selves as 'reliable' or 'unreliable' persons. In contrast to this, we cannot choose the character we play. We cannot choose our talents or temperament. The one who plays the role of the dim-witted guy remains stupid.[37]

There is a dialectical tension between *idem* and *ipse*. The reason is that it makes sense to talk about *ipse* even though the person changes quite a bit; at the same time the *idem* demands consistency: we want to say we are talking about the same thing. How can it be that we have certain permanence through time while changing all the time? It is narrative which solves this problem: it mediates between *idem* and *ipse*.

In all narratives there is both permanence and change – in Ricoeur's vocabulary 'concordance' and 'discordance;' the latter being unexpected events which disturb the sense of permanence. A story manages nevertheless to unite permanence and change. Analogously, it unites *idem* and its concordance, with *ipse* and its tendency towards discordance. It is a question of a synthesis of heterogeneous elements.

To understand this we must take a brief glance at Ricoeur's theory about the general function of narratives. Narratives, or more precisely *plots*, synthesise reality. A plot fuses together intentions, causal relations, and chance occurrences in a unified sequence of actions and events. Ricoeur seems to think that the plot creates a unified pattern in a chaotic series of events, ties them together, making them meaningful wholes. Thus, through the lens of the story we see things in a particular way, just as we can see the Jastrow figure as a duck, given a certain perspective. Another narrative could presumably give a rabbit perspective on things.

'Plot' plays an important role in creating the permanent aspects of human character. Just as in Ricoeur's scheme plot plays a constructive role for narratives, creating their permanent aspect, *mutatis mutandis* the same holds for human character. But despite unifying plots, narrative identities change all the time. They are not closed and static, but demand openness and freedom. In Ricoeur's own words, "Life is an activity and passion in search of a narrative." ('Life in Quest of Narrative') The self is not given; it is something that must be created. It must also be appropriated in communication with others and with the aid of stories: narratives can help make our lives meaningful. It seems that Ricoeur thinks that this meaningfulness is an essential part of the self.

According to Ricoeur, narratives are needed to bridge the gap between *idem* and *ipse*. We may hold that *ipse* (selfhood) is both permanent and changeable at the same time, in contrast to the *idem*, which is all permanence. This suggests that the idea of *idem* is superfluous, unless it is regarded solely as the permanence of the body (but it does seem that by '*idem*' Ricoeur means something more than just bodily permanence). The *ipse* already contains the moment of permanence, ascribed to the *idem*. There is both similarity and distinction between them. The narrative not only mediates between the *idem* and the *ipse*, but between the discordant and concordant moments of the *ipse itself*.[38]

Conclusion: Soul as the Experience of Mercy Trumping Justice
Following the insights from neurosciences and from narrative self, we may hold that soul is the centre of our spiritual experiences. It provides us with a focus(or centre) for our spiritual narrative, spiritual experiences. From a spiritual perspective, the soul may be considered as the narrative of our spiritual story.

Such a spiritual experience deals not only with the quest for meanings, wholeness, sense of adoration and wellness. It deals not only with a God who is our creator and destiny. It evokes in us not only a sense of wonder, mystery and surrender, but also redemption, grace and forgiveness,[39] as illustrated by a neurosurgeon, Paul Kalanithi.[40] Though brought up in a Christian family, he lost his faith as he grew up and became a highly successful neurosurgeon. But his story back to faith, as described in his best-seller book,[41] is an experience of the prodigal son, who has experienced mercy from God.

In the book, he recalls listening to the following verses from the Bible: Jesus answered and said to her, "Everyone who drinks this water will be thirsty again; but whoever drinks the water I shall give will never thirst; the water I shall give will become in him a spring of water welling up to eternal life." The woman said to him, "Sir, give me this water, so that I may not be thirsty or have to keep coming here to draw water." (John 4: 13-15). Meanwhile, the disciples urged him, "Rabbi, eat." But he said to them, "I have food to eat of which you do not know." So the disciples said to one another, "Could someone have brought him something to eat?" (John 4: 31-34)

It was passages like these, "where there is a clear mocking of the literalist readings of Scripture, that had brought me back around to Christianity after a long stretch, following college, when my notion of God and Jesus had grown, to put it gently, tenuous." He adds: "During my sojourn in ironclad atheism, the primary arsenal leveled against Christianity had been its failure on empirical grounds. Surely enlightened reason offered a more coherent cosmos. Surely Occam's razor cut the faithful free from blind faith. There is no proof of God; therefore, it is unreasonable to believe in God."[42]

Grown into the scientific worldview, he believed in the possibility of a material conception of reality, an ultimately scientific worldview that would grant a complete metaphysics, minus outmoded concepts like souls, God, and bearded white men in robes. He spent a good chunk of his twenties trying to build a frame for such an endeavor. The problem eventually became evident to him: "To make science the arbiter of metaphysics is to banish not only God from the world but also love, hate, meaning — to consider a world that is self-evidently not the world we live in. That's not to say that if you believe in meaning, you must also believe in God. It is to say, though, that if you believe that science provides no basis for God, then you are almost obligated to conclude that science provides no basis for meaning and, therefore, life itself doesn't have any. In other words, existential claims have no weight; all knowledge is scientific knowledge."[43]

He realises the paradox: "Yet the paradox is that scientific methodology is the product of human hands and thus cannot reach some permanent truth. We build scientific theories to organize and manipulate the world, to reduce phenomena into manageable units. Science is based on reproducibility and manufactured objectivity. As strong as that makes its ability to generate claims about matter and energy, it also makes scientific knowledge inapplicable to the existential, visceral nature of human life, which is unique and subjective and unpredictable. Science may provide the most useful way to organize empirical, reproducible data, but its power to do so is predicated on its inability to grasp the most central aspects of human life: hope, fear, love, hate, beauty, envy, honor, weakness, striving, suffering, virtue."[44]

Between these core passions and scientific theory, there will always be a gap. No system of thought can contain the fullness of human experience. The realm of metaphysics remains the province of revelation. For him atheism can be justified only on these metaphysical grounds.

So a prototypical atheist, then, is Graham Greene's commandant from *The Power and the Glory*, "whose atheism comes from a revelation of the absence of God." So for Kalanithi, the only real atheism must be grounded in a world-making vision. The favorite quote of many an atheist, from the Nobel Prize–winning French biologist Jacques Monod, belies this revelatory aspect of atheism: "The ancient covenant is in pieces; man at last knows that he is alone in the unfeeling immensity of the universe, out of which he emerged only by chance."[45]

This urged Kalanithi to return to the central values of Christianity – sacrifice, redemption, forgiveness – because he found them so compelling. There is a tension in the Bible between justice and mercy, between the Old Testament and the New Testament. And the New Testament says you can never be good enough: goodness is the thing, and you can never live up to it. The main message of Jesus, he believes, is that mercy trumps justice every time.[46]

Thus, we may hold that human soul is the focus of our experience of mercy. Of hope, fear, love, hate, beauty, envy, honor, weakness, striving, suffering, virtue! This would involve, like *idem* and *ipse*, some scientific and biological basis. But it goes beyond the neurological (or reductionist) understanding of the soul. It involves the emplotment of our experience of love, hatred, evil, goodness and mercy.

Endnotes

[1] This section is based on the many and outstanding writings of Dr ChackoNadakkevely. He has elaborately dealt with neurological implications of soul and spirituality.

[2] Matthew Alper, *The God Part of the Brain: A Scientific Interpretation of Human Spirituality and God* (New York: Rogue, 2001), p. 8.

[3] Mario Beauregard, and Denyse O'Leary. *The Spiritual Brain: A Neuroscientist's Case for the Existence of the Soul*(New York: HarperOne, 2008),p. 44.

[4] Alper, 56.

[5] Idem, p. 102.

[6] Idem, p. 123.

[7] Idem, p.134.

[8] Beauregard and Leary, *Spiritual Brain,*45.

[9] Idem,p.60.

[10] Idem, p.59

[11] Jeffrey L. Saver and John Rabin, "The Neural Substrates of Religious Experience," in *Journal of Neuropsychiatry and Clinical Neuroscience* 9 (1997), 498-510.

[12] Beauregard and Denyse, *Spiritual Brain,*pp.68-69.

[13] Orrin Devinsky, "Religious Experiences and Epilepsy," in *Epilepsy & Behavior* 4(2003), 76-77.

[14] Andrew Newberg,EugeneD'Aquili and Vince Rause, *Why God Won't Go Away* (New York: Ballantine Books, 2001), p.7.

[15] Idem, p.8.

[16] Dean H., Hamer. *The God Gene: How Faith Is Hardwired into Our Genes* (New York: Anchor, 2005).

[17] Beauregard and Leary, *Spiritual Brain,*p.48.

[18] As quoted by Jeffry Kluger, Jeff Chu, Broward Liston, et al., in "Is God in Our Genes?", *Time*, October 25, 2004. Hereafter referred to as "Is God in Our Genes?"

[19] Cytosine rather than an adenine is present at the position 33050 of this gene.

[20] Kluger, "Is God in Our Genes?"

[21] See, Mario and Denyse, *Spiritual Brain*, 52.

[22] See, idem, p.49.

[23] Carl Zimmer, "Faith-Boosting Genes: A Search for Genetics Basis of Spirituality," in *Scientific American* (September 27, 2004), 77.

[24] Barbara J. King, "Spirituality Explained? Reflections on Dean Hamer's *The God Gene,*" *Bookslut*, June 2005.

[25] Paul Rhodes, "Paul Ricoeur and Narrative Identity: Why We Are Our Story," Psychology Today (Apr 13, 2016), https://www.psychologytoday.com/intl/blog/post-clinical/201604/paul-ricoeur-and-narrative-identity?amp=. Hereafter 'Rhodes'.

[26] Rhodes.

[27] Rhodes.

[28] Rhodes.

[29] Rhodes.

[30] Mary Jean Walker, "Review, Joan Mccarthy, Dennett and Ricoeur on the Narrative Self" Metapsychology, 12, 26 (June 24th 2008)http://metapsychology.mentalhelp.net/poc/view_doc.php?type=book&id=4306. Hereafter McCarthy.

[31] McCarthy, 9.

[32] McCarthy, 223.

[33] Wilhelm Schapp: *In GeschichtenVerstrickt: ZumSein Von Mensch Un Ding.* Hamburg: R. Meiner, 1953.

[34] Stefán Snaevarr, "Don Quixote and The Narrative Self," *Philosophy Today,* 60(March-April 2007), https://philosophynow.org/issues/60/Don_Quixote_and_The_Narrative_Self

[35] Snaevarr.*Idem* may be considered *as sameness. It is identity. But Ipse is the being of oneself, that gives meaning, memory, continuity and significance, which is more than the physical identity. The narrative and unifying self emerges out of ipse.*

[36] Following Ricoeur we may distinguish two kinds of identities: identity as "sameness" (German: Selbigkeit; Latin: idem; French: mêmeté); on the other hand, identity as "selfhood" (German: *Selbstheit*; Latin: *ipse*; French: *ipséité*). Narrative identities are invariably ipse identities which are constantly reconfigured through the telling of stories.

[37] Ibid.

[38] StefánSnaevarr.

[39] Paul Kalanithi,"Why I Gave up on Atheism." Text Article. Fox News. Fox News, May 27, 2016. https://www.foxnews.com/opinion/paul-kalanithi-why-i-gave-up-on-atheism.

[40] Kalanithi, Paul, and A. Verghese. *When Breath Becomes Air* (New York: Random House, 2016).Hereafter Kalanithi and Verghese.

[41] Kalanithi and Verghese..

[42] Kalanithi and Verghese.

[43] Kalanithi and Verghese.

[44] Kalanithi and Verghese.

[45] Kalanithiand Verghese.

[46] Paul Kalanithi, "Why I gave up on atheism."

Chapter 8

Can Science Essentially Estrange Spirituality? Philosophy of Science Perspectives

Stephen Jayard

Abstract

While science and spirituality are generally seen as two different, even opposing, disciplines, having nothing in common, the recent inquiries in diverse fields of science seem to strongly challenge that age-old opinion; contemporary scientific investigations and insights even point to a possibility of collaboration between these two disciplines. Further, better awareness of the limits and limitations in the fields of science point to the greater need for humanity to reach out to the other domains of inquiries, say philosophy, religion, literature and so on, to get a more realistic picture of reality and of our own selves. In this context some pertinent questions are raised: Are science and spirituality foes or friends? Do they have anything in common? Does science necessarily have to antagonize spirituality? Or is there any common ground where they can meet? Is there any meaningful way whereby both are brought together for mutual enrichment? With this background, this short essay seeks to deal with one fundamental question: Can science essentially estrange spirituality? The notion of spirituality, among many others, involves two basic elements, namely, *mystery and faith*. Reflecting upon the role and relevance of mystery and faith in the fields of science, and spelling two important possible implications for the mutual enrichment of science and spirituality, the essay attempts to show that science cannot essentially estrange spirituality.

Keywords: Neuroscience, Consciousness, Scientific Methodology, Observation, Values, Rationality, Reasonableness

Introduction

The debates over the relationship between brain and consciousness are not new for both the worlds of science and philosophy. In the recent past, with more advanced knowledge and discoveries in the fields of cognitive and neurosciences and more interest in the domain of spiritual experiences, those debates and inquiries have narrowed down to focus more on the specific issues of the relationship between neuroscience and spirituality. Experts from diverse fields like cognitive sciences, behavioural neurology, metaphysics, biosciences and so on come together to investigate the nature of that relationship. Neuroscience does not deny the existence of God-experiences; it only argues that the origin for those experiences lie deep within the structures and functions of our brain. It also easily accommodates the fact that religions have pragmatic utility of social, psychological, communitarian and emotional impact upon our society.

Trying to locate God-spot in the brain has been taken very seriously by both the believers and the non-believers alike, to prove their own point; while the former tries to see the God-spot as the "scientific proof" for God's existence, the latter would take up the same discovery to argue that God is just a creation of our own brain and therefore it is more appropriate to say that we create God, rather than God creating us! Critics, however, would point out that both the positions are unwarranted. The changes that are observed in the brain during the states of deep meditations or mystical trance can only be taken as the manifestations of those religious experiences and not as the cause or source of those experiences. Computers use numbers, can we say that they create them? If we create a super intelligent machine, even if it has all the complexities of our brains, can it have spiritual or God-experience? The very fact that there are varieties of religious experiences shows that the brain captures, experiences God in very many different ways and the source of those experiences has to be somewhere outside of the brain. When we wipe our spectacles to see things better, does it mean that the spectacles has now created the reality outside with more clarity? Similarly the brain also at one point in its long evolution gets more refined or complex to capture those experiences which were not possible earlier! Further, revelations by the modern Cosmology and Astronomy can also make us realize how strange and big the universe is; it is not only bigger and stranger than we imagine, but more than what we *can* imagine! Cosmically we are very insignificant, though cognitively, in a way, indispensable. The universe is such that no matter how much our knowledge may advance in the future, we will never know how much we don't know. The deep awareness of our finitude and the infinitude of the universe, and thereby that of its Creator, can easily pave the way for spiritual experiences and convictions as well.

From all these discussions, one can show that it would not be wrong to conclude that science does not essentially estrange spirituality, and therefore it is highly likely that more and more interdisciplinary researches would enrich our understanding of science, metaphysics and religion, making humanity wiser and more holistic.

Science – A Hermeneutical Enterprise

Science is a hermeneutical enterprise; it has to interpret its investigations into the nature of matter. The 20th century Physics went through several conceptual revolutions; two pillars – *Quantum Physics* (revealing basic oneness of the universe) and *Relativity* (changed our concept of space and time). Both reveal our limits and limitations in understanding matter. Matter ceases to be material at its very bottom as it seems to be 'energy' dancing at its fundamental level. Heisenberg's Uncertainty Principle, De Broglie's 'wavicle' theory of light, Neils Bohr's Complementarity Principle and so on reveal that the full grasp of matter seems to be evading our understanding. We can never visualize matter to be out there and we look at it 'undisturbingly.' For, "Quantum physicists discovered that every act of observation made of an atom by a physicist disturbed the atom. The observer affects the observed.... A sudden, discontinuous change brought on by observer's act of observation. This change is sudden and noncausal. It cannot be predicted even by Quantum Mechanics. Therefore, it is outside the ability of Quantum Physics to predict the capricious behaviour of nature."[1] If every observation that we make is an interference with what is observed, then there is actually no independent observer, because "Our consciousness is part of every experiment and there is no clear boundary between the subject and the object."[2]

Nature is so complex and intricate in its structure, that we can't fathom its full picture. When we look at nature, we impose certain pattern upon it and force it to reveal accordingly. Unfortunately, we are not aware of this fact and even if we are aware of it, we can't do anything much about it. Immanuel Kant's twelve categories, including that of space and time, colours and determines what we see, so we can never see reality 'as it is.' Therefore "A physicistis looking at nothing but a set of highly abstract differential equations – not at reality itself but at mathematical symbols of reality. He deals with purely symbolic procedure, he can never understand what the facts are, so he limits himself to describing the patterns on mutilated facts in symbols, and quantum and relativistic physics deal with relative truth, a symbolic world."[3] Given these facts several of the quantum physicists are convinced that the long-cherished dividing lines between nature and human beings, subject and object, inner world and outer world, body and soul, are landing us into serious problems. Even the "dualism of space and time, energy and matter, and even space and objects"[4] are abandoned. Yes, the hitherto-held division of matter and energy is challenged because at the very fundamental level, matter ceases to be 'material' and "matter has lost its substance."[5]

Mysteries – Not Strangers to Science

Today sciences reveal the mysterious of nature. Just a word about *The Mystery of the 'Fine-tuning'* in the universe: The study of biotic coincidences and the anthropic principles seems to suggest that the universe has been very meticulously fine-tuned to be ready to receive conscious human beings; being convinced of this Dyson asserts that "the universe knew we were coming"[6] and Paul Davies declares that "We are truly meant to be here."[7] Recent studies in Cosmology and Astronomy reveal that the values of several constants in nature are so very finely and delicately tuned that had there been a very slight change in their values it would not have permitted the galaxies, stars, planets and life to emerge over the long period of evolution since the Big Bang; constants like the speed of light, Planck's Constant, Planck Mass-Energy, Mass of Electron, Proton and Neutron, Mass of Up, Down and Strange Quarks, Ratio of Electron-Proton mass, Gravitational Coupling Constant, Hubble's Constant, Higgs Vacuum Expectation value, etc., have very precise values. For instance, the force of gravity is determined by the Gravitational Constant, and if it were different even by one in 10^{60} parts, none of us would exist today! Similarly, the expansion rate of the universe after the Big Bang is determined by the Cosmological Constant, and if it were different even by one in 10^{120} parts, the universe would not have come into existence! Further, if mass and energy of the early universe were not evenly distributed to an exceedingly precise value of one in $10^{10 \times 123}$ parts, the universe would have been hostile to life of any kind![8] Further, the initial density of the universe had to be meticulously fixed to an accuracy of 10^{-60} and this precision is like an archer hitting a one-centimetre-square target placed fifteen billion light-years away.[9]

Several scientists-turned theologians, like John Polkinghorne, Arthur Peacock, Ilya Prigogine, etc., also find something more to the evolution process than mere chance. They have gone beyond reductionism and are open to mystical and metaphysical overtones in their approach to reality. Even great minds, like Einstein, are also convinced that such fine-tuning in the universe cannot be the outcome of mere chance. If one argues that all these fine-tunings are just fixed by laws of physics, the question arises: "Where do the laws of physics come from? And why *those* laws rather than some other set?"[10] Therefore the mystery still remains! Such a realization of mystery in nature makes the investigation of the universe meaningful and thereby gives meaning to our existence.[11]

The Role and Relevance of Faith in Science

Unless scientists are convinced of the worth of their scientific investigations, they will not be ready to invest their time and energy in them; unless they are convinced of the meaning and value of their researches, they will not be ready to undertake the challenging, risking and even life-threatening activities. It is a sort of *faith* which they have in the meaningfulness of their efforts that propels them to work further, and such inspiration to slog cannot be justified by the empirical world around us. The intelligibility of the universe is a fundamental assumption, which cannot be proved or touched or seen by empirical methods! Scientists constantly struggle to understand what it is; they look for the intelligibility of the universe and it is already a sort of *faith experience*. Many geniuses indeed marvel at the intelligibility (comprehensibility) of the universe and Einstein meaningfully wonders: "The most incomprehensible thing about the universe is that it is comprehensible!"[12] Scientific laws can only describe the situations but cannot go deeper to answer the questions about why only those situations, and not different ones, exist. Certain fundamental questions about the natural laws or the functions of the universe don't come under the purview of science. Scientific inquiry cannot answer them, though they are very much related to the scientific inquiry. When scientists raise questions like, why are there laws in the universe, and why these sets instead of different ones, or why these conditions and not some other conditions etc., we can see that they already implicitly speak about the Creator (God)!

Moreover, even "faith" in the religious sense (as related to the experiences of divinity) is not alien to the contemporary world of science. The better and deeper awareness of the unimaginable complex structure of the universe, paves the way for some religious experiences, in and through the exploration of this amazing universe. The same convictions are shared by physicists like Werner Heisenberg, Arthur Eddington and many other quantum physicists; they have strong mystical inclinations.[13] Albert Einstein is, as I have elsewhere elaborated, convinced that without the cosmic religious experience, which is the noblest driving force, no scientific research is possible.[14] This particular realization meaningfully paves the way for better interaction and integration between science and religion. In our present times both science and religion have become very strong forces affecting and shaping our society. They have great impacts upon both believers and non-believers and so they cannot be ignored. Both pursue to explore reality from their own perspectives. In fact, there are issues which bring them together. As Jean Staune explains, the coming together of science and religion is inevitable; for, "a) The outer boundaries of science are not clearly demarcated; b) there are areas in science that overlap with domains of religion, spirituality, and the quest for meaning; c) more scientific investigations into, say, the study of life and the study of consciousness have created a new possibility of 'the convergence of science and religion.'"[15] If these powerful enterprises are brought together in a healthy manner humanity will surely move towards holistic existence.

Realization of the Limits of Science

C. G. Hempel, in his thought-provoking paper "Science Unlimited?" enlightens us over the limits of science - limits in the reliability and potentiality of science. He further argues that these limits cannot be construed as the limitations of science, because either those aspects don't come under the competence of science or by its very nature science is not expected to handle those issues. For instance, he argues that science, or any other discipline for that matter, today or in future, will never be able to answer the question: 'Why is there anything at all and not rather nothing?' For, to answer this question is a logically inconsistent requirement, as "no theory, no conceptual scheme, can explain the existence of anything without assuming the existence of something."[16] To try to explain something in terms of nothing is an incoherent question.

It is true, as Hempel points out, that all these may not be limits of science as such, but I believe, they point out to a deeper lesson: that is, the powers of human cognition are not limitless. It seems that humans cannot see themselves as the masters of shaping their own destiny. It may be seen as a limit of human existence as a whole, as most of the Existential Philosophers have pointed out. Some of them, like Sartre and Nietzsche, have ended up with a pessimistic outlook towards the world, while some others, like Gabriel Marcel, have taken the fact of limits as something adding interest to the very human existence, opening up avenues of transcendence. After all, we cannot even know whether we know everything. That is why, Wittgenstein too rightly wonders, "We feel that even if *all possible* scientific questions be answered, the problems of life have still not been touched at all. Of course, there is then no question left, and just this is the answer."[17]

Some Reflections on the Notion of Spirituality

It is not easy to define what spirituality is and there are innumerable ways of understanding it. One way to understand it would be describing its features and the consequences of being spiritual or not. Religion in general may help one to go to the level of spirituality, but it cannot be identified with it. Among other things, religion is defined by its creed, cult and code; it is confined to the place of worship, the Holy Book and perhaps its founder(s). But spirituality is generally understood to be beyond all such confines and identifications.

- To be spiritual does not mean being always found at the places of worship, nor to be found carrying the Sacred Books. For, a goat that is housed in the library will certainly not become intelligent or wise! It is not the place where we are but with what dispositions we are, that matters.

- To be spiritual is not in performing the religious rituals all the time. One can perform them very diligently but still can be very far away from God. It is not uncommon to see people who attend the Holy Mass in the church (or the *Namaz* at the mosque or perform *Puja* at the temple) in the morning and during the very day getting bribe to do their duty or exploit the innocent in dealing with them. Their conscience does not prick them, probably because they may pacify God by offering something to God from the bribery that they receive!

- To be spiritual is not to be ignorant of the facts about life, world, scientific developments, one's self, religion, Sacred Scriptures, etc. It is a glory to God when one uses her / his reasoning power fully and equips oneself in every aspect.

- To be spiritual is not in hiding under the shield of "God-will-take-care-of' attitudes. God will, in fact, pity those, for having given them the intelligence which is one of the fundamental distinguishing characteristics of being human.

- Genuine spirituality does not depend on how long we pray, but how deep we pray! It is not in how holy we look, but in how holy we think! It is not in the good certificates given by people, but by God! Yes, perhaps the more spirituality is seen outside, the less likely that it is found inside.

Having seen, what spirituality is not, we can now see what spirituality can be:

- To be spiritual means to be consciously aware of God's presence, not only in the places of worship but also on the dusty streets of one's locality; it is the ability to see God in the suffering humanity, to see him who longs for consolation, who longs for a ray of hope and meaning in one's life. Yes, it is the ability to see God in all, and all in God.

- To be spiritual means to see God in people, not only in those, whom one loves, which is relatively easier, but also in those whom one does not like, or does not like even to think of. Charity begins at home. It is perhaps easier to love someone who is very far away, say, in the USA, as it costs nothing much, but it is a real challenge to love the ones with whom one has her/his daily living.

- To be spiritual implies being genuinely human and genuine humanness has certainly room for occasional stumbling and unintended mistakes. Yet, one is truly sorry for the sins, and is determined not to repeat them with the strength that comes from God. We need to be practical in having expectations about ourselves; being over-angry for our mistakes,or being scrupulous or pre-occupied about our sins are, in fact, signs of not trusting the forgiving mercy of God; or it may even be the indication of our arrogance that makes us think of ourselves too big to sin!

- To be spiritual means being firm, without being harsh; being principle-oriented, without being arrogant; being compassionate without being compromising and being humble without reducing oneself to nothingness. Genuine humility means the constant awareness of my dependence on God, others and nature for my very living.

- To be spiritual means to be cool, calm and serene even in the midst of the moments of uncertainty and anxiety. Such a person is convinced of doing one's best and leaving the rest to God; she/he never doubts the fact that God always gives the best to those who leave the choice to him; it is easy for such people to drop their ego; dropping one's ego is, in fact, a real challenge, even to a sage, who has dropped everything else.

In short, spirituality, in its genuine sense,would keep us virtuous, and therefore we can be free from anxiety;it would keep us wise and therefore we can be free from perplexity; it would keep us brave and therefore we can be free from fear; and it would certainly keep us faithful and therefore be free from meaninglessness in life. [18]

Scientists are not stranger to faith or religious feelings. Several of the quantum physicists do have mystical inclinations. For instance, Albert Einstein, the man of the last millennium, is convinced that"The most beautiful and most profound experience is the sensation of the mystical. It is the sower of all true science. He to whom this emotion is a stranger, who can no longer wonder and stand rapt in awe, is as good as dead. To know that what is impenetrable to us really exists, manifesting itself as the highest wisdom and the most radiant beauty which our dull faculties can comprehend only in their primitive forms - this knowledge, this feeling is at the center of true religiousness."[19]The marriage between science and spirituality will surely strengthen humanity, both therapeutically and culturally. "It leads to perception of the wholeness which bestows insight or intuition. Perception of the wholeness ends all misery, pain and sorrow, and every man will revel in peace, freedom and bliss. The leads to the emergence of a new global civilization."[20]

Science can enable us to move towards being humble in our achievements, honest in our dealings, modest in our claims, human in using our knowledge, thoughtful in our commitment to humanity, grateful to the supreme designer and wise in our researches. Spirituality can thus be seen as a fundamental experience of human existence. There is a natural longing in our hearts for permanence and stability; therefore, what is contingent and passing does not really satisfy this longing. Only God who is permanent and eternal can satisfy that longing. That is why the wise words of St. Augustine of Hippo make sense: "Our hearts are restless until they rest in you."[21]

Two Important Implications of Mutual Enrichment of Science and Spirituality

Making Sense of (hitherto) *Non-sense*!

The hitherto assumptions that emotions and psychological aspects have nothing to do with strict scientific and objective endeavours seem to be shaken at the core with more insights / discoveries at the level of neuronal level of our bodies. Intuition, seen in opposition to the faculty of reason, is usually not taken to play any role in the strict scientific enterprises. But we now know how intuition, and women's intuition at that, which is normally downplayed, plays a significant role in science. Taking intuition seriously in science leads, as I have elaborated elsewhere,[22] to very many substantial implications in enriching science. There seems to be a tension between what is empirical and rationality (logic) in science. For, the empirical experience, which is always instantaneous, does not give us universality. For our daily lives too, we need to transcend our immediate environment to think about the past and to plan for future for which rationality is essential. If rationality is left alone it would be empty having nothing to think of either! Therefore, science needs to include a-rational and non-rational elements too in its purview.

Big strides have been made in the process of creating 'Artificial Intelligence.' We have seen *intelligent* computers, like Deep Blue, which have overpowered the world chess champion Kasparov in demonstrating the power of artificial intelligence. Various types of robots, cyborgs and intelligent devices seem to overtake humans at least in certain aspects. But eyebrows are raised, besides the ethical implications of such projects, about the very possibility of imitating human intelligence completely. It is highly doubtful whether the so-called thinking machines can use its common sense (if it has one!), whether they can be creative, whether they can dream and so on. No final word is given as yet whether such machines can be conscious. Given the complexities of the issue of consciousness, in my opinion, which is certainly not infallible, we can never create consciousness in the machines. In spite of all the techniques of the modern neurobiology we are not able to map the area of the brain which contributes to consciousness. Prof. R. C. Pradhan also wonders whether we would ever be able to achieve reductionism of consciousness to physical phenomena: "All elimination strategies are built upon the assumption that consciousness is a product of the material causes in the brain.... (But) The conscious states have certain properties which cannot be traced back to the brain states. Therefore, we have to admit a gap between the functions of the brain and the conscious phenomena. Elimination of the conscious states into brain states fails because conscious states are themselves presupposed rather than explained by the deconstruction procedures."[23] Thus, not limiting scientific enterprises to direct observations strictly seems to help in having a better understanding of the world around us and to make sense of what has been thought to be *non-sense* till recently.

Moving Towards a New Vision of Life

Scientists are now almost sure of the extinction of humans, even the very biological life in the universe, due to some natural reasons and conscious decisions of humanity. Natural reasons like immunodeficiency, decreasing sperm count, the threat of Andromeda Galaxy's collision with our Milky Way (in about next three billion years!) and the human-made reasons like the enormous degradation of the environment, perforation of the Ozone layer, increase in the global temperature, the genetic manipulations (on advanced humans) with the danger of resulting in extinction of human race as such – all these seem to usher us into the extinction of the evolution. In spite of such threats, humanity can now decide to act creatively and collectively, wisely and responsibly, to handle the natural threats and to avoid the humanly-created ones. It is high time that we acted swiftly to preserve, not just human life, but the whole planet earth and to take evolution further.

Further, contemporary science has helped humanity to realize its proper position in the whole of the universe. Darwin, Marx and Freud, for the reasons well-known, have drastically changed the conception of the position of humans in the universe. Humans, thought to be absolute and the top of the creation, were pushed to the periphery, as it were, to be a speck in one of the solar families in the neighbourhood of a second-rate galaxy, one among the 100 billion of the known ones thrown out there in the dark space. We can no more afford to have domineering attitude towards nature. Taking us beyond strict determinism, reductionism and mechanism of the modern science, the contemporary scientific enterprises take us to an entirely new vision of the world, within us and around us. Similarly, quantum physics teaches us that "The physical world in which we live is not ontologically sufficient. Time and space are not the only frame of reality, the observer plays an undefined role but a role in the aspect that our environment takes. Even if they do not seem to have practical applications, the existence of connections of non-specific character shows that the world is more 'holistic' than reductionist."[24] We need to ask questions of deeper dimensions, like "Did we appear by chance in a Universe devoid of meaning? Are we 'neuronal beings' who 'do not care about spirit?' Or is our existence – and even that of the whole Universe – part of a process or a goal?"[25] Hence, we are given a new insight into the deeper aspects of life to make life more meaningful.

Conclusion

With deep awareness of the serious limits and limitations of our abilities, not only in exploring nature, but also in the very abilities of our thinking and conceptualizing, several of the hardcore scientists feel humbled in their scientific inquiries. They encounter amazing and unimaginable nuances in nature, both at the sub-atomic and astronomical levels; as we explore into the distant and deep regions of the universe, we are taught that what is reachable by us is only very small portion of the universe, while the invisible and unreachable universe is much larger than what we can imagine. One calculation reveals that the visible (accessible) universe is extremely small and insignificant compared to the invisible universe; it is estimated to be about 150 sextillion times (150×10^{21}) times smaller than the invisible universe.[26] Several of such revelations lead the world of science to be sober and humble about its own achievements. Humility is, thus, no more a spiritual virtue, which is being spoken of only in the domains of religion and spirituality, rather it has solemnly entered the turf of science as well.

As Blasé Pascal has it, "Man is only a reed, frailer than nature, but he is a thinking reed. It does not need the whole universe to wipe him out; a breath, a drop of water, is enough to kill him." But still humans are more powerful and noble than the universe, because, "he knows that he dies and knows the advantage the universe has over him,"[27] whereas the universe that kills him does not, cannot know anything. That is why the words of the Psalmist become more significant and meaningful as science develops to reveal our insignificance in the cosmos, while at the same time the importance of ours as thinking beings: *What is man, that thou art mindful of him? and the son of man, that thou visitest him? For thou hast made him a little lower than the angels, and hast crowned him with glory and honour* (Psalm 8:4 & 5). True, sciences help us to have a better grasp of life and its mechanisms, at its micro and macro levels. But no matter how these sciences advance, they cannot assure us that life is meaningful. *Sciences, can offer good tools to fathom the mystery of life a little more, but to allow them to define life or its dignity and meaning, would lead to the risk of making life a commodity.* Without the spiritual dimensions of life, which enable us to work towards meaning and meaningfulness of life, goal and purpose of life, life would perhaps end up as Shakespeare has it in his *Macbeth:* "Life's but a walking shadow, a poor player, that struts and frets his hour upon the stage, and then is heard no more: it is a tale told by an idiot, a sad tale, told by an idiot, full of sound and fury signifying nothing!"[28]

Endnotes

[1] N. K. Singh, ed., *Science and Spirituality* (New Delhi: Global Vision Publishing House, 2005), pp. 170-71.

[2] Ibid.,p. 172.

[3] Ibid.,

[4] N. K. Singh, ed., *Science and Spirituality*, pp. 180.

[5] Thierry Magnin, "Moral Philosophy – A Space for Dialogue between Science and Theology," in Jean Staune (Ed.), *Science and the Search for Meaning – Perspectives from International Scientists* (Philadelphia, USA: Templeton Foundation Press, 2006), p. 146.

[6] Freeman Dyson, *Disturbing the Universe* (NY: Harper & Row. 1979), p. 250

[7] Paul Davies, *The Mind of God* (NY: Simon & Schuster, 1992), p. 232.

[8] See: https://www.youtube.com/watch?v=Q3jvfvho3CE

[9] Trinh XuanThuan, "Science and Buddhism," in Jean Staune (Ed.), *Science and the Search for Meaning*, p.184;

[10] Paul Davies, "Glimpsing the Mind of God" in Jean Staune (Ed.), *Science and the Search for Meaning*, p. 31.

[11] I have elsewhere elaborated on this: "Can We Ever Know What We Don't Know? – Lessons from Contemporary Sciences", in *Magis – Xavierian Journal of Education*, Vol VII, January 2018, pp. 33 – 42.

[12] See: http://www.phnet.fi/public/mamaa1/einstein.htm.

[13] More on this, Stephen Jayard, "Mysticism and Quantum Physicists – Friends or Foes?", in *Omega – Indian Journal of Science and Religion*, Vol. 3 (2004), pp. 89 – 106.

[14] Stephen Jayard, "Learning to Learn – Dudley Shapere's Invitation to Learn from the Contemporary Science," in Augustine Pamplany (ed.), *Mastery Meets Mystery – Intersecting Science, Philosophy, Religion and Culture, Interdisciplinary Essays in Honour of Prof. Job Kozhamthadam* (New Delhi: Serials Publications Pvt. Ltd., 2015), pp. 62-85.

[15] Jean Staune, ed., *Science and the Search for Meaning*, pp.4-5.

[16] C. G. Hempel, "Science Unlimited?", in *The Philosophy of Carl G. Hempel – Studies in Science, Explanation and Rationality*, ed. James H. Fetzer (Oxford: Oxford University Press, 2001), p. 341

[17] L. Wttgenstein, *Tractatus Logico-Philosophicus* (London: Keganpaul, Trench, Trubner& Co., Ltd. New York: Harcourt, Brace & Company, 1933), 6.52.

[18] For more reflections on the notion of spirituality, please see my book, *A Book That Cannot Be Titled – Spiritual Insights and Reflections on Deeper Dimensions of Life* (New Delhi: Christian World Imprints, 2018).

[19] **Albert Einstein,** "The Merging of Spirit and Science", See:http://www.spaceandmotion.com/albert-einstein-god-religion-theology.htm

[20] N. K. Singh, 2005, p. 185.

[21] See: http://www.piercedhearts.org/theology_heart/teaching_saints/hearts_restless_st_augustine.htm

[22] Stephen Jayard, "The Role of Intuition in Science", in *Together Towards Tomorrow – Interfacing Science and Religion* in India, ed. Kuruvilla Pandikattu, SJ (Pune: Association of Science, Society and Religion, 2006), Pp.145-170

[23] R. C. Pradhan, "Why Consciousness cannot be Deconstructed: Towards a Positive Theory of Consciousness," in *Science and Metaphysics: A Discussion on Consciousness and Genetics*, eds. Sangeetha Menon, Anindya Sinha and B. V. Sreekantan (Bangalore: National Institute of Advanced Studies, 2002), p. 104.

[24] Jean Staune, p.48

[25] Ibid., p. 44

[26] See: https://www.youtube.com/watch?v=Iy7NzjCmUf0.

[27] Blasé Pascal, *Pensees*, Philippe Sellier, ed. (Paris: Mercure de France, 1976).

[28] See:http://everything2.com/title/A+tale+told+by+an+idiot%252C+full+of+sound+and+fury%252C+signifying+nothing

Chapter 9

The Soul – The Missing Link: A Psychiatrist's Perspective on Avenues of Interfacing the Soul, Psychiatry and Neuroscience

Sally John

Abstract

The study of brain, mind and soul has engaged some of the finest researchers of yesteryears, and many more today. It remains an ennobling pursuit, worthy of such captivating interest of studies although the mind and the soul remain fascinating enigmas still. For many, the soul comprises all human emotions, awareness, constructive thought, drive, state of mind and spirit, representing the essence of human persons. For many, soul is the principle of life or the breath of life. But for some others, soul is an imaginary concept, without having any existential value. There were several attempts to find neurological correlates of soul and to scientifically prove or disprove its existence.

The word psyche comes from the Greek word meaning 'soul.' Considering mental illnesses, Hippocrates concluded that madness originated in the brain, while Plato felt that folly was a disease of the soul. Descartes localized the soul in the pineal gland as it lay deep within the brain. Following their footsteps, neuro-scientists have delved deeper to find the soul within the brain and often equated the soul with consciousness. The religious and spiritual understanding of the soul goes transcending physical constraints and boundaries of consciousness and other faculties of the mind and brain. Many believe that this realm does not exist because it is inaccessible to human experiments and research pursuits.

Already while I was a medical student, within me an essential curiosity arose from our anatomy dissection days: 'where in this body is the soul?' Naturally the period of studies and the clinical exposures opened more avenues for this search, inspiring the mind to look beyond biological pursuits for a fascinating realm unprovable by experiments in the labs. Advancing research in the field of neuroscience and psychiatry has been successful to crack through and interlink most normal and abnormal behaviors to physiological variations within the brain and body. The search for the soul has definitely deepened the scientific knowledge about the neuro-biological aspects of human beings especially mental illnesses. Placing the soul into psychiatry may seem esoteric as the concept of the soul or spirituality remains beyond data and statistically analyzable parameters at a realm of experiential understanding and so subjective in itself. Down the lane, as a clinician dealing with diseases of the mind and disorders of behaviour patterns, I realized that a pure biological understanding could not explain or satisfactorily answer many of the clinical situations and dilemmas I encounter daily. The close relation between the provable physical and unprovable spiritual concepts seem to have a significant influence on both the diagnostic and therapeutic interventions in a medical field like Psychiatry. Despite the major advances in the field of neuro-psychiatry, there is an apparent soul loss or a missing link in the current approach of understanding and managing mental illness. It seemed vital to search newer avenues, trying to see an interlink between the soul, spirituality and neuro-biology. This paper is a result of such a quest to find the missing link addressing the possible interphase between the soul, psychiatry and neurosciences.

Key words: Soul, Psychiatry, Neurosciences, biology, consciousness

Introduction

Human desire to know and understand the soul is as old as the development of their reasoning skills. Questions like what is the meaning of life and what happens after this life have always been intriguing realms of human search. Infirmities and sufferings needed an explanatory understanding to see life as something meaningful. The lack of it meant lack of direction and purpose of one's actions. The volition to do better and redefine life is also intrinsically connected with this knowledge. It can also mean an increase in the perception of the depth of suffering in disease conditions and connected essentially with morality and spirituality. This search to understand the purpose of life need not be part of religious beliefs or affiliations although its nuances are intertwined deeply with spirituality.

Mental illnesses always cause significant distress to the sufferer. The understanding of the world and himself/herself change due to the illness,causing disconnection with the real world. The structural and behavioural changes in the brain contribute to this. The impact on the family and care-takers can be high since the illness poses challenges to the way things were perceived so far. It can break the whole meaning system which once gave purpose and direction to life as a whole. Therefore, an alternative way of meaning-making becomes necessary when dealing with mental illness. To have such an understanding without the influence of religious and socio-cultural forces is the challenge in the mental healthcare. The neuro-biological underpinnings and a structure-based understanding lead to the development of psycho pharmacology to relieve suffering in mental illness, which indeed is a path-breaking development. The psychological understanding lead to interventions based on cognitive and behavioural modifications and various psycho-social models of care. Yet the area of the spiritual realm is left without attracting much significance in the mainstream mental health care system. It is a fact that pure biological or psycho-social interventions cannot address many existential questions and longings of a sufferer. Persons with mental health issues need more coherent and holistic explanatory model to deal with the illness. As a mental healthcare professional with religious affiliations, I set out on a challenging journey trying to understand the concept of the soul in an unbiased manner from available resources. It was a pursuit to find if there is any interlink between the soul and psychiatry. In many ways this search is a deeper exploration of the interlacing of spirituality, morality and psychiatry. This article is a synopsis of my research findings.

Various Ways of Understanding the Concept of the Soul

Soul being unseen, abstract and difficult to perceive has always been a subject of interest for researchers from the fields of science and spirituality. Studies are undertaken on this topic in great detail. Most of them were efforts to find if the soul exists at all, and if it does, what its nuances are. Various approaches to understand this concept and its implications are dealt with briefly in the following pages.

Dualistic Approach to the Soul

Pythagoras was a dualist, holding the view that mind and body co-exist, but neither could be explained in terms of the other. He believed in the eternal nature of the soul even pointing towards the possibility of incarnations. Aristotle, on the other hand, believed that mind and soul are one and the property of each other. Rene Descartes was the proponent of mind body dualism in modern times, who propagated the idea that mind and body were two separate entities. According to him, human beings consisted of two quite distinct substances which could not exist in unity. Mind was considered an un-extended, immaterial but thinking substance and body an extended, material but unthinking substance. The mind was more or less equated to the soul concept, and according to him the body and not the mind was subject to mechanical laws.[1]Later, Newton who attempted to explain the laws of nature and transformed the understanding of the physical universe,regarded positively the existence of a divine essence(soul). He considered expressions of the physical world as the creative handiwork of God.[2]

Neuro-biological Approach

There were attempts to restrict the soul as an emergent property of the brain. Anatomical and physiological understandings of the structure and functions of the brain have tried to establish it as the "seat of the soul." As an organ of reflection and memory, brain became identical with the "self" through the existence of consciousness – of mind. Thus, brain has been associated with a range of transcendent concepts – soul, spirit, mind and consciousness. Also, all relate to each other in terms of their perceived location within the brain and the way each works to define the person. Although not everything about the functions of the brain is fully understood, there are efforts to prove that neuro-biology and soul are closely linked.[3,4] Well-known brain scientist Ramachandran believes in the universal spirit of the cosmos, but denies the existence of a soul in human beings.[5] The idea of rejecting whatever cannot be proved physically or considering them as unreal persists as majority of the researchers support this view. Some tend to equate physical senses as reality, throwing away the possible existence of spirituality, soul and God.[6]Examples are people like Bertrand Russell, a Nobel laureate and famous British philosopher who argued against the existence of the soul. According to him, what cannot be proved is possibly non- existing. He argues that even if the existence of the soul can't be disproved, belief in the soul is irrational unless positive evidence or argument can be given in favour of its existence.[7]

Scholars like Ken Wilber has a different approach. As for him, asking about the science of the soul is pointless because it is not a subject science can address. He was regularly asked, "what do you say as a scientist about the soul?" His answer was, "as a scientist, I have nothing to say about the soul. It's not a scientific idea."[8]

Soul is nothing but the sum total of genes and their expressions is another school of argument. The function of the soul is considered to be an emergent property of DNA, the base pairs constructing and constituting properties of soul. This group of researchers consider evolution through genetic chances, changes and combinations as the basis for all forces of life connecting it to natural selection.[9]The vital question, as Pollack asks, is: "Does the capacity of DNA to express novelty through natural selection extend to encoding souls, or is DNA perhaps nothing more than the Golden Calf of the day, worshipped precisely by those too impatient to consider their souls?"[10]Along the same line, there is the view that human beings are beyond what can be defined by their brain, body or DNA, and reducing them to pure biology or physiological functions could be another way of pursing reductionism. According to this view, the very capacity to rise beyond this mere reductionistic constraints can be considered the real function of the soul.

Physical experiments were done to find the soul at various stages in the past. It was with the objective of measuring the physical property of the soul as matter that can be quantified. Interestingly there have been attempts to weigh the soul-substance in a fine balance. It was a search for a space occupying substance, responsible for continuation of personal identity and consciousness which researchers called as 'soul.' Such experiments couldn't be repeated due to moral and ethical implications. All such researches were inconclusive.[11]

Religious Understanding of the Soul

The term soul is often used in religious terms to describe the spiritual or immaterial aspect which enlivens every human being. The perception and meaning attributed to the soul are influenced and shaped by culture and one's belief systems. It is mostly envisioned as the part of one' spiritual self. Some hold that the soul is constant, unchanging and perfect in its essence while others see the soul as making an evolutionary journey. As Agamben points out, the human soul has both philosophically and theologically been associated with the essence of the individual; the soul is what makes the person more than a machine, what constitutes individuality. What ancient writers called the "animal spirit" similarly provided the "vital principle" that animated life.[12]

Soul and Psychological Interlay

The word 'psyche' comes from the Greek word meaning 'soul.' Many use the term soul to mention mind and vice versa based on the unmeasurable realms of mind and soul.[13]The mind has been variously defined as that which is responsible for one's thoughts and feelings; the seat of faculty of reason. Also, as the aspect of the intellect and consciousness experienced as combinations of thought, perception, memory, emotion, will and imagination. Hence, soul is also used to denote these functions of the mind, indirectly meaning dynamics of consciousness. It is also understood as the sum and substance of higher cognitive and affective functions. But the quality of subjective experience of one person differs quite drastically from another. It is to be noted that despite improved understanding of synaptic transmissions, neurotransmitter chemistry, and neuronal computation, there is no accounting for the conscious experience, the "self," free will or "qualia" – the essence of experienced perceptions.[14]

Paranormal Events and the Soul

The field of paranormal experiences is also a well-researched area. Although 'paranormal' events defy the laws of space and time and are immeasurable, they are believed by many to be true. There is a database of verified paranormal findings both naturally occurring and experimental. These include near death experiences, afterlife/reincarnation, past life regression, out of body experiences, precognition, telepathy, remote viewing and healing by means of prayer. Research is still going on about near death experiences and afterlife.

Reported cases of persons experiencing strange events at the point of death are described in literature,vividly remembered and narrated after regaining consciousness. Many of these encounters point to the importance of exploring the spiritual realm in lives of patients during psychological therapies. Some of these can have huge impact on their healing itself as researchers like Shlotterbeck point out.[15]

Stevenson et al claims to have authentic information from a long-term research in the field of reincarnation. Children who claimed to remember previous lives were found and their cases were investigated in different countries and cultures.[16]Pasricha and Stevenson made comparative studies of 54 variables in two groups of Indian cases two generations apart.[17] Repeated investigations in this line by other investigators seem to reproduce his findings which are claimed as authentication of this matter.[18] These investigations show the interest and attempt along with the entwining belief in the existence and expressions of the soul in various forms.

Avenues of Soul and Psychiatry

The definition given by WHO for health encompasses not just physical or mental wellbeing, but intellectual, social and spiritual as well.[19] Over the past century the growth journey of psychiatry as a medical branch had literally been a roller-coaster journey. Before the medical era, symptoms were explained in terms of evil possessions, superstitions like sorcery, enchantment, shamanisms, spiritualization of symptoms and over-involvement of faith healers. Psychiatry also went through the era of social ostracism where the mentally ill were isolated and restricted to asylums and subjected to inhuman treatments. Mental illness attracted significant stigma and apathy in the process, isolating mentally ill from the mainstream society. One's meaning making system is jeopardized in mental illness. Poor insight into the root cause of the illness and difficulty in accepting the illness and prevailing stigma complicated the picture. However, in recent times the explosion of research in the field of neurology has enabled to understand the biological underpinnings of mental illness. Unlike earlier times, advancing research in the field of neuroscience and psychiatry is able to crack through and interlink most normal and abnormal behaviours to the physiological variations within the brain and body. But this process has also caused an extreme separatism of viewing mental illness from a purely biological angle resulting in a loss of soul/essence in psychiatry. For,biological approach alone cannot explain adequately the plethora of subjective experiences in psychiatric illnesses.

Down the lane, as a clinician dealing with diseases of the mind and disorders of behavior patterns, I comprehended this loss of the soul leading to a lack of adequate explanation or having satisfactory answer for many of the clinical dilemmas I encounter daily. The close relation between the provable physical and unprovable metaphysical concepts was found to have a significant influence on both the diagnostic and therapeutic interventions of our daily psychiatric practice. The varied experiences of patients with psychosis or mania with similar chemical or genetic and cultural background, severe unremitting illnesses improving to normalcy when unchartered areas of their belief system get adequately addressed, victims of severe traumatic events regaining wholeness without the aid of any modern therapies, development of resilience even after catastrophes capable of shattering one's meaning system are some of the examples.

Introducing the soul into psychiatry is not an esoteric undertaking.[20] When dealing with patients it means being open, interested, asking the relevant questions and letting the answers come naturally. It means giving enough space and trying to understand what he/she tries to convey. It means having a therapeutic empathy that helps in exploring together the strange experiences and beliefs the person holds strongly. It is more important to find the right question than getting the right answer. Those simple enquiries may reveal the breathtaking story of consciousness and enduring spiritual values and aspirations.[21]Most text books while describing a bio-psycho-social model for psychiatric illnesses conveniently omit the spiritual realm, owing to the difficulty in assessing or objectively commenting on it. "Persons and families feel devastated because a part of their being is lost in the process of illness. Today, clinical practice suffers a soul loss more than mere physical or mental pain caused by the illness. When treatment lacks a holistic approach in modern medicine, the course of recovery is experienced as incomplete or partial." Some prefer to see mental illness as a soulful compensation for the society's soul loss where practices like faith healing, more than medicines, seem to work better with knowledge and experience of the sicknesses, wanderings, longings and fragmenting fate of the soul.[22] This view is totally contradicting to those held by modern medical practice.

Certainly, there is a paradigm shift in the approach of care for mentally ill persons today. It has come a long way forward from isolation in old mental asylum or institutionalization model to a more humane approach of reintegrating the person with a community-oriented care plan.[23] Helping the person regain the lost meaning is the primary responsibility in mental healthcare. Healing is mediated by empathy and a heartfelt understanding of the other. It means entering another's world with sensitivity and respect towards beliefs and values of the person. Thus, the role of spirituality, specifically a deeper search to inner realities that one may call as soul search, is indubitably an intrinsic part of Psychiatry.

Searching for a missing link in psychiatric interventions doesn't specifically target the finding of a soul. One cannot prove the existence or non-existence of the soul through a reality test. But it offers a more effective model when the divine or spiritual element that gives meaning to one's existence is infused into the healing process. Evidence clearly shows that a spiritual integration promotes the furtherance of physical and psychological well-being. Many rehabilitation centres and hospitals in India adopt a conducive atmosphere for spiritual recovery or regaining the lost soul. It becomes most effective in a community fostering freedom of expression and a desire to be well again, making the recovery more personal and lasting. Individual and group activities like meditation, yoga, spiritual exercises,sharing and learning from the mistakes and strengths of others aid in this process. Better renewal occurs when treatment schedule incorporate activities aimed at vocational, spiritual, physical and social well-being of the person.

The Soul and Ethical Implications

There are occasions when one as a mental healthcare professional is confronted with matters of choice in life like using embryos for stem cell research, abortion, euthanasia, human cloning, and dealing with end of life care. Belief in the soul can influence one's ethical decision making. Much research has addressed the strong relationship between one's religious and spiritual background and his/her decisions about ethical issues.[24]An intriguing finding was that one's concepts of soul predicted that person's ethical decision making, independent of religious affiliation.[25]

Concept of the Soul and Abortion

In psychiatric practice, we come across pregnant women asking advice or assurance before undergoing abortion. The situation may be at times complicated with the medication involved in the first trimester of pregnancy or a finding suggestive of a congenital malformation further challenging the decision making. Patient autonomy more than ethical considerations is given importance by many clinicians although their religious or spiritual dispositions do have a bearing in such situations. The question that has been repeatedly debated in many circles is: Does the fertilized ovum possess a soul? If it does, is there a particular stage in the development of the fetus when it acquires a human soul (ensoulment) such that abortion before that stage is not legally prohibited? According to Polkinghorne, the human soul is surely what expresses and carries on the continuity of personhood.[26] Ethics of abortion in the clinical setting is closely interlinked with the idea of personhood. Many believe that a fetus becomes a person only at the time of birth and so the abortion of a fetus doesn't become an offence any time prior to its birth. For patients, religious affiliations more than spirituality have a greater influence on the choice of abortion.[27]

The delayed ensoulment theory dates back to the time of Aristotle. He argued that ensoulment for males was after 40 days and for females, 90 days of conception.[28]Thomas Aquinas was among the Christian philosophers who affirmed delayed ensoulment.[29] The immediate ensoulment theory goes in accordance with current Church teachings. It says that the soul begins to be present from the moment of conception when the sperm fuses with the ovum. Christianity clearly looks at personhood as happening from the time of meeting of two cells. And so, any attempt to hamper the growth and development of the embryo at any stage is considered as a sin. Whereas in Islam the personhood is largely believed to be achieved after four months of conception when the ensoulment happens. By virtue of the possession of the human soul, a person's life is deemed sacred and is to be preserved by all means.[30]Most of contemporary Shiite jurists do not allow abortion at any phase of fetal life without ample reason. But abortion, especially before 4 months, on grounds of fetal or maternal conditions that bring extreme difficulties for the mother or family is allowed.[31] Hinduism has traditionally taught that a soul is reincarnated and enters the embryo at the time of conception. According to the Charaka Samhita, the soul is joined with matter at the time of conception. Soul is described as descending "into the union of semen and (menstrual) blood in the womb in keeping with the psychic disposition of the embryonic matter." In Rig Veda, Vishnu is called "protector of the child-to-be," emphasizing that the fetus deserves even divine reverence. But, the Garbha Upanishad, claims that ensoulment takes place in the seventh month, but this view is not generally part of mainstream Hindu thought. The concept of reincarnation lays it down that the soul in the womb is not a new soul but a continuation of its previous births. The purpose of life is regarded as a progress made by human beings towards liberation from rebirth. The most important thing for each soul is the unfolding of its karmic destiny. Abortion obstructs this unfolding. Therefore, it is condemned.[32]

Aspect of the Soul in Death, Suicide/Euthanasia

The enduring quest of human being is to find something lasting, beyond death and decay. Here it is pertinent to think about how the belief in the soul and death are interconnected. Belief in something permanent gives meaning to direct one's actions in the best possible way. One's belief system acts as a protective factor in such a case, as in the case of Hinduism where the belief in Karma that if one doesn't complete one's Karma or hampers life in any way, there is rebirth in which one has to complete the cycle of life. Likewise, in Christian faith one attains salvation as a reward for the good done in the present life. Here, belief in the soul can become a protective factor from engaging in irresponsible activities.

Here, the question of autonomy over one's life becomes relevant. The case that sparked a lot of debate was about the couple asking for euthanasia in Mumbai because they felt their Kama in this life was over. Some choose to end life because of the fear of prolonged, intractable pain and not willing to burden the family financially or socially. A case was reported from Burari in Delhi where 11 members in a family committed suicide at the same time. It is said to be due to a shared delusional belief or on a cult practice that prescribed a performance of a particular ritual for the salvation of their souls. It is often hard to investigate what drives people to such drastic ends. But their belief systems influence such decisions to a great extent. Belief in possession by the spirit of a dead person is commonly seen in psychiatric clinics as part of cultural belief. Understanding the ethos, traditions, customs and belief systems become essential in the management of such presentations.

The Soul and Terminal illness

Death is the only unchangeable reality. People with end stage diseases face existential questions like what the meaning in life is and what will happen afterdeath. A person diagnosed with terminal illness, having only a few days to live will be distressed by existential questions like, "Will I meet my loved ones after death? How long till I meet my creator or attain salvation and will I be judged for the wrong I have done?" These apprehensions certainly cannot be answered by a biochemical approach to human sufferings. A belief in the existence of the soul or something beyond the earthily life is important in such cases. Essentially it is here, that the spirituality and inner dispositions of the suffering person and the healthcare team become vital.[33]

Conclusion

The information gathered over the course of the past research and enclosed in this review reveal numerous underpinnings to the soul from diverse viewpoints although the understanding of the soul still remains an enigma, outside the realm of any such research. Understanding the neurobiological, psychological and religious explications of the soul can help us better appreciate the divine element guiding humanity since the dawn of time until now. The pursuit to understand the soul will continue as long as human aspirations exist and the directions of such pursuit will depend on the dispositions of the seeker. Psychiatry as a medical branch has much more to explore and learn. Research on the central nervous system and the intricacies of the human brain and its functions will bring much light in the future. Amidst all these searches, whether one will be able to pinpoint the seat of the soul is a question we need to wait and see. But one thing can be said for sure as a concluding remark. None of the future endeavors or neuro-scientific quests to find the soul will be able to separate God from human beings. Irrespective of the path taken in the pursuit of the soul, it will certainly prove to be a powerful guide in shaping humanity's subjective perception of reality, self, God and other existential considerations.

Endnotes

[1] See Douglas C. Long, "Descartes' Argument for Mind-Body Dualism," in *Philosophical Forum* 1, 3 (1969), 259-273.

[2] See T. Millon, *Masters of the Mind: Exploring the Story of Mental Illness from Ancient Times to the New Millennium* (New York: John Wiley & Sons, 2004).

[3] E. Thompson, E., & Varela, F. J., "Radical Embodiment: Neural Dynamics and Consciousness," in *Trends in Cognitive Sciences,* 5,10 (2001), 418-425.

[4] W. Penfield, *Hippocratic Preamble: The Brain and Intelligence. The History and Philosophy of the Brain and Its Functions* (Oxford: Blackwell Scientific, 1958), p. 3.

[5] C. Dean, "Science of the Soul? 'I think, Therefore I Am' Is Losing Force," in *The New York Times,* 2007.

[6] R.A. Sorensen, *Thought Experiments* (Oxford: Oxford University Press on Demand, 1998).

[7] See B. Russell, *The Philosophy of Leibniz.* (Philadelphia: Routledge, 1992).

[8] See Ken Wilber, "The Marriage of Sense and Soul: Integrating Science and Religion," in *Harmony,* no. 120 (1999).

[9] See D. Nelkin, D., & M.S. Lindee, *The DNA Mystique: The Gene as a Cultural Icon*(Ann Arbor: University of Michigan Press, 2010).

[10] R. Pollack, *The Faith of Biology and the Biology of Faith: Order, Meaning, and Free Will in Modern Science* (New York: Columbia University Press, 2000).

[11] Duncan MacDougall, "Hypothesis Regarding the Soul Substance together with Experimental Evidence of Existence of such Substance," *Journal of American Society for physical Research,* 1907.

[12] G. Agamben, *The Coming Community,* Vol. 1 (Minneapolis: U of Minnesota Press, 1993).

[13] P. Macdonald, *History of the Concept of Mind:* Volume 1: *Speculations about Soul, Mind and Spirit from Homer to Hume* (Philadelphia: Routledge, 2017).

[14] P.A. Zizzi, "Emergent consciousness: From the early universe to our mind." Retrieved, from http://arxiv.org/abs/gr-qc/0007006 on 25.4.2018.

[15] Karl Schlotterbeck, *Living Your Past Lives: The Psychology of Past-life Regression,* Universe, 2003.

[16] I. Stevenson, "Reincarnation: Field Studies and Theoretical Issues," in *Handbook of Parapsychology*, 1977, pp. 631-663.

[17] S. Pasricha, S., & I. Stevenson, "Indian Cases of the Reincarnation Type Two Generations Apart," in *Journal of the Society for Psychical Research*, 1987, pp.54, 239.

[18] Keil Jorgen & Stevenson, "Do Cases of the Reincarnation Type Show Similar Features over Many Years? A Study of Turkish Cases a Generation Apart," in Journal *of Scientific Exploration*, Vol. 13, No. 2, 1999, pp. 189–198.

[19] D. Callahan, "The WHO definition of 'health,'" *Hastings Center Studies*, 1973, pp.77-87.

[20] E.P. Shafranske, Religious involvement and professional practices of psychiatrists and other mental health professionals. *Psychiatric Annals, 30*(8, 2000), 525-532.

[21] A. Powell, "Spirituality and Psychiatry– Crossing the Divide. *Spirituality, Values and Mental Health (2007),* 161-171

[22] R. Noll, "Shamanism and Schizophrenia: A State Specific Approach to the 'Schizophrenia Metaphor' of Shamanic States, *American Ethnologist, 10*(3, 1983), 443-459

[23] W.A. Anthony, "Recovery from Mental Illness: The Guiding Vision of the Mental Health Service System in the 1990s," *Psychosocial Rehabilitation Journal, 16*(4, 1993), 11.

[24] R.A. Richert., & E. Smith, "The Essence of Soul Concepts: How Soul Concepts Influence Ethical Reasoning across Religious Affiliation," *Religion, Brain & Behavior,* 2, (2, 2012), 161-176.

[25] C.B. Cohen, "Promises and Perils of Public Deliberation: Contrasting Two National Bioethics Commissions on Embryonic Stem Cell Research," in *Kennedy Institute of Ethics Journal*, 15 (3, 2005), 269-288.

[26] Polkinghorne, J. (2003). *The God of Hope and the End of the World*. Yale University Press.

[27] W. Glannon, "Tracing the Soul: Medical Decisions at the Margins of Life," in *Christ Bioeth* 6 (2000), 49–69.

[28] Aristotle, A. (1991). *History of Animals* (pp. 487b-488a). Cambridge, MA: Harvard University Press.

[29] Jones, D. A. (2005). The human embryo in the Christian tradition: a reconsideration. *Journal of medical ethics, 31*(12), 710-714.

[30] Hussain, A. A. (2005). Ensoulment and the Prohibition of Abortion in Islam. *Islam and Christian–Muslim Relations, 16*(3), 239-250.

[31] Hedayat, K. M., Shooshtarizadeh, P., &Raza, M. (2006). Therapeutic abortion in Islam: contemporary views of Muslim Shiite scholars and effect of recent Iranian legislation. *Journal of medical ethics, 32*(11), 652-657.

[32] Coward, H. G., Lipner, J., & Young, K. K. (1989). *Hindu ethics: Purity, abortion, and euthanasia.* SUNY Press.

[33] Moad, E. O. (2004). Hindu ethics on the moral question of abortion. *Eubios J Asian Int Bioethics, 14*(4), 149-50.

Chapter 10

The Biology of Violence: Ethico-Philosophical Response

Victor Ferrao

Abstract

Violence is not just triggered by the stimuli from outside; it also irrupts from our biology. The dominant model to understand violence for the most part of the twentieth century was exclusively based on sociological and psychological models. Bruce Lipton's *The Biology of Belief* which teaches that our belief has a significant role in our genetic expression also seems to support these models to some extent. But today we have new developments in science that add information that calls us to understand violence in a new light. These new findings chiefly arise from two important branches of science today. Molecular and behaviour genetics are demonstrating that most of our behaviour has in part their basis in genetics. Along with these developments, we can also find that some revolutionary techniques of brain imaging are opening a new window into the biological basis of crime. This study aims to understand the findings of these principles and techniques to understand our anti-social/violent behaviour. These new developments raise several ethical questions and legitimate social fears. They seem to force us to leap into an eugenic society and hence, challenges us to strive to evolve appropriate ethico-philosophical response to these bold findings.

Key Words: Bruce Lipton, molecular genetics, behavioural genetics, brain imaging, biological basis for violence

Unearthing the Biology of Violence

Socio-biology of Violence

The scientific study of the biology of violence is said to have started in the work of Ceasre Lombroso in 1871.[1] He was an Italian army medical officer working as a psychiatrist and prison doctor at an asylum for the criminally insane in the town of Pesaro. While doing a routine autopsy he noticed an unusual indention at the base of the skull that he interpreted as reflecting a small cerebellum. He then proposed a theory based on these observations that the basis of the criminal behaviour was in the brain and the criminals were evolutionary throwback to more primitive species. He suggested that criminals could be identified on the basis of a large jaw, sloping forehead, and singular palmar crease. He in fact created an evolutionary hierarchy that portrayed his eugenic orientation which placed the Jews and northern Italian on top and southern Italian, Bolivians and Peruvians at the bottom. He seems to be tilting to a theory that claimed that criminals are born.[2] But in the twentieth century Lombrosian thinking fell into disrepute and was replaced by the socio-psychological perspective of human behaviour. Thanks to new scientific fields like socio-biology, we can trace as a new and refined presentation of the biological basis of violence and crime. Besides, developments in genetics and neuroscience have revealed the anatomy of violence and it has become possible to hold that there is, in part a biological basis of violence and crime. Like violence, altruistic behaviour that leads us to cooperate with each other is learnt though the evolutionary process because of its benefits.

Genetic Basis of Violence

In evolutionary terms human capacity for anti-social and violent behaviour was not a random occurrence. It is said that this capacity is present among the early hominids who exhibit an ability to reason, communicate and cooperate. At this evolutionary phase, violence may have been employed as a strategy to take away resources from others. The females were also attracted to the brave and resourceful males. Though in our days, we perceive violence as maladaptive and aberrant, social biologists seem to suggest that violence may have been our vital survival strategy. Besides being offensive aggression to gain hold over the resources of others and to attract female, violence was also a defensive mechanism to ward off others who were competitors for their resources and females. Today we are socialized against these violent instincts and we seem to have been domesticated by the civilizing process. Along with the sociologists, the radical genetic basis of our life and behaviour is taught by geneticist like by Richard Dawkins in his 1976 book, *The Selfish Gene.*[3] His thesis is that genes are ruthlessly selfish in their struggle for survival giving rise to selfish human behaviour. He makes genes the basic unit of selfishness and presents a gene-eye-view of violence and crime.

Neuroscientific Basis of Violence

PET (Positron Emission Topography) allows us to measure the metabolic activity of different regions of the brain simultaneously. It is found that prefrontal cortex (that part of the brain which is above our eyes and bellow the forehead) is the chief site in the brain to understand violence. A study of a sample of 41 persons revealed that prefrontal cortex of some persons who were involved in murders showed a striking lack of activation. They did not exhibit any such problems with the occipital cortex which houses our vision system as it manifested strong activation (glucose metabolism). It seems to indicate that a poor functioning of the prefrontal cortex would dispose someone to violence. Although these brain imaging techniques does not necessarily establish causality, we are led to move towards it in this context. This is so because reduced prefrontal functioning can result in loss of control of the functioning of some evolutionary primitive parts of the brain such as the limbic system that generates raw emotions such as rage and anger. A more sophisticated prefrontal system keeps a control on these limbic emotions. If prefrontal cortex is dysfunctional, these emotions will boil over.[4] Besides, research on neurological patients who had damaged prefrontal cortex exhibited tendencies to take risks, irresponsible behaviour and rule breaking. This means such people are already tilting to violent behaviour. At the personality level, any damage at the orbitofrontal cortex triggered impulsivity, loss of self-control, inability to adapt and inhibit behaviour appropriately.[5]

Biology of Violence and Nature/ Nurture Tangle

The Violence as a Public health Problem

Deep down in the brain, bellow the civilized upper crust of the prefrontal cortex we have the limbic system that is the site of our emotion and more primitive parts of our neural makeup. It is here that the amygdale that fires up our emotions that trigger both predatory and affective attack is placed. The hippocampus regulates aggression and when stimulated sets in motion predatory attack. Thalamus is a relay station between emotional limbic system. Mid brain when triggered gives expression to full-blooded affective emotional aggression. Studies on murderers, both reactive and proactive ones, exhibit a higher activation of the sub cortical limbic regions. Thus, behind the apparent innocent face of the criminal there is a lot bubbling under the deeper sub cortical cauldron of the brain functioning.   Some researcher have also tried to demonstrate that a poorly functioning hippocampus and a dysfunctional posterior cingulate that lies more towards the rear of the head and deep inside the middle of the brain are predisposing some people to violent anti-social and criminal behaviours.[6] These studies seem to indicate that violence and crime is a public health problem and as such can be treated. Hence, we need to think of violence in medical terms.

Biosocial Factors of Violence

Violence is not only grounded in biology. The biological disposition for violence coupled with social dysfunctional upbringing has shown that the rate of crime increases four times more in such cases than those who had normal social upbringing but has biological disposition.[7] Further, it has been found that biosocial interaction leads to the unset of violence early in age.[8] But these studies somehow did not explain violence that started later in life. The social factor that aggravates the already biological disposition for violence was found to be maternal rejection like attempts to abort the foetus, as found in Copenhagen studies, or those that were exposed to famine, starving and malnutrition, as found by the studies of New York State Psychiatric Institute. Such factors were more prone to exhibit violent criminal behaviour.[9] Here one also can trace that a mother who had an unwanted pregnancy, but did not take any action that suggests rejection did not seem to affect the violent behavioural outcomes of the child. It was found that maternal rejection seems to be more responsible for the launching of particularly violent careers.[10] All this shows that the hand that rocks the cradle is ruling the world as the early period when connected with the mother really counts,[11] and any damage to this child-mother bond can produce a psychopath adult.[12] This means some of us are born with markers of violence but social factors can aggravate our violent behaviour.

Food and Violence

The link between nutrition and violence has been studied by several researchers. Some have broadened it to include larger factors like social deprivation but found that malnutrition leads to increased aggressive behaviour.[13] Within the malnutrition deficiency of iron was found to be more prone to facilitate aggressive behaviour.[14] It is found that children below the age of three afflicted by malnutrition also exhibit low IQ at that age and also at the age of 11 years.[15] The decreasing scores of IQ increase aggressive behaviour. Some studies have shown that people with high fish diets do not exhibit hostile and aggressive behaviour. People with low levels of Omega-3 have been shown to be more aggressive.[16] Omega-3 has two important components: DHA (docosahexaenoic acid) and EPA (eicosapentaenoic acid). These are known to play a vital role in neural structure and function.[17] Like iron, zinc deficiency has been shown to be igniting possibilities of increased violent behaviour. Micronutrients like iron and zinc are necessary for the production of neurotransmitters and are important for brain and cognitive development.[18] Similarly it is said that high tryptophan diet reduces aggressive behaviour. Some studies have revealed that low blood sugars lead people to both physical and verbal violence.[19] More studies reveal that lead is lethal to our brain. It is found to be neurotoxic. The toxic effects of lead are documented by several brain-imaging studies among workers exposed to lead. It has been shown that these workers manifest considerable amount of brain volume reduction. It has been demonstrated that people who are in an atmosphere of lead exposure are at risk to violent behaviour.[20] Hair samples of violent offenders in U.S have shown high levels of cadmium, and have also been linked to aggressive behaviour among children living close to cadmium mines.[21] Some say that excessive manganese can result into lowering brain functioning and lower IQs.[22] Mercury is toxic to the brain and other bodily organs but despite its toxicity, it has been shown that it does not necessarily predispose humans to violent behaviour. This has been shown by some studies on individuals with high levels of mercury in their blood, but there are also other studies that have shown conflicting results regarding the propensity of mercury to induce aggressive behaviour.[23] It has been studied that it is selenium that latches on to mercury molecule and keeps it from binding with brain tissue in some cases preventing brain damage.[24]

Deepening the Nature /Nurture Puzzle

The Biosocial Enlargement

It has been well accepted that social factors do influence criminal behaviour. Now with the studies on the biology of violence, we have to talk about biosocial factors of criminal behaviour – social upbringing, peers, etc. There is body politics irrupting from the bodies as they are radicalised, marked by caste/race, medically named as disabled/diseased/unfit, etc. Neighbourhoods, poverty, dysfunctional brain can increase violent behaviour among humans. Biological dispositions get a social push and we find mindless human violence. Scientists have shown the link between the genes, brains and violence. But social factors cannot be kept out from these biological inclinations that convert into full-blooded psychopathology that triggers antisocial and violent behaviours among humans. Besides, changes in gene expression (Epigenetics) have been studied and environmental along with psycho-social factors also have been shown to play a role in the proteomics that will also affect the genomics.[25] Such factors have led to the consideration of biological factors in criminal behaviour leading to the emergence of neural-law in USA.[26]

The Question of Agency

The reduction of violent behaviour to biosocial factors takes away human agency. Such a view does question the existence of human freedom and seems to indicate that we are all determined by our biology and sociology and we cannot do anything about it. This simply means that the freedom that we think we have is a delusion. Therefore, our legal and justice system that is dealing with crime and its punishment is fundamentally flawed and we are punishing innocent and helpless people. This also reduces into a disease that may be cured by effecting biological changes in our brain. Primatologists like Travis Rayne Pickering teach that primates like Chimpanzees also rape murder and wage rudimentary wars.[27] Hence, we have the challenge to respond to new biological determinism. This means we are faced with biology of unfreedom that seems to take away all moral responsibility in the context of human criminality.

Dangers of Neo-eugenics

These new findings seem to have resurrected the age old racists divide. The biology of violence seems to draw a line between those who enjoy good birth and those who are born with biological predispositions for violence. We seem to be re-inaugurating the dangerous brave new world of Aldous Huxley riving the 'us and them' divisions even more strongly than before. These prospects produce legitimate fears and raise ethical questions that we have to face in the context of this rising neo-eugenics.

Facing the Biology of Violence

Crime and Biological Cure

With the arrival of the biology of violence, there is optimism among some regarding the possibilities of treating violence as a disease. Attending to the biological factors that induce violence has shown that conduct disorder and violence can be controlled to a large extent. While we attend to the biological pathways to violence, we have to heal the socio-psycho pathways to violence also. Besides, some reformists have used extreme interventions like castrations to reduce violent behaviours among some unmanageable people – paradoxically healing violence with violence. This makes us think how what we call biological intervention is not free from violence. Yet, these studies are important to prevent individual as well as human collective violence and even total human extermination.

Neuro-scientific Evidence and Law

The new findings of the biology of violence have literally put human brain on trial. The neuro-scientific evidence seems to be interrogating our well-established tradition of justice and brings mercy to the fore. As the findings of genetics and neurobiology gain wider circulation and social acceptance, the current legal system has begun to look cruel, and the need of its review has begun to look more urgent. This attention to the biological evidence to human violence is welcome and can be emancipative.

Biology of (Un) freedom

The biology of violence has given a hard blow to human freedom. It seems that it has put hard determinism on solid scientific footing. While we face these findings of what may be also called the science of (un)freedom, we cannot blindly accept this physicalist and positivist reductionism of human behaviour as merely brain driven. Besides brain, humans also have a mind and are spiritual beings. While we embrace these important findings, we cannot fall into the reductive traps that merely impoverish and dehumanize humans. Hence, we may tilt to compatibilism (existence of freewill and determinism together), if not libertarianism as regards the existence of human freedom. This way we can still consider moral responsibility of the human person for both good and evil behaviour. This means we have to critically accept the findings of the biology of violence.

Conclusion

The biology of violence seems to be constructing a portrait *of Homo Pugnax*, the violent species. The basis of violence in our biological factors, without taking away the social factors, is enlightening and insightful; yet it has a great challenge to the existence of human agency, and consequently to moral culpability to violent and aggressive crimes. While these findings push us towards a denial of human freedom and as such the biology of violence becomes a form of biology of (un)freedom, we resist this temptation of philosophical suicide, and wish to overcome the reductive anthropology of science that does not recognize the mind and the soul. This reductive anthropology fixes human behaviour into the genes and brain mechanisms, but we try to open these findings to the synergy that mind and soul brings in human life.

Endnotes

[1] D.G. Horn, *The Criminal Body and Lombroso and the Anatomy of Defiance* (New York: Routlege, 2002)

[2] Adrain Raine, *The Anatomy of Violence: the Biological Roots of Crime* (London: Penguin Books,2013) 11-13.

[3] Richard Dawkins, *The Selfish Gene* (New York: Oxford University Press, 1976).

[4] A. Damasio, *Decartes' Error:Emotion, Reason and Human Brian* (New York: G. P. Putmam's son, 1994)

[5] Adrain Raine, *The Anatomy of Violence*, 67-69.

[6] Ibid., 76-83.

[7] Ibid., 186.

[8] Ibid.

[9] Ibid., 207.

[10] Ibid., 187.

[11] Ibid., 191.

[12] Ibid., 192.

[13] Ibid., 209.

[14] Ibid 210.

[15] Ibid. 211.

[16] Ibid., 215.

[17] Ibid.

[18] Ibid., 218

[19] Ibid., 222.

[20] Ibid., 223-225.

[21] Ibid.,227-228

[22] Ibid., 229-230.

[23] Ibid., 230-231.

[24] Ibid.,231.

[25] Ibid., 364-265.

[26] S.A. Barnett, *Biology and Human Freedom: an Essay on the Implication of Human Ethology* (Cambridge: Cambridge University Press, 1988), 41.

[27] https://www.the-scientist.com/?articles.view/articleNo/34795/title/The-Roots-of-Violence/ accessed on 17th Nov. 2017.

Chapter 11

Spiritual Dimension of Humans in the Light of Sri Aurobindo and the Limitations of Science

Ramesh Bijlani

Abstract

There are three principal routes to the deeper truths of existence: mystic experience, metaphysical speculation, and scientific research. True to the Hindu tradition, Sri Aurobindo considered experience to be the most reliable route to Truth. But since he was not only a seer but also an intellectual genius, in The *Life Divine* he rationalized the Truth as experienced by him and other mystics. He also dealt with the extent to which science can go into metaphysical enquiry. While acknowledging the contributions made by science to spirituality, he also pointed out the limitations of the scientific method in addressing questions on the subject. His reservations about science are fundamental, and continue to be valid in spite of recent advances in science. What recent advances have done is to temper the earlier denial of the spiritual worldview by science because research in physics, neurophysiology and medicine has observed facts and phenomena that are consistent with the corollaries and implications of mystic experience.

While experience is supreme, it is possible to rationalize it, and build a philosophy on the basis of experience. That is the origin of the major Indian systems of philosophy. But in the process of building a philosophy on the basis of experience, the mind can go into its characteristic speculative excursions. That is how we can get several philosophies from essentially the same experience. Among the older interpretations of Vedanta, Sri Aurobindo's philosophy comes closest to the qualified non-dualistic version, but is unique in a variety of ways. First, it has a strong world-affirming and life-embracing tilt. Secondly, it is couched strongly in terms of evolution. Finally, it also goes considerably at length into the course evolution is likely to take, and the role human beings can play in shaping the future of the world. Not all these aspects are within the realm of science, but some of the aspects where science and spirituality can interact will be discussed, primarily in terms of recent advances in neurophysiology and clinical medicine.

Briefly, that the spiritual experience is not a hallucination is supported by brain imaging studies which show a characteristic pattern associated with the experience. Thus the brain is wired for manifesting the spiritual experience in some individuals under certain conditions. Secondly, the basic interrelatedness of all creation is consistent with the effects of mind over matter not only in the human body but also in plants, microorganisms and enzymatic reactions. That a human being can evolve is consistent with the structural and chemical changes in the brain resulting from long-term spiritual practices. But science can only talk in terms of associations, correlations and facts that are consistent with spiritual truths. Science can neither prove nor disprove these facts.

One fundamental point on which it is difficult to reconcile science and spirituality is the genesis of consciousness. Treating matter as primary, science considers consciousness to be an emergent property of the brain. On the other hand, in spirituality, consciousness is primary, and the brain is only an instrument that channelizes consciousness.

It is possible to support or contradict both points of view on rational grounds, and further scientific research is unlikely to give us a definitive conclusion.

Introduction

There are some difficult questions about the universe in which we live, which have not been answered with certainty in spite of receiving attention from some of the best minds for several millennia. These are questions such as how the material universe was created; what is the relationship between the Creator, if any, and its creation; what is the role of individuals in the universe; and what is the purpose of human life. Traditionally, there have been two principal methods that have been used to explore these questions.

One is the method used by the mystics. This method consists of a combination of intense concentration and extreme degrees of self-purification. The answers have come in the form of experiences, which have been called mystical or spiritual experiences. These experiences are completely outside, and sometimes contradictory to,ordinary sensory experiences. But those who have received these experiences are very sure that the answers they have received correspond to the Truth. Even among the masses who generally construct their picture of reality on the basis of sensory experiences, the predominant tendency has been to trust the mystics, and consider them to be the enlightened ones. Although mystics have not been many at any given time and at any given place, over thousands of years, there have been a large number of them all over the world and they have been drawn from all religious traditions. To this select group belong the *rishis* (those who have seen, or the seers) of the Hindu tradition, the Sufis of the Islamic tradition, and the mystics of the Christian and Judaic traditions. Some of the mystics have tried to describe in words what they have experienced, and on the basis of their experiences,their perception of the Truth. Many comparable descriptions available from the works of *Rishis*, Sufis and Mystics have been brought together at one place by

Aldous Huxley in his book, *The Perennial Philosophy*. The remarkable similarity seen in these descriptions, in spite of the enlightened authors being separated by time, tradition and geography, suggests that their experiences do correspond to the Truth.

The second method is that of philosophers. Philosophy is based on rational analysis. Rational analysis is based on mental activity. On the other hand, what we are trying to understand is the genesis of the universe, of which mental activity is itself only a small fraction. It is difficult for anything to understand what is larger than itself. Therefore, rational analysis is an inadequate and inappropriate tool for exploring the deeper truths of existence. However, that has not prevented philosophers from dealing with this issue. The outcome of such intellectual effort is metaphysical speculation. Aristotle is the father of metaphysical speculation.

In the Hindu tradition, spiritual experience is considered the most reliable route to the highest Truth. But the Truth discovered through experience can be rationalized. Rationalization of spiritual experience gives a spiritual philosophy. Thus, the Upanishads, which are descriptions of the spiritual experiences of *rishis*, form the basis of Vedanta, which is the best known spiritual philosophy of the Hindu tradition and is based on Badrayana's *Vedanta Sutra*. But the intellect is so versatile that rationalization of the same basic truths can give us many philosophies. That is how the Hindu tradition not only has philosophies other than Vedanta, it also has many interpretations of Vedanta, ranging from non-dualism (Sankara) through qualified non-dualism (Ramanuja) to dualism (Madhavacharya). True to the Hindu tradition, Sri Aurobindo considered experience to be the most reliable route to Truth. But since he was not only a seer but also an intellectual genius, in *The Life Divine* he rationalized the Truth as experienced by him and other mystics. *The Life Divine* may be considered a modern interpretation of Vedanta in the English language. His interpretation is close to qualified non-dualism, but goes beyond it in its emphasis on evolution of consciousness. In *The Life Divine*, Sri Aurobindo provides his roadmap and vision of the future of the human race based on the evolutionary thrust that characterizes the creation on earth.

To the two traditional methods of exploring the mysteries of existence has been added scientific research. Modern science has had a chequered history since its beginnings with the European Renaissance in the sixteenth century. Starting with conflict with religion, it emerged 'triumphant' within three hundred years.[1] Partly because of this historical factor, and partly because of its preoccupation with the physical universe, science distanced itself from metaphysics. It not only did not try to address the deeper truths of existence, it considered metaphysics and its close cousins such as religion and spirituality to be meaningless unverifiable superstitions. Its approach was, 'if I do not see it, it does not exist,' a stance that Sri Aurobindo calls 'denial of the materialist.' However, this division between science and spirituality started getting blurred with developments in quantum physics. Physicists discovered truths that were completely contrary to common sense. They also came up with findings which were consistent with spiritual philosophies. After the physicists, neurophysiologists took interest in exploring states of consciousness, mapped brain activity during meditation, and found patterns of brain activity which were specifically associated with peak experiences. The last among the scientists to get on to the bandwagon are physicians who interpret the observations made in the experiments related to non-local healing as consistent with spiritual philosophies.

So successful has the scientific enterprise been in a relatively short period of five hundred years that the word 'scientific' has come to be seen as a synonym for 'true, valid and worthwhile.' Therefore, society is so enamoured by science at last condescending to get involved in spirituality that scientific experiments are quoted enthusiastically in support of spiritual truths, sometimes even at the expense of interpreting the findings of science in an unscientific manner. Even today, science deals with a sphere much narrower than spirituality, and its methods have limitations in exploring the deeper truths of existence. Everything that science explores can be a part of spirituality; all of spirituality on the other hand cannot fit into science. Spirituality deals with the Whole Truth, science deals with a part of the Whole Truth. The validity of the Whole Truth does not depend upon certification by its part. What we need is a dispassionate view of the details that science is adding to some aspects of spirituality, as well as the limitations of science in dealing with spiritual truths. With this background, we can now see the view that Sri Aurobindo had on the interactions between science and spirituality.

Search for Truth

Both science and spirituality seek truth. Their methods also have a basic similarity. But there are different layers of truth. Sri Aurobindo says:

> It is necessary to distinguish between the essential Reality, the phenomenal reality dependent on it and arising out of it, and the restricted and often misleading experience or notion of either that is created by our sense-experience and our reason. ... The physical scientist probing into phenomena erects formulas and standards based on the objective and phenomenal reality and its processes ... The psychologist ... discovers another domain of realities, subjective in character, ... But there is a deeper probing which brings up the truth of the self and spirit and establishes a greater order of the real ... it is the reason accustomed to deal with the finite that makes these exclusions; it cuts the whole into segments and can select one segment of the whole as if it were the entire reality. ... When we come to the experiences of the spiritual which is itself the whole or contains the whole in itself, our mind carries there too its segmenting reason and the definitions necessary to a finite cognition; it cuts a line of section between the infinite and the finite, the spirit and its phenomena or manifestations, and dubs those as real and these as unreal. But an original and ultimate consciousness embracing all the terms of existence in a single integral view would see the whole in its spiritual essential reality and the phenomenon as a phenomenon or manifestation of that reality. ... When thus seen integrally, the phenomenal reality ... would have another deeper reality ... it would put on another reality of a spiritual character; the finite would reveal itself as a power, a movement, a process of the Infinite. ... What our mind sees as contraries may be to the infinite consciousness not contraries but complementaries: essence

and phenomenon of the essence are complementary to each other, not contradictory.[2]

Thus, science, treating material as the basis of phenomena of nature, discovers the laws governing the phenomenal or pragmatic reality. On the other hand, spirituality looks upon the phenomenal reality as the manifestation of an Absolute Reality which is imperishable, constant, all-embracing, and free of any contradictions. Perception of this spiritual Truth requires for its realization tools higher than sense-organs and reason. While realization of the highest, most comprehensive, unifying Truth requires a tool higher than reason, the Truth itself can be rationalized, and can even be arrived at by rational analysis.

Contributions of Science to the Search for Truth

While the Truth cannot be realized by the tools of science, science has aided the recognition of spiritual truths in ways more than one. First, science has helped sharpen the intellect. What the intellect perceives and accepts after critical examination is also a part of the spiritual truths. Science has helped avoid distortion of these truths by superstitions, dogmas and pre-conceived notions. Sri Aurobindo says:

> It is well that we should recognize the enormous, the indispensable utility of the very brief period of rationalistic Materialism through which humanity has been passing. For that vast field of evidence and experience which now begins to reopen its gates to us, can only be safely entered when the intellect has been severely trained to a clear austerity; seized on by unripe minds, it [intellect] lends itself to the most perilous distortions and misleading imaginations and actually in the past encrusted a real nucleus of truth with such an accretion of perverting superstitions and irrationalizing dogmas that all advance in true knowledge was rendered impossible. It became necessary for a time to make a clean sweep at once of the truth and its disguise in order that the road might be clear for a new departure and a surer advance.[3]

Another important contribution of science is the logic and detail that knowledge of the physical universe brings to spirituality. Sri Aurobindo says, "The touch of Earth is always reinvigorating to the son of Earth, even when he seeks a supraphysical knowledge. It may even be said that the supraphysical can only be mastered in its fullness – to its heights we can always reach – when we keep our feet firmly on the physical."[4] Science also inspires awe and wonder by revealing to us the knowledge of the physical universe, and we start admiring, adoring and worshipping the Higher Power that designed the universe. For example in life sciences, we learn how processes are coordinated like an orchestra, using signals at sub-microscopic level which seem to depend on the electrical charge that a molecule carries or the shape it has. The electrical charge and shape are only the visible indicators of an infinite intelligence packed in each electron. As Sri Aurobindo says, "Science reveals to us how minute is the care, how cunning the device, how intense the absorption it bestows upon the smallest of its works as on the largest."[5]

Human Search for Truth Is Unstoppable

Since the soul of science is search for knowledge, it was only to be expected that it will not be able to stop with discoveries of the material universe. Science, with its conscientious approach to remain open to new knowledge, was destined to reach a point where it will overcome its own self-imposed limitations, and open itself up to even knowledge that challenges some of its own assumptions. Referring to modern science based on materialism, Sri Aurobindo says, "… since its very soul is the search for Knowledge, it will be unable to cry a halt; as it reaches the barriers of sense-knowledge and of the reasoning from sense-knowledge, its very rush will carry it beyond … We see already that advance in its obscure beginnings. … Science confirms in the domain of Matter the conceptions and even the very formulae of language which were arrived at, by a very different method, in the Vedanta, – the original Vedanta, not of the schools of metaphysical philosophy, but of the Upanishads."[6] And elsewhere, he says, "The intellect itself, having reached near to the natural limits of the capacity of physical discovery, … has begun, still tentatively and hesitatingly, to direct an eye of research on the deeper secrets of the mind and the life-force and on the domain of the occult which it had rejected *a priori*, in order to know what there may be in it that is true."[7]

Scientific Studies That Have Redefined Science

The first among the scientists to become open to spiritual truths were the physicists. It all started with the theory of relativity. Einstein turned not only Newtonian mechanics but also commonsense upside down.Some of the observations that prompted a shift in the attitude of scientists were that first, an observed phenomenon is affected by the observer; and secondly, the spin of an electron in New Delhi can affect the spin of another electron in New York. These observations are consistent with interconnectedness between the observer and a material phenomenon, and between two material objects separated by a long distance. Interconnectedness of all creation, animate and inanimate, and the continuity of consciousness are spiritual truths. These ideas prompted physicists like Fritjof Capra to write classics such as *The Tao of Physics.*

The next among the scientists to investigate spiritual matters were neurophysiologists. Among the pioneers were Prof. B.K. Anand, Prof. G.S. Chhina and Prof. Baldev Singh of the All India Institute of Medical Sciences, New Delhi, who demonstrated in 1961 that the electroencephalographic records of advanced yogis had a predominance of alpha waves, the waves associated with being awake but totally relaxed. Further, during the meditative state, these waves could not be disturbed even by sensory stimuli such as a bang or a touch.

Recently, brain has been imaged during spiritual practices with sophisticated techniques which can tell us about the regional distribution of brain activity. The activity does follow a characteristic pattern. The classical studies are those of Andrew Newberg and Eugene d'Aquili, who observed that the peak of spiritual experiences in meditating Buddhist monks and Christian nuns coincides with dramatic reduction in the activity of the brain's left parietal lobe. This is the part of the brain which processes sensory information, and helps define the boundary between the individual and the rest of the universe. Silence of this area at the peak of meditation is not surprising because reducing and ignoring sensory inputs is an important component of meditation. Further, since this is the area which enables the individual to identify himself/herself as separate from the rest of the universe, inactivity of this area is likely to erase this boundary. A feeling of unity with the universe, a feeling of being a drop in an ocean, is the core of spiritual experiences. Newberg and d'Aquili have hypothesized that the brain is so wired that the vacuum created by inactivity of the area which thrives on 'normal' sensory experiences is filled in by the transcendent experience. The experience is indeed real; the question that has not been, and probably cannot be answered is whether the experience corresponds to a reality that really exists. Since science is incapable of proving a negative, it is unreasonable to expect from science proof for the nonexistence of a supraphysical reality. Andrew Newberg, has merely said: "The possibility of such a reality is not inconsistent with science." Since these studies by Andrew Newberg and Eugene d'Aquili, there have been other similar studies, and some of them have also shown, besides the activity pattern in the brain, also an increase in neuronal connections and an increase in the cortical thickness of the regions of the brain that are more active in experienced meditators.[8]

After the neurophysiologists, the next group of scientists that has made observations consistent with the spiritual worldview are the clinicians. The first major group of studies in this category were those which discovered a positive, although weak, effect of intercessory prayer on healing.[9] That the positive healing emotions of the healer or a well-wisher could really help suggests a connection between the healer's mind and the patient's body. Spiritually speaking, the effect is easy to explain. The healer's mind and the patient's body are two modes of the same Supreme Consciousness. Therefore, changes in one mode of Consciousness can affect another mode of the same Consciousness. But the scientific explanation of the phenomenon has been rather skeptical. It has attributed the effect to the patient believing in the power of somebody praying for him. Thus the patient gets better because he expects to. Hence, the studies are thought to depend on the power of the patient's mind on his own body. Studies on animals and other forms of creation have helped clarify this objection.

A frequently cited study was done on experimentally produced surgical wounds in two groups of mice. In the experimental group, a spiritual healer held the cages for 15 minutes twice daily for 15 days. The wounds healed faster in the experimental group than in the control group, which did not receive any such treatment. It might be argued that the effect was due to the extra attention that the experimental mice received, once again demonstrating only the mind-body connection within the individual. Several studies have been done on microorganisms. Positive results have frequently been reported regarding the healer's ability to influence (positively or negatively) the growth of fungi, bacteria or cancer cells, and the rate of mutation of *Escherichia coli*. A study examined the effect of psychosomatic power emitted through Zen meditation by a Zen master on prostate cancer cells. It was found that the experimental treatment significantly reduced the growth rate and enhanced the expression of a differentiation antigen in the cancer cells.[10]Even the velocity of the reaction between a substrate and an enzyme in a test-tube can be influenced by wishing, willing or intending. Several such studies have been compiled by Benor.[11]What all these studies suggest is an unmediated, unmitigated and instantaneous effect of one mode of consciousness (the mind of a person) on a variety of other modes of consciousness, including the mode represented by chemicals in a test tube.

A Balanced View of Science-Spirituality Interaction

While the science-spirituality interaction adds to human knowledge and understanding of the universe, it is good to keep in mind a few fundamentals. Spirituality deals with the whole, while science deals with only a part. Spirituality uses the method of intense concentration and self-purification, and realizes Truth by identity. Science uses a combination of sensory perception, sometimes magnified enormously by instruments, and logic. In spirituality, consciousness is primary; in science, matter is primary.

Reception of Scientific Studies by the Spiritually Inclined

Because of the prestige that science enjoys today, the reception of scientific studies by the spiritually inclined has been rather over-enthusiastic. They seem to be grateful to the scientists who have condescended to look at spiritual matters. The result has been unfortunate in at least two ways.

First, there has been a tendency to misinterpret results, to see in the results of scientific studies what is not there. When a physiologist says that a specific pattern of brain activity is associated with a specific experience, he is only talking of an association. An association does not prove a cause and effect relationship. The maximum one may conclude from the association is that the experience of the meditator is genuine. The scientific study does not prove that the experience corresponds to something that really exists. When a clinical study shows that prayer helps healing, it only shows that prayer works. The study does not prove that the prayer works through divine intervention. In fact, scientists have alternative explanations for how it might work irrespective of divine intervention. When the scientists only assert that certain observations are consistent with the spiritual worldview, the spiritually inclined tend to interpret the observations as scientific proof of the spiritual worldview. Being consistent only means that there is no inevitable conflict between the scientific observations and the spiritual worldview. The scientific observations neither prove nor disprove the spiritual worldview, and are incapable of doing it because the methods of science are not only inadequate, but also inappropriate for the task. The methods are inappropriate because science explores the physical universe, the universe that can be perceived objectively. Modern physics accepts that observations of the physical universe may be affected by the observer, but the exploration is nevertheless directed at the physical universe.

The second unfortunate result of misplaced enthusiasm of the spiritually inclined is that they themselves try to do some 'research' that may be at best be called 'pseudoscience.' Without any clarity about the question being asked, and the scope of the techniques used, a lot of data is collected, and presented as 'proof' of the spiritual truths. The amount of data, the sophistication of the techniques used, and the elegance of graphic representation does not constitute proof; often it does not even constitute a scientific study.

What the spiritually inclined should remember is that spirituality is not dependent upon a certificate from science for the validity of its truths. Spiritual truths will remain subjective in character, and will be real only to the one who has experienced them. For the rest, these truths will be a matter of faith, which is optional. Spiritual masters were, and continue to be, satisfied to get their answers by a route higher than the mental. They do not look for validation of these truths by the mental methods used by scientists.

Those who are passionate about spirituality also have a tendency to attribute many discoveries of modern science to spiritual masters, which creates needless and unjustified antagonism between spirituality and science. While it is true that many scientific discoveries were anticipated by spiritual masters, there are a few caveats to consider. First, the spiritual masters were not seeking scientific truths; for them, these truths were part of the whole Truth that they discovered. Secondly, pride based on precedence fosters complacency. It is possible to arrive at the same truths independently by different routes at different points in time – that, by itself, does not confer superiority on the one who discovered it first. Thirdly, spiritual masters are at a level of consciousness too high to care for such superiority, even if it is justified. Finally, it has to be conceded that the scientific truths that had been hinted at by spiritual masters have acquired considerable additional depth and detail as a result of the efforts of modern science. In short, spiritual enthusiasts have to guard against two common but opposing tendencies: one, trying to glorify spirituality by saying that spirituality gave us all of modern science long ago; and two, seeking a certificate from science that it has validated spiritual truths. If we are sure that spirituality gave us long ago all what modern science is saying today, why do we have to get, somehow or the other, a scientific proof for spiritual truths? It would be better to simply accept that spirituality can give us some scientific truths but not objective evidence; on the other hand, science may touch the periphery of spirituality but can neither prove nor disprove spiritual truths.

Strictly speaking, spiritual truths do not need scientific proof, because although both spirituality and science seek truth, they seek it in different domains. Science deals with finite truths, whereas spirituality reaches out to the Infinite. Further, spiritual truths may include scientific truths, but the converse is not true. The Whole is not dependent on its parts for the proof of Its existence.

The Attitude of Scientists

While science has stretched its limits, many hard-core scientists continue to have a dismissive attitude to spirituality. Among those who are critical of the spiritual worldview, there is a tendency to interpret the inability of science to find evidence in its favour to be proof of the worldview being false. First, absence of proof is not proof of absence. Secondly, being a scientifically derived fact is not synonymous with being true. Scientific facts are tentative; that is the weakness of science. Scientific facts are open to revision by better research; that is the beauty of science. Finally, the refusal to entertain the very possibility of something that science does not know is in itself unscientific. It is important to understand that verification of scientific discoveries depends on using the same methods as the discoverer, and having faith in the methods. Scientific verification of the presence of cells in a leaf is impossible if the leaf is examined with the naked eye. Using the same yardstick, spiritual truths cannot be questioned unless we have examined them using the same method that the rishis and mystics have used – the method of intense concentration and an extreme degree of self-purification.

Limitations of Science

The fundamental limitations of science arise from its basic instrument, the mind; and its basic assumption to treat matter as primary.

The mind is an instrument, which is very well developed in humans, but is still inadequate for direct perception of the whole Truth. It is like a torch that can show us the next few feet of the path, but cannot illumine the entire route to the goal. Its method is linear, logical, analytic and calculative. On the limitations of the mind, Sri Aurobindo says, "[the mind] cannot get beyond the limits of this mathematics. If it goes beyond and tries to conceive a real whole, it loses itself in a foreign element; it falls from its own firm ground into the ocean of the intangible … … Mind cannot possess the infinite, it can only suffer it or be possessed by it; it can only lie blissfully helpless under the luminous shadow of the Real cast down on it from planes of existence beyond its reach. The possession of the infinite cannot come except by an ascent to those supramental planes, nor the knowledge of it except by an inert submission of Mind to the descending messages of the Truth-Consciousness-Reality.[12]

The basic tool that the mind uses is reason. Reason can reduce error; it cannot eliminate it. Using reason, it is possible to arrive at more than one conclusion from the same data, and sometimes none of these conclusions may be right. That is why all scientific conclusions are expressed in terms of probability; and these conclusions are accepted tentatively so long as the probability of their being right is more than 95 percent (P<0.05). On the limitations of reason, Sri Aurobindo says, "... this limping action of reason is a movement of Ignorance searching for knowledge, obliged to safeguard its steps against error, to erect a selective mental structure for its temporary shelter ..."[13] That is what makes the process of research slow, and still not fool-proof. Sri Aurobindo has summed up the process of research and the tentative nature of its conclusions in these words: "Advancing tardily from a limping start,Crutching hypothesis upon argument,Throning its theories as certitudes,It reasons from the half-known to the unknown, Ever constructing its frail house of thought,Ever undoing the web that it has spun."[14]

The second fundamental weakness that imprisons science is its assumption that all knowledge can be derived from the laws governing matter. Thus, matter is primary so far as science is concerned. How this limits science has been explained by Sri Aurobindo in these words: "All insistence on the sole or the fundamental validity of the objective real takes its stand on the sense of the basic reality of Matter. But it is now evident that Matter is by no means fundamentally real; it is a structure of Energy."[15] In spite of Einstein having linked matter and energy in a two-way relationship, the tendency to treat matter as "fundamentally real" continues. In spiritual terms, both matter and energy are two modes – one gross and the other subtle – of the same Supreme Consciousness. Sri Aurobindo sums it up when he says, "The supraphysical is as real as the physical; to know it is part of a complete knowledge"[16]

The net result is that while scientific knowledge has enabled us to land a man on the moon, the basic existential questions about the totality of man and the purpose of his life remain outside the scope of science. As Sri Aurobindo says in poetic language, "And sciences omnipotent in vain/By which men learn of what the suns are made, Transform all forms to serve their outward needs, Ride through the sky and sail beneath the sea, But learn not what they are or why they came.[17]

A Continuing Controversy

Before concluding this essay, a fundamental divergence between the scientific and the spiritual might be mentioned in passing. In science, consciousness is considered an emergent property of the brain. The neuronal activity in the brain, which can be detected and monitored with instruments, is assumed to *somehow* lead to the subjective awareness called consciousness. Correspondingly our thoughts and feelings, which are subjective in nature, are *somehow* assumed to lead to the physico-chemical processes detected as neuronal activity in the brain. The 'somehow' conceals ignorance regarding the link between the subjective and the objective. But that does not stop science from treating the origin of consciousness in the brain as axiomatic. In spiritual terms, consciousness is primary and universal. Brain is an instrument that is designed to channelize a certain fraction of this consciousness and manifest it in a certain way. Even non-living matter, living cells, plants and animals are instruments designed to manifest the same consciousness in a certain way. For example, the same electricity can manifest as heat in a heater, and as cold in a refrigerator; in a fan, it manifests as motion. So far as the brain is concerned, the instrument has been growing in complexity in the course of evolution to allow a greater fraction of the universal consciousness to manifest as mental processes. It is something like a computer scientist coming up with a better processer to design a faster computer. It is sometimes argued that if there is no functional brain, there is no consciousness. Therefore, science is right in treating consciousness as an emergent property of the brain. But this argument is flawed. Without a bulb, there can be no light. But the bulb is not the generator of light; it is only an instrument that allows electricity to manifest as light. In the same way, the secret of light can be understood by understanding the nature of electricity, not by dissecting a bulb. These are ideas which need a radical change in the paradigms of modern science. Sri Aurobindo had said nearly a hundred years ago that science believes consciousness to be the product of the senses and the brain. This contention is no longer able to hold the field against the tide of increasing knowledge. It is becoming more and more obvious that brain is an instrument of consciousness, not its generator. It is no more logical to explain consciousness on the basis of physical structures than to explain the motive power of steam on the basis of the structure of the steam engine.[18] Today the results of many well-designed experiments convincingly show that the explanations of reductionistic materialism are indeed "becoming more and more inadequate and strained," as Sri Aurobindo had said.[19]

Closing thoughts

It seems the Divine guards its secrets carefully, and reveals them only to the single-minded, persistent, patient and prolonged search and unconditional surrender of the believers. The scientists, who start with skepticism and a misplaced confidence in the capacity of the mind to find what lies beyond the mind, are in the meantime kept amused with facts, which according to Sri Aurobindo, are the husks of Truth[20]. The superficial nature of knowledge revealed to science as a poor but glamorous substitute for Truth has been described in elegant poetry by Sri Aurobindo in the following lines from his sonnet, 'Discoveries of Science':

> "The surface finds, the screen-phenomenon,
> Are Nature's offered ransom, while behind,
> Her occult mysteries lie safe, unknown,
> From the crude handling of the empiric Mind."

Endnotes

[1] The "Conflict" theory of science-religion relationship has been challenged, and shown to be highly questionable, if not incorrect, by many contemporary thinkers in the field. (Editor)

[2] Sri Aurobindo, *The Life Divine* (Puducherry: Sri Aurobindo Ashram Publication, fifth edition, 1970), pp. 472-474.

[3] Idem, p.10.

[4] Idem. p.11.

[5] Idem, p.71.

[6] Idem, pp.13-14.

[7] Idem, p.868.

[8] See Sara W. Lazar, Catherine E.Kerr, Rachel H. Wasserman, Jeremy R. Gray, Douglas N. Greve, Michael T. Treadway, MettaMcGarvey, Brian T. Quinn, Jeffery A. Dusek, Herbert Benson, Scott L. Rauch, Christopher I. Moore, and Bruce Fischld, "Meditation experience is associated with increased cortical thickness," *Neuroreport* (2005 Nov 28 16(17), 1893–1897. PMCID: PMC1361002, NIHMSID: NIHMS6696. See also Eileen Luders, Arthur W. Toga, Natasha Lepore, and Christian Gaser, "The underlying anatomical correlates of long-term meditation: Larger hippocampal and frontal volumes of gray matter, *Neuroimage* (2009 Apr 15; 45(3), 672–678. PMCID: PMC3184843, NIHMSID: NIHMS90659. See also Alice G. Walton, " 7 Ways Meditation Can Actually Change The Brain," *Pharma and Healthcare* (9 Feb 2015). https://www.forbes.com/sites/alicegwalton/2015/02/09/7-ways-meditation-can-actually-change-the-brain/#19ceeb3a1465

[9] WS Harris, M Gowda, JW Kolb, CP Strychacz, JL Vacek, PG Jones, A Forker, JH O'Keefe, BD McCallister, "A randomized, controlled trial of the effects of remote, intercessory prayer on outcomes in patients admitted to the coronary care unit," *Arch Intern Med* (1999; 159), 2273-2278.

[10] T Yu, HL Tsai, ML Hwang, "Suppressing tumour progression of in vitro prostate cancer cells by emitted psychosomatic power through Zen meditation,"*Am J Clin Med*(2003; 31), 499-507.

[11] DJ Benor, "Survey of spiritual healing research," *Complementary Med Res* (1990; 4), 9-33.

[12] *The Life Divine*, pp.162-23.

[13] Idem, p.940.

[14] Sri Aurobindo, Savitri (Puducherry: Sri Aurobindo Ashram Publication, 3rd edition, 1970), Book 2, Canto 10, p.240.

[15] *The Life Divine*, p. 652.

[16] Idem, p. 651.

[17] *Savitri*, Book 10, Canto 4, pp. 644-645.

[18] See *The Life Divine*, pp. 85-86.

[19] See M. Miovic, "Non-local studies – implications for health," *New Approaches to Medicine and Health (NAMAH)* (2003; 11(1), 7-21.

[20] See *Savitri*, Book 2, Canto 10, p. 253.

Chapter 12

Chan Consciousness and Enlightenment &
the Spiritual Dimension of Humans

Jijimon Alakkalam Joseph

Abstract

Chan (Zen) Buddhism is a fast growing spiritual tradition in the contemporary world. The influence of *Chan* ideals and concepts on the lives of its followers is comprehensive. A browse through the titles of books on *Chan* on the internet or in bookstores proves it. In recent times, *Chan* teachings on concentration, consciousness, enlightenment and meditation have attracted the attention of academics and practitioners. There is a plethora of academic and non-academic writings on the ties between *Chan* and psychology that consider them as partners in liberation. There is no doubt that psychological analysis of *Chan* consciousness and meditation has helped practitioners to deal with their patients. This paper looks at *Chan* consciousness and enlightenment from the spiritual dimension of humans. Such an approach further expands the possibilities of *Chan* ideals and concepts. *Chan* teachings on enlightenment and transformation of consciousness (into wisdom) can contribute not only to psychological wellbeing, but also to the interpretation of the spiritual dimension of human life and harmonious coexistence of spiritual traditions in the contemporary world.

Keywords: *Chan*, Consciousness, Enlightenment, Transformation, Wisdom.

Introduction

The *Chan* (transliteration of the Sanskrit *dhyāna)* tradition is often called the meditation school of Mahāyāna Buddhism.[1]*Chan* Buddhism has its origin in Buddha, the founder of the Buddhist tradition. Although we know very little about the historicity of Buddha with certainty[2] his enlightenment experience stands out preeminently in the thought and practice of *Chan*. The *Chan* tradition has it that once during his sermon on the Vulture Peak, Śākyamuni wordlessly raised a flower. Only Kāśyapa understood the profound meaning and smiled. The World Honored One said, "I possess the true Dharma eye. The wondrous mind of nirvāna, the subtle dharma gate born of the formlessness of true form, independent of words and transmitted beyond doctrines. I entrust it to Mahākāśyapa."

A central Asian meditation monk called Bodhidharma,[3]who was the 28th Indian patriarch and also the first Chinese patriarch, transmitted *Chan* to China. Signifying the direct transmission of the mind, Bodhidharma passed on his robe successively to HuiKe, Seng Can, Dao Xin, Hong Ren and HuiNeng, who was the 6th patriarch. The *Chan* tradition developed in China from 6th century CE onwards, and became very dominant and extremely influential during the Tang and the Song dynasties. During the Tang dynasty *Chan* split into the 'Five Houses' (*wujia*) and then into the 'Seven Schools' (*qi zong*) during the Song dynasty, two of which – the Rinzai School[4] and the Sōtō School[5] – still remain.

A detailed history of the *Chan* tradition is not within the scope of this paper. Our interest here is to analyze the *Chan* understanding of consciousness, its transformation, attainment of *wu* and their significance for the interpretation of the spiritual dimension of humans in the contemporary world.

Roots of *Chan*

For a better analysis of the origin, development and influence of the *Chan* understanding of consciousness and enlightenment, it is necessary that we take a brief look at what preceded *Chan*. Buddha's teaching was a very practical and humane way to attain liberation with *nirvāna* as its goal. He did not attempt to establish a philosophical system. He maintained a 'noble silence' when irrelevant questions that did not lead to actual experience of liberation were asked. But later, the Indian minds, unsatisfied with that silence, gave themselves up to metaphysical speculations and epistemic concerns that in turn gave birth to various movements within Buddhism. Hīnayāna[6] and Mahāyāna are two of them.

The Mahāyāna (the Great Vehicle/the Great Path) tradition[7] distinguished itself from the Mainstream (the Lesser Vehicle/the Inferior Path) Buddhism that emphasized personal liberation accessible only to monks through intensive meditation. Mahāyāna Buddhism is presented as a rejection of this selfish, old and conservative tradition. Mahāyāna is a bundle of different trends, developed over many centuries, and is united by the bodhisattva ideal. Unlike the Mainstream Buddhist monk who works for personal liberation, the bodhisattva tirelessly works for the liberation of all sentient beings. "Although perfectly enlightened and in possession of the omniscience of a Buddha, the bodhisattva forgoes final entrance into nirvāna in order to aid sentient beings on their path to enlightenment.... The idea of bodhisattva is thus related to the basic teaching of Mahāyāna, namely that of the Buddha nature within all living things."[8]

Here it is worth mentioning the self-definition of Mahāyāna found in the *Bodhipathapradīpa* of Atiśa, an eleventh century Indian Buddhist scholar and missionary to Tibet. Atiśa divides Buddhist practitioners into three hierarchical classes depending on their motivation.[9] Those of lowest motivation attain *saṃsāra*. Those of middle motivation attain *nirvāna* and are called the Arhats (the saintly purified one who transcended all desires, conditioning and defilements in personal enlightenment) who are the followers of the 'Inferior Path.' Those with highest motivation attain the perfect Buddhahood. Their goal is the freedom of all sentient beings from suffering. They are the followers of the 'Great Path.' For Atiśa "*Mahāyāna is not as such an institutional identity. Rather, it is an inner motivation and vision, and this inner vision can be found in anyone regardless of their institutional position.*"[10]It is the motivation, the intention, and the vision that makes a follower of Mahāyāna, not the robes, rules or doctrines. Mahāyāna is a spiritual movement, and it is all about an alternative and distinctive vision of what Buddhism and the intentions of the Buddhist practitioners should ultimately be.[11] The concepts of bodhisattva and Buddha nature are central to the *Chan* tradition as well.

It was during the first half of the 8th century CE that the *Chan* movement "first became conscious of its own tradition."[12] The four-line declaration describing the principles with which *Chan* distinguished itself from other schools of Buddhism was:

1. A special transmission outside the teachings, *jiaowaibiechuan*,

2. Not established on words and letters, *bu li wen zi*,

3.   Pointing directly to a person's mind, *zhizhirenxin*,

4. Seeing one's nature and achieving Buddhahood, *jianxingchengfo*.

We do not know about the author and the time of these slogans[13] although the *Chan* tradition has erroneously ascribed it to Bodhidharma.[14]Individual phrases of this four-line aphorism appear in several early *Chan* texts but as a set formula it appeared first in a collection of the Recorded Sayings of the *Chan* master Huai (992-1064) contained in the *Zu ting shiyuan* compiled by Mu An Shan Qing in 1108.[15] But the general opinion is that this aphorism dates from the Tang dynasty. These slogans are generally accepted as the self-definition of *Chan*, but the question remains unanswered: who decided/decides this definition of *Chan*?

The first two lines of the above-mentioned aphorism speak of a spiritual transmission that is especially entrusted to the *Chan* tradition. This 'special transmission' is said to be a 'transmission of mind by mind/mind-to-mind' (*yixinchuanxin*). This special transmission implies that "at the moment the disciple's mind reaches the same state of intuitive understanding as that of the master, a fusion of minds takes place, and the understanding of the disciple becomes one with that of the master, or, in the traditional words, the master 'transmits' his mind to the disciple. No words are employed in this transmission."[16] These slogans were taken to imply the inadequacy of language and also the rejection of traditional Buddhist scriptures. But did the *Chan* tradition really negate language? Does *Chan* transcend language? Modern scholarship on the philosophy of language challenges the *Chan* neglect of letters.

The third slogan – pointing directly to a person's mind– speaks of the unique teaching methods used by the *Chan* masters to awaken the innate nature. Non-verbal signs such as shouts, blows, gestures, etc., are the devices used in this method. This "rhetoric of immediacy," an expression that Faure (1991) uses, led *Chan* to reject all forms of mediations – meditation, rituals and scriptures. However, contemporary scholarship on *Chan* is very critical of the *Chan* iconoclasm and the *Chan* rhetoric of immediacy.

Seeing one's nature (*jianxing*) is one of the important doctrines accepted by almost all schools of Mahāyāna Buddhism, and is not unique to the *Chan* tradition. This doctrine holds that all sentient beings intrinsically possess the Buddha-nature. The most developed statement of this doctrine could be that of Dōgen, who said that all beings are intrinsically Buddhas. Dōgen says, "Sentient beings are Buddha-nature. Grass, trees, and lands are mind; thus they are sentient beings. Because they are sentient beings they are Buddha-nature. Sun, moon, and stars are mind; thus they are sentient beings; thus they are Buddha-nature."[17]

The *Chan* tradition invented the above-mentioned self-definition to emphasize its uniqueness within the Buddhist tradition and to claim superiority over other schools of Buddhism. This four-line aphorism has also influenced later interpretations of the *Chan* tradition. "Zen is not a systematic explanation of life, it is not an ideology, it is not a worldview, it is not a theology of revelation and salvation, it is not a mystique, it is not a way of ascetic perfection, it is not mysticism as this is understood in the West, in fact it fits no convenient category of ours."[18] "What Zen communicates is an awareness that is potentially already there but is not conscious of itself. Zen is then not Kerygma but realization, not revelation but consciousness."[19]

The *Chan* claims of its uniqueness can be debated. But its attempt to retrospect and renew the tradition from within is worth paying attention to. Some sort of transcendental or mystical experience forms the foundation of every spiritual tradition. "'God' must be an experience before 'God' can be a word."[20] As a spiritual tradition develops, it creates philosophies and theologies to protect its mystical experiences from their counterfeit and to claim superiority. Eventually, scriptures, doctrines and rituals become dominant, and significance of experience receives less attention. So, from time to time, there emerge revolutionary movements within that to force spiritual traditions to pay more attention to its foundational experience. The emergence of *Chan* within the Buddhist tradition, if reflected on seriously, can have immense impact on the harmonious co-existence of various spiritual traditions. The best way to assert the identity and rejuvenate the fading spirit of a tradition is to renew it from within, inviting the adherents to return to the tradition's foundational spiritual experience – the experience of the immanent presence of the Ultimate in every living being.

Structure of Consciousness and its Transformation

The Buddhist view of consciousness, though very elusive, is the subject of numerous scholarly studies in recent years. Consciousness is the translation of the Sanskrit word *vijñāna*, which means discernment. Buddhism in general speaks of eight layers of consciousness. They are:

(1)   *caksurvijñāna* Eye/Sight consciousness

(2)   *śrotravijñāna* Ear/Hearing consciousness

(3)   *ghranavijñāna* Nose/Smell consciousness

(4)   *jihvavijñāna* Tongue/Taste consciousness

(5)   *kāyavijñāna* Body/Touch consciousness

These five correspond to our five senses with which we gather information from outside of ourselves.

(6)   *manovijñāna* Mental/Conscious/Thinking mind consciousness or empirical self-consciousness that integrates the information received from the five senses.

(7)   *kleshavijñāna* Afflicted/Deluded/Subconscious mind consciousness or transcendental self-consciousness is the realm of motivation and intention where we form judgments.

(8)   *ālayavijñāna* Ground/Store consciousness[21] or the ontological origin of all consciousness where all our experiences of present and past lifetimes filtered through the initial seven layers of consciousness are stored.

In the context of this paper, the important aspect of the *Chan* philosophy of consciousness is the transformation of consciousness into wisdom. Enlightenment consists in transforming delusions into wisdom that is the realization of Buddhahood in everyday life. True Suchness is not a goal to be realized through the acquisition of any conceptual understanding. Rather it is the end product of the internal transformation of all mental activity, achieved through various meditation practices. "Zen meditation is a process of unification in which the whole personality is harmonized in a oneness which reaches its climax with a complete absence of subject-object consciousness in satori."[22]

Different levels of consciousness transform themselves into various wisdoms. "The eighth consciousness is transformed into mind/heart corresponding to the wisdom of the grand perfect mirror…the seventh consciousness into mind/heart corresponding to the wisdom of equality… the sixth consciousness into mind/heart corresponding to the wisdom of marvelous observation. Finally… one could transform the five actual consciousnesses into the wisdom of achieving all deeds."[23] The great mirror wisdom (*adarshana-jnana*) contains the wisdom of equality (*samata-jnana*) or the fundamental wisdom (the perception of oneness), the wisdom of marvelous observation (*pratyaveksana-jnana*) or the subtle observation wisdom (the perception of differences), and the wisdom of achieving all deeds (*krityannusthana-jnana*) or the spontaneous action wisdom (the perception of the refined functioning of the five senses)."The Mirror Wisdom represents the omnipresent, absolute Buddha-Mind containing all relative, localized, particular phenomena, including the mentalities and subjective experiences of sentient beings. The Equality Wisdom reveals that all these relative phenomena in turn contain the one absolute reality as their essence. The Analytical Wisdom and the Accomplishment of Works Wisdom represent the liberating work through which the Buddha-Mind reveals itself to human minds, or in other words, through which the absolute takes particular form and communicates itself to the relative." [24]

Asanga, a major exponent of the *Yogacara* (Consciousness-Only) school of Buddhism, relates this transformation to four ways of knowing: mirror knowing, universal knowing, observing knowing and the perfection of action.[25] One of the famous Zen masters, Hakuin, associated these four ways of knowing to four gates on the Buddhist Path: The gate of Inspiration, of Practice, of Awakening and of Nirvana.[26]

Wisdom is not within the realm of mind-consciousness. Wisdom is at the level of mind-spiritual.[27] The individual who has reached the realm of the Grand Perfect Mirror Wisdom is no longer bound by consciousness. *Chan* consciousness is often compared to a mirror that reflects everything that comes to it as it is, without distinguishing and categorizing.[28] "Zen is consciousness unstructured by particular form or particular system, a trans-cultural, trans-religious, trans-formed consciousness."[29]

The *Chan* discussion on transformation of consciousness brings home some important aspects of spiritual practices. It stresses the 'Ultimate' element that envelops the entire universe and the existence of the Ultimate in every being and that makes us all equal. *Chan* also stresses the uniqueness of every existence and the need to engage with the world. These teachings, if studied seriously, force us to question the purpose of all our spiritual practices. What is the final goal of all spiritual activities: to affirm the identity, uniqueness and superiority of one spiritual tradition over others? Or is it to help humanity together with the entire universe to embark on a pilgrimage towards the Ultimate?

It is good news that modern studies and discussions on spirituality somehow affirm the teachings of *Chan*. Let us analyze a few recent definitions of spirituality. "Spirituality is now commonly regarded as an individual phenomenon and identified with such things as personal transcendence, supraconscious sensitivity, and meaningfulness" and "has recently acquired a specific positive connotation through its association with personal experiences of the transcendent."[30]Spirituality is described as "a quality that goes beyond a specific religious affiliation"[31] Sandra M. Schneiders defines spirituality "as the experience of conscious involvement in the project of life-integration through self-transcendence toward the horizon of ultimate value one perceives."[32] "The generally-agreed-upon characteristics included in this definition are the notions of progressive, consciously pursued, personal integration through self-transcendence within and toward the horizon of ultimate concern …. This definition, while excluding the organizing and orienting of one's life in dysfunctional or narcissistic ways (e.g., alcoholism or self-centered eroticism), includes potentially any spirituality, Christian or non-Christian, religious or secular."[33] Claire E. Wolfteich understands spirituality "as a way of life embedded in a tradition and woven together with relationships with God, self, neighbor, community, and the created world.[34] David B. Perrin summarizes the four key characteristics of spirituality contained in these definitions as follows:

> Spirituality refers to a fundamental capacity in human beings. It is expressed within human experience before people identify that experience with a particular religious or spiritual set of beliefs, rituals, or ethics. Spirituality, as an innate human characteristic, involves the capacity for self-transcendence: being meaningfully involved in, and personally committed to the world beyond an individual's personal boundaries. This meaningful involvement and commitment shapes the way people live and allows them to integrate their lives. Spirituality can be clearly identified and studied in human events and written texts, or other forms of expression, such as art and music, desires and motivations. Spirituality is also an academic discipline. Using interdisciplinary methods, the dynamics of the spiritual dimension of life can be analyzed.[35]

Chan Understanding of Enlightenment

The *Chan* understanding of enlightenment beautifully summarizes the above-mentioned purposes of spiritual practices. As mentioned already, some sort of mystical experience lies at the very foundation of every spiritual tradition. In the context of this study, religious/mystical/spiritual/ transcendental experience needs some clarification. "Religious experience might be the most fundamental lived experience of humankind in a double sense. First, it is related to our ultimate concern. Second, it is the condition of the possibility of all other lived experience"[36] "It is an experience of metaphysical or mystical self-transcending and also at the same time an experience of the 'Transcendent' or the 'Absolute' or 'God' not so much as object but

Subject. The Absolute Ground of Being … is realized so to speak 'from within' – realized from within 'Himself' and from within 'myself,' though 'myself' is now lost and 'found' 'in Him.'"[37]

Enlightenment has always been the goal of every school of Buddhism. Buddhism has its foundation in the enlightenment of Buddha. Enlightenment in *Chan* is called *wu,* which means seeing into the essence of things. "There is no Zen without satori, which is indeed the Alpha and Omega of Zen Buddhism."[38] It "is the goal, the meaning and the heart of Zen."[39] However, the *Chan* tradition places a special emphasis on the 'Great Experience,' not on Buddha. In the kōans[40] and in the collections of sayings of various *Chan* masters, the person of Śākyamuni does not have a significant role as the great founding figure on whom the religious tradition is centered. In *Chan,* it is the enlightenment experience that has the last word. The *Chan* sayings like 'if you find Buddha, kill him!,' 'there is no Śākyamuni in the past and in the future no Maitreya,' 'the good old Śākya has given us a village comedy,' etc., speak about the insignificant role the person of Buddha plays in the *Chan* tradition.[41]

Chan has several names for *wu,* such as "'the mind that has no abode,' 'the mind that owns nothing,' 'the homeless mind,' 'the unattached mind,' 'mindlessness,' 'thoughtlessness,' 'the one mind.'"[42] In all these, we find a stress on 'mindlessness,' because mind is dualistic in nature and prevents one from properly understanding oneself. "Zen mediation is a process of unification in which the whole personality is harmonized in a oneness which reaches its climax with a complete absence of subject-object consciousness in *satori.*"[43] *Wu* opens the way for us to see into the suchness or pureness of everything. "No longer 'I' and 'it' or 'I' and 'thou,' but only 'is.'[44]

For *Chan,* it is next to impossible to describe *wu* in words because it is one of the most innate of all personal experiences.[45] But an attempt must be made to describe *wu* somehow, however inadequately. The *Lankavatara Sūtra* speaks of *wu* as "the state of consciousness in which

Noble Wisdom realizes its own inner nature."[46] "Satori may be defined as an intuitive looking into the nature of things in contradistinction to the analytical or logical understanding of it. Practically, it means the unfolding of a new world hitherto unperceived in the confusion of a dualistically-trained mind."[47] William Johnston describes enlightenment as "an experience of absolute unity; it is beyond subject and object; the empirical ego is so submerged that there is no longer 'I' and 'it' but pure existence or 'is-ness.'"[48] It is inner and creative. It is a kind of inner perception not of individual objects but of reality itself. Very often it is compared to the blooming of a flower and the singing of a bird, which happen out of inner necessity. It is not pre-meditated: rather, it is an inner overflowing.

Now let us analyze some of the characteristics of *wu*.[49]

1. *Irrationality, inexplicability and incommunicability*: The personal and subjective nature of satori makes a coherent and logical explanation of it difficult. An explanation of satori mutilates its content. However irrationalities cease to be such when satori is attained. Satori is beyond the limits of reasonable demonstration.

2. *Intuitive insight*: "meaning 'to see essence or nature', which apparently proves that there is 'seeing' or 'perceiving' in satori"[50]But there is no dualism of the one who sees and that which is seen."Zen insight is not our awareness, but Being's awareness of itself in us."[51] Zen uses expressions like 'no-self,' 'no-mind,' 'no-thought,' and 'nothing to do' to indicate this intuitive experience.

3. *Authoritativeness*: It means, "that the knowledge realized by satori is final, that no amount of logical argument can refute it."[52]

4. *Affirmation*: Satori is essentially an affirmative attitude towards all that exists. It accepts all as they are regardless of their moral values. But because of this kind of an approach, calling satori pantheistic is incorrect.

5.   *Sense of the beyond*: The satori is one's own personal experience, but one feels it to be rooted elsewhere. Zen followers would say it is like "'coming home and quietly resting.'"[53]"To call this the Beyond, the Absolute, or God, or a person is to go further than the experience itself and to plunge into a theology or metaphysics."[54]

6.   *Impersonal tone*: Satori is "thoroughly impersonal or rather highly intellectual."[55]It does not mean that satori is merely intellectual. It is existential. Satori, as well as the occasion that inspires it, are said to be very unromantic, barren and lacking in super-sensuality compared to Christian mystic experiences that are often considered very romantic and personal.

7.   *Feeling of exaltation*: This feeling arises because satori breaks up "the restriction imposed on one as an individual being,"and thus results in the "infinite expansion of the individual."[56]There is a feeling of self-contentment.

8.   *Momentariness*: Satori comes upon one as a flash of lightning, at a single stroke. "If it is not abrupt and momentary, it is not satori."[57]

Scholars and the faithful in general can welcome the fact that today religion and spiritual traditions are studied and interpreted more and more in terms of subjective, intersubjective, existential and experiential dimensions. "While the academic study of religion has largely moved away from essentialist understandings that religion has some common, perhaps transcendent, essence, it has only begun to take seriously the claim that religion cannot be abstracted from its cultural matrices,"[58] which "implies a theoretical as well as an empirical discourse concerning the relationships between 'self,' 'body,' 'culture' and 'transcendence' and concerning wider political issues of the relation between 'self' and 'other,' 'first world' and 'third world,' 'world capital' and 'ecosystem,' and between 'global' and 'local.'"[59]Today, the ways of viewing religion and spiritual traditions are discernibly different from the confessional and apologetic ways. This change heralds "a move away from the idea of understanding any objective truth towards relativism and perspectivalism; that objectivity is relative to the contexts of its occurrence and to perception."[60]

Conclusion

In this paper we have made an attempt to throw some light on the practical applications of *Chan* analysis of consciousness and enlightenment for the interpretation of the spiritual dimension of humans in the modern world. The *Chan* determination to return to its foundational spiritual experience of enlightenment, and its emphasis on the final goal of all the spiritual activities, invite us not to see different realities, but to see reality differently, and thus experience the ultimate liberation. Being free, one experiences that one is free and the mountains are once more mountains.

"How can we attain freedom?" the master was asked.

"Who put you under restraint?" was the reply.

Endnotes

[1] Heinrich Dumoulin, *Zen Buddhism: A History, Vol. 1, India and China* (Bloomington: World Wisdom, 2005), p.27.

[2] Rupert Gethin, *The Foundations of Buddhism* (Oxford: Oxford University Press, 1998), p.9.

[3] Scholars like Bernard Faure interpret Bodhidharma "as a textual and religious paradigm and not ...as a historical figure or a psychological essence" (Faure 1986, 190).

[4] The Rinzai School is one of the two (the other is the Sōtō school) major Japanese Zen Sects. It is an extension of the Chinese school *Lin jizong.* Eisai Zenji (1141-1215) brought this school to Japan.

[5] The Sōtō School is an extension of the Chinese school *Cao dongzong,* and Dōgen Zenji (1200-1253) brought this school to Japan.

[6] At times it is also called Sectarian Buddhism, Conservative Buddhism, Śrāvakayāna, Nikāya Buddhism and recently Mainstream Buddhism. Contemporary scholarship seldom uses the term 'Hīnayāna', since it is pejorative. Hereafter, we will use 'Mainstream Buddhism' to denote 'Hīnayāna' Buddhism.

[7] There are many theories about the origin of Mahāyāna tradition. For more, see Paul Williams, Paul and Antony Tribe,*Buddhist Thought: A Complete introduction to the Indian Tradition* (London and New York, Routledge. EBook, 2000). See also Williams, *Mahāyāna Buddhism: The Doctrinal Foundations, 2nd edition*(London: Routledge, 2009, EBook).

[8] Dumoulin, p. 29.

[9] Paul Williams, and Antony Tribe,*Buddhist Thought: A Complete introduction to the Indian Tradition*(London and New York, RoutledgeEBook, 2000), pp.101-102 .

[10] Idem, p.102.

[11] Idem, p.3.

[12] SeizanYanagida, "The *Li-Tai Fa-Pao Chi* and the Ch'an Doctrine of Sudden Awakening."In *Early Ch'an in China and Tibet*, edited by Whalen Lai and Lewis R. Lancaster (Berkeley: Asian Humanities Press, 1983), p.17.

[13] Daisetz Teitaro Suzuki, "Zen Buddhism," *MonumentaNipponica*, Vol. 1, No. 1 (Jan 1938), 48-57.

[14] Isshū Miura and Ruth Fuller Sasaki, *Zen Dust: The History of the Koan and Koan Study in Rinzai (Lin- chi) Ch'an*(New York: Barcourt, Brace and World, 1966), p.230.

[15] Albert Welter, "Mahākāśyapa's Smile: Silent Transmission and the Kung-an (Kōan) Tradition," in *The Kōan. Texts and Contexts in Zen Buddhism*, edited by Steven Heine and Dale S. Wright (Oxford: Oxford University Press, 2000), p.79.

[16] Miura, Isshū Miura and Ruth Fuller Sasaki, *Zen Dust: The History of the Koan and Koan Study in Rinzai (Lin- chi) Ch'an* (New York: Barcourt, Brace and World, 1966), p.231.

[17] KōsenNishiyama, *trans. A Complete English Translation of Dōgen Zenji's Shōbōgenzō: The Eye and Treasury of the True Law*, Vol. IV. Tokyo: Nakayama Shōbō, 1983), p.134.

[18] Thomas Merton, *Zen and the Birds of Appetite*(New York: New Directions Books, 1968), p.35.

[19] Idem, p. 47.

[20] Paul F Knitter,*Without Buddha I could not be a Christian* (Oxford: Oneworld Publications, 2009), p. 15.

[21] The Mahāyāna tradition calls it ālaya (Sanskrit), and the Theravāda tradition calls it *bhavanga* (Pali). Sometimes it is also called root consciousness (*mulavijñana* in Sanskrit) or *sarvabijaka*, which means totality of the seeds.

[22] William Johnston,*The Still Point: Reflections on Zen and Christian Mysticism* (New York: Fordham University Press, 1970), p.4.

[23] Vincent Shen,"Appropriating the Other and Transforming Consciousness into Wisdom: Some Philosophical Reflections on Chinese Buddhism," *Dao: A Journal of Comparative Philosophy*, Vol. III, No. 1 (2003), 15-16.

[24] J.C. Cleary, *trans,A Tune Beyond the Clouds: Zen Teachings From Old China*(Berkeley: Asian Humanities Press, 1990), pp.34-35.

[25] See Low, Albert Low., *ed, Hakuin on Kensho: The Four Ways of Knowing*(Boston: Shambhala, 2006), p.22.

[26] See Idem, pp. 32-39.

[27] Here it is worth noting that in Chinese philosophy the 'mind' has a very broad connotation. The mind has four levels: Blood-energy, mind-consciousness, mind-intellectual, and mind-spiritual (Wu 2011).

[28] See Merton, p.6.

[29] Idem, p.4.

[30] Zinnbauer, Brian J.Zinnbauer, Kenneth I. Pargament, Brenda Cole, Mark S. Rye, Eric M. Butter, Timothy G. Belavich, Kathleen M. Hipp, Allie B. Scott and Jill L. Kadar, "Religion and Spirituality: Unfuzzying the Fuzzy," in*Journal for the Scientific Study of Religion* 36, No. 4 (December 1997), 551.

[31] Turner, Robert P. Turner, David Lukoff, Ruth Tiffany Barnhouse, and Francis G. Lu, "Religious or Spiritual Problem: A Culturally Sensitive Diagnostic Category in the DSM-IV," *Journal of Nervous and Mental Disease* 183, No. 7 (1995), 437.

[32] Sandra M.Schneiders,"Approaches to the study of Christian Spirituality," in *The Blackwell Companion toChristian Spirituality*, edited by Arthur Holder(Boston: Blackwell PublishingLtd, 2005), p.16.

[33] Sandra M.Schneiders, "Spirituality in the Academy,"*Theological Studies,* 50(1989), 684.

[34] Claire E. Wolfteich, "Spirituality," in *The Wiley-Blackwell Companion to Practical Theology*, 1ˢᵗ Edition, edited by Bonnie J. Miller-McLemore (Boston: Blackwell Publishing Ltd. 2012), p.331.

[35] David B. Perrin,*Studying Christian Spirituality* (New York: Routledge. 2007), p.20.

[36] (Chan 2010, 38).Wing-Cheuk Chan, "No-Mind and Nothingness: From Zen Buddhism to Heidegger," *Canadian Journal of Buddhist Studies* 6 (2010), 38, aAccessed on November 22, 2017, *http://jps.library.utoronto.ca/index.php/ cjbs/article/view/15224/12262*

[37] Merton, p.71.

[38] William Barrett,*ed,Zen Buddhism: Selected writings of D. T. Suzuki*(New York: Image Books, 1996), p.84.

[39] Humphreys, Christmas Humphreys,*Zen Buddhism*(London: Unwin Books, 1961), p.108.

[40] Literally, the word kōan (Chinese: *gong an*) means "a combination of graphs that signifies 'public notice' or 'public announcement'" (Dumoulin 2005, 245). In *Chan*, kōan is "'a public document setting up a standard of judgment', whereby one's Zen understanding is tested as to its correctness" (Suzuki 1958, 86). Kōan could be a story, dialogue, question or statement told by *Chan* masters. It is estimated that there are 1700 kōans in the *Chan* tradition. The English titles of some of the famous kōan collections are the *Blue Cliff Record*, the *Book of Equanimity* (also known as the *Book of Serenity*) both of which were collected during the 12th century; the *Gateless Gate* (also known as the *Gateless Barrier*) which was collected during 13th century.

[41] Dumoulin, p.11.

[42] Suzuki, p.66.

[43] Johnston, p.4.

[44] Idem, p.7.

[45] Scholars like C. Lawson Crowe (1965) are very critical of the so-called 'irrational, inexplicable, and incommunicable' nature of satori.

[46] Suzuki, p. 18

[47] Barrett, p.84.

[48] Johnston, p.21.

[49] For this section, I depend almost totally on Suzuki 1958, 30-6.

[50] Suzuki, p.31.

[51] Merton, p.17.

[52] Suzuki, p.32.

[53] Idem, p.33.

[54] Ibid.

[55] Idem, p.34.

[56] Idem, p.35.

[57] Idem, p.36.

[58] Gavin Flood,*Beyond Phenomenology: Rethinking the Study of Religion* (London: Cassell, 1999), pp.2-3.

[59] Idem, p.15.

[60] Idem, p.13.

Chapter 13

Human Soul: A Biblical Perspective

Thomas Karimundackal, SJ

Abstract

The biblical perception of human person is not a bipartite creature of the divine and human, of soul and body. Instead of splitting a person into body and soul, the Bible sees it as a unified being. In the biblical view, a person "does not *have* a soul, but *is* a soul". The "soul" (*nepēš* and *psūchê*) is integral to physical life itself. It is therefore not a good idea to assume that any of the meanings of *nepēš* and *psūchê* involve "having", since such an interpretation would lead to a misunderstanding of the anthropological nature of *nepēš* and *psūchê*. Both *nepēš* and *psūchê* points to the vital self of the person which is lived only in the body. They stand for human needs, desires and feelings, including thought, memory and consciousness. Thus, it can be the locus of joy and sorrow and love and hate etc. As the vital self, individuated life and part of the body *nepēš* and *psūchê* points to the whole person.

Key Words

Human person, soul, *nepēš*, *psūchê*, living soul, vital self, individuated life, physical life etc.

Introduction

The traditional concept of an immaterial and immortal soul distinct from the body is not found in ancient Hebrew beliefs,[1] but developed as a result of interaction with the Hellenistic philosophy.[2] The only Hebrew word traditionally translated as "soul" in the Hebrew Bible *nepēš* refers to a living, breathing conscious body, rather than to an immortal soul.[3] In the Greek Septuagint *psūchê* is used to translate each instance of *nepēš*.[4] The Greek word *psūchê* traditionally translated as "soul" in the New Testament also has basically the similar meaning of *nepēš* in the Hebrew Bible.[5] Both these terms - *nepēš* and *psūchê* - carry a similar range of meanings in the OT and the NT and can designate the person or the person's life as a whole.[6] In modern parlance we can say *nepēš* or *psūchê* is the life-principle, or simply is the self or person. In short, in the biblical view, a person "does not *have* a soul, but *is* a soul".[7]

1.   *Nephesh* in the Old Testament

The noun *nepēš* occurs 754 times, and its verbal form in the *niphal* 3 times in the Hebrew Bible (Exod 23:12; 31:17; 2 Sam16:14).[8] The Hebrew term *nepēš*, although translated as "soul" actually has a meaning closer to the-life principle of a living being or simply a living being or the vital self. In the second creation account in the book of Genesis we see both man and animal as *nepēš*:

- "The Lord God formed man of the dust of the ground, and breathed into his nostrils the *breath of life*; and man became a living soul [*nepēš hayyâh*]" (Gen 2:7).

- "And out of the ground the Lord God formed every beast of the field, and every fowl of the air; and brought them unto Adam to see what he would call them: and whatsoever Adam called every living creature [*nepēš hayyâh* "living soul"], that was the name thereof" (Gen 2:19).

Therefore, the term *nepeš* in the Hebrew Bible is applied to animals as well as human beings (cf. *nepeš hayyâh* Gen 1:20.24.30; Ezek 47:9).

Although the term נֶפֶשׁ has various shades of meaning in the Old Testament[9], the word comes to stand for the individual, personal life, the person, with two distinct shades of meaning which might best be indicated by the Latin *anima* and *animus*.[10] As *anima, nepeš* is the life inherent in the body, the animating principle in the blood (cf. Deut 12:23 "Only be sure that thou eat not the blood: for the blood is the soul (*nepeš*); and thou shalt not eat the soul (*nepeš*) with the flesh"). As *animus, nepeš* is the "mind", the centre of our mental activities. Thus we read of "a longing soul" (Ps 42:2), "a hungry soul" (Ps 107:9), "a weary soul" (Jer 31:25), "a grieved soul" (Job 30:25), "a loving soul" (Cant 1:7), "a snaring soul" (1Sam 28:9; Prov 18:7) etc.

1.1. *Nepeš* as the 'Vital Self'

Frequently in the Old Testament *nepeš* designates the individual person:

- Lev 17:10: "I will set my face against that *soul* (*nepeš*) that eats blood."

- Lev 23:30: "As for any *soul* (*nepeš*) that does any work on this same day, that soul I will destroy from among his people."

Nepeš is simply another word for "person" and these persons die:

- Num 35:11.15: "that the slayer who kills *any soul* (*nepeš*) unintentionally may flee there."

- Ps 105:18: "they afflicted his feet with fetters, his *soul* (*nepeš*) was laid in irons."

Nepeš may also indicate a number of individuals such as:

- Abraham's party: Gen12:5: "And Abram took Sarai his wife and Lot his nephew, and all their possessions which they had accumulated, and the *souls* (*nepeš*) which they had acquired in Haran."

- The remnant left behind in Judah: Jer 43:6: "the men, the women, the children, the king's daughters and every *soul* (*nepēs̆*) that Nebuzaradan the captain of the bodyguard had left with Gedaliah".

- The offspring of Jacob: Gen 46:15: "… all the *souls* (*nepēs̆*) of his sons and his daughters *were* thirty and three.

As life in the physical sense, the *nepēs̆* can be 1) taken by God: Job 27:8 → For what is the hope of the godless when he is cut off, When God requires *his life* (soul *nepēs̆*)? 2) or be forfeited by a person: Hab 2:10 → "You have devised a shameful thing for your house by cutting off many peoples; so you are sinning against *your life* (*soul nepēs̆*)."

As vital self the *nepēs̆* also stands as the object of salvation and redemption:

- Ps 116:4 → "then I called upon the name of the Lord: 'O Lord, I beseech you, save *my soul!*" (*nepēs̆*)

- 2 Sam. 4:9→ "As the Lord lives, who has redeemed *my life* (*my soul nepēs̆*) from all distress."

Nepēs̆ in the Physical sense can even be saved from Sheol or from the state of death:

- Ps 86:13 → "For your loving kindness toward me is great, and you have delivered *my life* (*my soul nepēs̆*) from the depths of Sheol."

In many instances the *nepēs̆* denotes as the 'vital self' of a person in relationship with other individuals.

- In Gen 12:13 Abram says to Sarai: "Say you are my sister, so that it may go well with me because of you and *my soul* (*nepēs̆*) may be spared on your account".

- In Gen 19:19-20 Lot is speaking to Yahweh: "You have shown me great kindness in keeping my נֶפֶשׁ alive; …. Look, that city there is nearby; … let me take refuge there, that my *soul* (*nepēš*) may be saved".

- The plea "let my *soul* (*nepēš*) *live!*" in 1Kings 20:32 is indeed referring to the vital self itself.

- In Num 23:10 Balaam cannot help speaking God's word, and so he cries out: "Let my *soul* (*nepēš*) die the death of the upright".

- The summons to one's *nepēš* praise Yahweh speaks for itself: "Bless the Lord, O my soul…" (Ps 103:1,2,22; 104: 1,35; cf. Isa. 61:10; Ps. 34:3[2]; 35:9; 71:23; 146:1).

As the vital self the *nepēš* is the precise subject of lamentation:

- It despairs and is disquieted → "And my *soul* (*nepēš*) is greatly dismayed…" (Ps 6:3); "When I remember these *things*, I pour out *my soul* (*nepēš*) in me" (Ps 42:5); "Why are you in despair, O my soul? (*nepēš*)…" (Ps 43:5).

- It is exhausted and feels defenseless → "Woe *is* me now! For *my soul* (*nepēš*) is wearied because of murderers" (Jer 4:31).

- It feels itself weak and despondent → "When *my soul* (*nepēš*) fainted within me I remembered the Lord…" (Jonah 2:7).

- It is afflicted → "You have known the troubles of *my soul* (*nepēš*)" (Ps 31:7; cf. Gen 42:21).

- It suffers misery → "He shall see of the travail of *his soul* (*nepēš*)" (Isa 53:11).

The *nepēš* is often described as being bitter, that is to say embittered through childlessness ("And she was in bitterness of *soul* (*nepēš*)…" 1 Sam 1:10), troubled because of illness ("Let her alone; for her *soul* (*nepēš*) is vexed within her…" 2Kings 4:27), enraged because it has been injured ("lest fierce men fall upon you and you lose *your soul* (*nepēš*), with the lives (*nepēš*) of your household" Judg 18:25; 2 Sam17:8)".[11]

The expression "man/men of bitter soul (*nepēš*)" cf. Jdgs 18:25; 1Sam 22:2; 2 Sam 17:8 is a stock phrase meaning extremely dangerous fighters ready for anything.[12] It is not their soul but their whole being that displays their bitterness. When in Gen 42:21 Joseph's brothers say that they saw the anguish of his *soul* (*nepēš*; not simply *his* anguish), it must be understood as the anguish of the very being of Joseph. The same is true in the case of the servant of Yahweh in Isa 53:11 when it speaks of "the anguish of his soul (*nepēš*).[13]

The Deuteronomic expression "with all your heart and with all your soul" (cf. Deut 4:29; 6:5.6; 10:12; 11:13.18; 13:4; 26:16; 30:2.6.10; Josh 22:5; 23:14; 1Kings 2:4; 8:48 // 2 Chr 6:38; 2 Kings 23:5) is particularly significant in describing the entirety of the person. Only very rarely we see *nepēš* referring directly to God and an individual (e.g., Ps 63:9[8]: "My *nepēš* clings to Yahweh; his right hand upholds it"), and the reason is given in Eccl 5:1 [2]: "God is in heaven, and you upon earth", i.e., a direct relationship would obscure the distance between profoundly ephemeral mortals and God. Therefore, *nepēš* does not require to love God with all its heart and might. Instead, people are required to love God with all their נפש and all their might.[14] Thus, the phrase "with all your soul" shows the intensity of the involvement of the entire being. This can be further substantiated by Moses' exhortation in Deut 11:18: "write these my words in the heart and in the soul". Here *nepēš* has become something present in the person" and not outside of the person.[15]

Nepēš as vital self makes expressions denoting repulsion appear more vivid:[16]

- hatred → "He who is a partner with a thief hates *his own soul*" (Prov 29:24).

- abhorrence → "and *my soul* shall not abhor you" (Lev 26:11.15.30.43; cf. Ezk 25:6, 15; 36:5).

- loathe → "has *your soul* loathed Zion?" (Jer 14:19; cf. Job 10:1).

- detest → "and *our soul* detest this miserable bread" (Num 21:5; Ps 106:15) etc.

In short, as in Gen 2:7 a person does not *have* a vital self but is a vital self.[17] It is therefore not a good idea to assume that any of the meanings of *nepēš* involve "having",[18] since such an interpretation would lead to a misunderstanding of the anthropological nature of *nepēš*.[19] Therefore, *nepēš* is not like a person as though he/she exists outside of the "soul", but the "soul" is the person. The "soul" is what each person is as a human being.

1.2. *Nepēš* as Individuated Life

In many instances *nepēš* takes the meaning of individualized life. Here I merely take a few instances to show that *nepēš* denotes not life in general but life inherent in individuals, animal or human.

In many instances *nepēš* is clearly mentioned as the life of an individual:

- In 1Sam 26:21 Saul's *nepēš* was precious to David and he preserved it ("because my life (*nepēš*) was precious in your sight this day..." (cf. 2 Kings 1:13,14; 1Sam 26:24).

- In 2 Sam 23:17 (// 1 Chr 11:19) we read of David's unwillingness to drink water brought by his followers at the risk of their lives (*nepēš*): "*is not this* the blood of the men that went in jeopardy of their lives (*nepēš*). Therefore, he would not drink it".

- Similarly in Lam 5:9 we read how the Israelites risk their lives (*nepēš*) to earn their bread: "We get our bread at the risk of our lives (*nepēš*) because of the sword in the wilderness" (cf. Jdgs 12:3; 1Sam 19:5; 28:21; Job 13: 14).

- In Jdgs 5:18 we read how the people of Zebulun and Naphtali despise their lives to death ("Zebulun was a people who despised their lives to death, and Naphtali also...").

In many instances *life* (*nepēs̆*) is placed where it poses threats to life: " Escape for *thy life*; look not behind thee, neither stay thou in all the plain; escape to the mountain, lest thou be consumed" (Gen 19:17; cf. Deut 4:15; Josh 23:11; 1 Kings 19:3; 2 Kings 7:7; Jer 17:21; Prov 7:23; Lam 2:19; Est 7:7; 8:11; 9:16). In this connection, the formula 'to seek after someone's life' (*nepēs̆*) also reveals the individuated life inherent in the persons, cf. 1Sam 20:1; 22:23[2x]; 23:15; 25:29; 2sam 4:8; 16:11; l Kings 19:10.14; Jer 4:30; 11:21; 19:7,9; 21:7; 22:25; 34:20f.; 38:16; 44:30[2x]; 46:26; 49:37; Ps 35:4; 38:13[12]; 40: 15[14]; 54:5[3]; 63: 10[9]; 70:3[2]; 86:14; Exod 4:19.

1.3. *Nepēs̆* as Part of the Body

נֶפֶשׁ is also used to designate parts of the body, primarily to stress their characteristics and functions, for example "throat, gullet"[20] as the organ used for eating and breathing. Although in such instances נֶפֶשׁ denotes the parts of the body to denote their characteristics and functions, in fact נֶפֶשׁ points to the whole person.

1.3.1. *Nepēs̆* as an Organ for Eating and Breathing

- Isa 5:14 speaks of the mouth of Sheol: ("therefore Sheol has enlarged its *nepēs̆* [*throat*]: Isa 5:14).

- Hab 2:5 transfers the image to the gluttonous individual, who is like Death and never has enough ("He enlarges his *nepēs̆* [*throat*] like Sheol, and he is like death, never satisfied" Hab 2:5).

- Similar references can be seen in the book of Proverbs: "The Lord will not suffer the *nepēs̆* [*throat*] of the righteous to hunger" (Prov 10:3); "The righteous eats to the satisfying of his *nepēs̆* [*throat*]: Prov 13:25); "*As* cold waters to a thirsty *nepēs̆* (*throat*), so *is* good news from a far country" (Prov 25:25).

- The meaning "desire, appetite" is obviously closely related to the meaning "throat".

- Thus *nepēs̆* can denote simple hunger, as in Hos 9:4: "for their bread is for their *souls*.

- Deut 23:25 allows grapes to be eaten for one's *appetite* (*nepēs̆*) in a vineyard, but they must not be carried away.

- Isa 29:8 uses the image of a hungry person who dreams of eating but wakes up with empty נפש and dreams of drinking but wakes up with thirsty *nepēs̆*.

- Prov 27:7 says that "a sated נפש loathes honey, but to a famished *nepēs̆* any bitter thing is sweet".

- Prov 16:26 is a very dense saying: "The *nepēs̆* (*hunger*) of the worker works for him; his mouth drives him on".

In all these instances *nepēs̆* points to the whole person because the hunger or thirst is experienced by the whole person and the person does not have an existence when his/her throat is cut off.

1.3.2. *Nepēs̆ as an Organ for Breathing*

Nepēs̆ as throat also denotes as an "organ of breathing" or "breath":[21]

- In Exod 23:12 Moses stresses that the home-born slave and the resident alien should 'breathe easily' (*nepēs̆* verb *niphal* imperfect) on the seventh day: "so that the son of your female slave, as well as your stranger, should breathe easily" (Exod 23:12).

- Exod 31:17 also applies this usage to Yahweh, who 'breathed easily' after the six days of creation: "and on the seventh day he rested, and he breathed easily" (Exod 31:17).

- In a similar way Gen1:30 speaks of all the creatures that can move about, in which there is breath: "and to everything that creeps upon the earth, wherein there is breath (Gen 1:30).

- Jer 2:24 probably goes along with this line: "A wild ass used to the wilderness, *that breaths* up the wind at her pleasure" (Jer 2:24; cf. Job 41:13).

In all these instances, while *nepēs̆* focusing on a single part of the body and its function, by synecdoche the whole person is represented.

1.4. *Nepēs̆* as Totality of Human Life

Nepēs̆ can stand for human needs, desires and feelings, including thought, memory and consciousness.

1.4.1. *Nepēs̆* as Desire Involving the Whole Person

The synthetic view of life always thinks of 'desire' as involving the whole person. Thus,

- Gen 34:3 says that Shechem's *nepēs̆* "was cleaved to" Dinah.

- Gen 34:8 goes on to say that his *nepēs̆* "loved" her.

- In Ezk. 23:l 7f. we see that after her prostitution, Oholibah's *nepēs̆* turned away from her lovers, and in like fashion Yahweh will turn away from Oholibah, just as he turned away from the *nepēs̆* of Oholah (cf. 23:22,28).

- Erotic desire, however, is only one form of passionate attachment and love. For example, Gen 44:30 records that Jacob's נֶפֶשׁ was bound up with Benjamin, Joseph's only full brother.

- The same is said of Jonathan in l Sam 18:1, his *nepēs̆* was so bound up with David: "and the soul of Jonathan was knit to the soul of David, and Jonathan loved him as himself."

- However, the most passionate attachment known is that between man and woman so that in Cant 1:7; 3:1-4 it is hardly possible to distinguish between the individual and the longing *nepēs̆*.

Nepēš is also used to denote excessive desires: 1) gluttony ("And put a knife to your throat, If you are a man of *appetite*" Prov 23:2), 2) and of unfulfilled desires like barrenness ("And Hannah answered and said, No, my lord, I *am* a woman of a sorrowful spirit: I have drunk neither wine nor strong drink, but have poured out my soul before the Lord" (1 Sam 1:15).

Spiritual yearning/desire is also assigned to *nepēš*, such as the desire for God:

- "As the deer pants for the water brooks, so *my soul* (*nepēš*) pants for you, O God" (Ps 42:1).

- "*My soul* thirsts for Thee ..." (Ps 63:2).

- "*My soul* longed and even yearned for the courts of the Lord (Ps 84:3).

- "*My soul* is crushed with longing after thine ordinances at all times" (Ps 119:20).

- "At night *my soul* longs for Thee ..." (Isa 26:9).

Nepēš is also used to denote desires like evil ("The soul of the wicked desires evil..." (Prov 21:10), and political power ("and that thou may reign over all that thine heart desires" (2 Sam 3:21).

In all these instances where *nepēš* designates the desire of the person we see the state of consciousness of the entire person.

1.4.2. *Nepēš* as Human Need

Nepēš is often used to express physical needs such as hunger and thirst:

- Deut 12:20 → "and you shall say, I will eat flesh, because *your soul* longs to eat flesh; you may eat flesh, whatsoever *your soul* lusts after";

- Num 21:5 → "for *there is* no bread, neither *is there any* water; and *our soul* loathes this light bread;

- 1 Sam 2:16 → "And *if* any man said unto him, let them not fail to burn the fat presently, and *then* take *as much* as *your soul* desires";

- Hab 2:5 → "Furthermore, wine betrays the haughty man, so that he does not stay at home. He enlarges his hunger (*nepēš*) like Sheol."

- Num11:6 → "But now *our soul* dried away: there is nothing at all, beside this manna, before our eyes" (Num11:6).

- Prov 25:25 → "*As* cold waters to a *thirsty soul,* so *is* good news from a far country.

In all these occurrences *nepeš* points to the entire person who feels hunger and thirst.

1.4.3. *Nepēš* as Emotions and Experiences

Nepēš is also used to express human emotions and experiences. It can be sad, grieve, weep, rejoice, and be distressed and loved.

Grief:

- Jer 13:17 → "*my soul* shall weep in secret places for *your* pride"; Ps 44:25 → "For our soul has sunk down into the dust."

- Gen 42:21→ "because we saw the distress of *his soul* when he pleaded with us."

- Deut 28:65 →　"failing of eyes, and despair of *soul.*"

- Job 30:25 → "Was not my soul grieved for the needy?"

- Ps 6:4 → "and *my soul* is also sore vexed: but thou, O Lord, how long?"

Joy and exultation:

- Ps 35:9 → "And *my soul* shall rejoice in the LORD; It shall exult in His salvation."

- Ps 42:5 → "When I remember these *things*, I pour out *my soul* in me…"

- Ps 103:2→ "Bless the Lord, O *my soul*, and forget not all his benefits"

Love:
- 1 Sam 18:1 → "and the soul of Jonathan was knit to the soul of David, and Jonathan loved him as himself (*soul nepēs*)."

Will as well as Moral Action:
- Gen 49:6 → "Let *my soul* not enter into their council; Let not my glory be united with their assembly; because in their anger they slew men, and in their self-will they lamed oxen".

- Num15:27→ "And if any *soul* sin through ignorance, then he shall bring a she goat of the first year for a sin offering".

Nepēs **as the seat of memory:**
- Lam 3:20 → "Surely *my soul* remembers and is bowed down within me."

In all these instances *nepēs* points to the entire person who feels sad, grieved, distressed, rejoiced, and loved. The ability to discern and to act morally also involves the whole person. Likewise, the capacity to remember affects the entire life of a person and not merely his/her cognitive faculty.

1.5. The *Nepēs* of God

There are also instances in the OT which speak of the *nepēs* of God. It is used sporadically in the sense that God, too, has a relationship with himself and with his people because it is otherwise absurd to think of God having a soul in the Hellenistic perspective.

- In Am 6:8 and Jer 51:14, he swears by his *nepēs*, i.e., by his own self: "The Lord God has sworn by his soul …" (Amos 6:8); "The Lord of hosts has sworn by Himself…" (Jer 51:14).

- The character of the servant of God in Isaiah springs from the same the root: "in whom *my soul* delights" (Isa 42:1).

- The same idea appears in 1 Sam 2:35: instead of the sons of Eli, Yahweh will "raise up a faithful priest, who shall do according to my heart and according to *my soul.*

- In Isa 1:14 *nepēš* expresses God's utter rejection of Jerusalem's festivals and prayers, extending to the utmost depths of God's living being: "Your new moons and your appointed feasts my soul hates."

- In Jer 6:8 God warns Jerusalem: "lest my *nepēš* turn from you" (Jer 6:8), and this rejection is confirmed in Jer 15:1: "My *nepēš* would not be with this people (cf. 5:9.29; 9:8; Ezk 23:18; Zec 11:8; Lev 26:11.30).

- In Ps 11:5 God tests the righteous and the wicked, and the one who loves violence *his soul* hates" These texts (Isa 1:14; Jer 6:8; 15:1; Ps 11:5) all articulate God's disgust against the disobedient Israel. However, in Jer 32:41 we see God's renewed passion towards Israel: "I will plant them in this land with all my heart and with all *my soul*" (Jer 32:41).

2.   Soul in the New Testament

The New Testament counterpart to the Old Testament word for *nepēš* is *psūchê*,[22] and it has substantially the same meaning as the Hebrew *nepēš*. Compared to *nepēš* in the Old Testament, *psūchê* appears relatively rare in the New Testament because it is used only where πνεῦμα would be out of place.[23] Besides this, *pneûma* stands in quite a different relation to God from the *psūchê*. The *pneûma* is the out breathing of God into the creature, the life-principle derived from God,[24] whereas the *psūchê* is the vital self, that which distinguishes one individual from another.

2.1. *Psŭchê* as Life

The term *psŭchê* has a range of meanings similar to *nepēs̆* in the Old Testament. It frequently designates life:[25] While in Acts 20:10 *psŭchê* is the life which remains in Eutyches, Acts 27:22 says that there will be no loss of life (*psŭchê*).

- o Acts 20:10 → "Do not be troubled, for his life is in him."

- o Acts 27:22 → "for there shall be no loss of life among you, but *only* of the ship."

- Acts 27:10 refers to the danger not merely to the ship and cargo but also to the *psŭchê* of the passengers. The plural shows already that *psŭchê* can individualise very strongly.

- o Acts 27:10 → "not only of the cargo and the ship, but also of *our souls*"

Moreover, we see instances where one:

- gives his life (*psŭchê* cf. Matt 20:28; Mk 10:45; Jn. 10:11.15.17;13:27f.; 15:13; 2 Cor 12:15; 1Thess 2:8; 1 Jn 3:16; Rev 12:11):

- o Matt 20:28 → "just as the Son of Man did not come to be served, but to serve, and to give His life (*psŭchê*) a ransom for many"

- risks his life (*psŭchê* cf. Matt 2:20; Lk 12:20; Jn 13:37; acts 15:26; Rom 16:4);

- o Matt 2:20 → "Arise and take the Child and His mother, and go into the land of Israel; for those who sought the Child's life are dead"

- lays down his life (*psŭchê* cf. Jn 10:15.17-18; Rom 16:4);

- o Jn 10:15 → "…and I lay down *my life* for the sheep"

- forfeits his life (*psūchê* cf. Matt 16:26);

  ○ Matt 16:26 → "For what will a man be profited, if he gains the whole world, and forfeits *his soul*? Or what will a man give in exchange for his soul?"

- bearing witness to life (*psūchê* cf. Phil 2:30);

  ○ "because he came close to death for the work of Christ, risking his life …"

- hates his life (*psūchê* cf. Lk 14:26).

In Lk 12:20 life (*psūchê*) is demanded from the man: "But God said to him, 'You fool! This *very* night *your soul* is required of you; and *now* who will own what you have prepared?" In Matt 16:25 Jesus says: "Whoever wants to save his life will lose it, but whoever loses his life (*psūchê*) for me will find it" (Matt 16:25).

In all these instances *psūchê* refers to physical life of a person, a life that God intended for every individual.

2.2. *Psūchê* as Vital Self

As we have seen, *psūchê* is in the first instance denotes the physical life, however, this does not indicate the phenomenon of life in general but the life which is manifested in the vital self. Therefore, *psūchê* can indicate the entire person as in Acts 2:41.43; 27:37; Rom 2:9; 13:1.

- Acts 2:41→ "…and the same day there were added *unto them* about three thousand *souls*"

Psūchê also serves as the reflexive pronoun designating the self ("I will say to myself" (*psūchê*) Lk 12:19; "as my witness" (*psūchê*) 2 Cor 1:23; "share our lives" (*psūchê*) 1 Thess 2:8).

- Lk 12:19 → "And I will say to *my soul* (*psūchê*), 'Soul, you have many goods laid up for many years *to come*; take your ease, eat, drink *and* be merry.'"

2.3. *Psūchê* as Seat of Emotions and Feelings

Psūchê as the place of feeling can express emotions such as:

- Grief (Matt 26:38; Mk 14:34):

  - Matt 26:38 → "*My soul* (*psūchê*) is deeply grieved, to the point of death …"

- Anguish: Jn 12:27→ "Now *my soul* (*psūchê*) has become troubled"

- Sorrow: Lk 2:35 → "and a sword will pierce even your own soul (*psūchê*) - to the end that thoughts from many hearts may be revealed"

- Exultation: Lk 1:46 → "And Mary said: '*My soul* (*psūchê*) exalts the Lord'"

- Pleasure: Matt 12:18 → "…My Beloved in whom *my soul* (*psūchê*) is well-pleased…"

- In Lk 12:19 the *psūchê* is addressed in soliloquy. It has goods, can take its ease, can eat, drink and be merry.

2.4. *Psūchê* as True Life

In certain places, *psūchê* stands for more than physical life that ceases at death:

  - In Jn 12:25 Jesus says, "The man who loves his life (*psūchê*) will lose it, while the man who hates his life (*psūchê*) in this world will keep it for eternal life".

  - Those who endure suffering without a loss of faith will "keep their *souls*" (Heb 10:39).

Although *psūchê* can never be sundered from the purely physical life, it is not identical with it, but a true life in distinction from purely physical life (Mk 8:35; Matt 10:39; Lk 17:33).

- Mk 8:35 → "For whosoever will save his life (*psūchê*) shall lose it; but whosoever shall lose his life (*psūchê*) for my sake and the gospel's, the same shall save it".

- Matt 10:39 → "He who has found his life (*psūchê*) shall lose it, and he who has lost his life (*psūchê*) for my sake shall find it"

- Lk 17:33 → "Whoever seeks to keep his life (*psūchê*) shall lose it, and whoever loses *his life* shall preserve it".

An analysis of these passages will show that "the awakening to eternal life is not a magical change, for the believer already has *psūchê*. Again *psūchê* is not an immortal soul, for otherwise we should not be called upon to hate it. *Psūchê* is the life which is given to man by God and which through man's attitude towards God receives its character as either mortal or eternal."[26]

2.5. *Psūchê* as Totality of Human Life

However, in certain instances of Paul's use of "soul", "spirit" and "body" may cause confusion over the meaning and significance of these words or the influence of its Hellenistic thought. For example, in 1Thess 5:23 Paul says: "May God himself, the God of peace, sanctify you through and through. May your whole spirit (*pneûma*), soul (*psūchê*) and body (*sôma*) be kept blameless at the coming of our Lord Jesus Christ." In recent times, most scholars have come to view these terms as differing aspects of one human reality, which is personhood.[27] In Heb 4:12 the word of God is said to penetrate so deeply that it divides "soul and spirit." Here again the terms "soul and spirit" simply means that the word of God probes the deepest parts of our personhood, or human self. Therefore, mostly the use of "soul", "spirit" and "body" in the NT is a way of perceiving the totality of human life.

Therefore, in all variant meaning of *psūchê*, *psūchê* is the physical life given by God that cannot be limited by death, but to be cherished as God intended it. *Psūchê* is the vital self of the person which is lived only in the body.[28]

Conclusion

The biblical view of man is not a bipartite creature of the divine and human, of soul and body. Instead of splitting a person into body and soul in the Hellenistic thought, Hebrew thought sees it as a unified being. According to the Old Testament understanding of *nepēs̆* human person is a living soul (*nepēs̆ hayyâh*) rather than having a soul, and *nepēs̆* is integral to his/her vital self. As Seebass explains, "human beings in the OT do not think of themselves in a subject-object relationship (spirit and soul). On the basis of being alive, of individuation within life, of perceiving life as an in-and-out rhythm (breathing?), they find themselves to be living quanta with respect to *hayyim,* life."[29] Similarly *psūchê* in the New Testament indicates the entire person. *Psūchê* is always the vital self, never the phenomenon of life as such but as a whole, a person. Thus, both נֶפֶשׁ and *psūchê* refer to person's vital self and his/her individuated life. It can stand for human needs, desires and feelings, emotions and experiences, including thought, memory and consciousness. Accordingly it can be the locus of person's hunger and thirst, joy and sorrow, lamentation and exultation, love and hate etc. It describes the individual person from the standpoint of inward participation in the fellowship with God and with the fellow beings in the midst of his/her earthly existence. In short, the biblical understanding of human person is not like the Hellenistic view of a person i.e. a union of soul and body, but a living soul animated by God's breath (Gen 2:7). *nepēs̆* or *psūchê* is not part of a person, rather it is person him/herself viewed as a living being.

Endnotes

[1] T. James, "The ancient Hebrews had no idea of an immortal soul living a full and vital life beyond death, nor of any resurrection or return from death", What the Bible says about Death, Afterlife, and the future, https://jamestabor.com/what-the-bible-really-says-about-death-afterlife-and-the-future. (Accessed on Jan 15, 2018). For an overview of human soul in the Old Testament, cf. H. Seebass, *nepēs̆* in: *Theological Dictionary of the Old Testament*, vol. IX, 497-519;

C. WESTERMANN, nepēš in: *Theological Lexicon of the Old Testament*, vol. II, 743-759; H. W. WOLFF, *Anthropology of the OT*, Philadelphia, 1974; C. A. BRIGGS, "The Use of nepēš in the Old Testament", in: *JBL* 16 (1897), 17-30.

[2] Cf. T. ANN, *Bodies of thought: science, religion, and the soul in the early Enlightenment*, (Oxford2008), 42. For an overview of the Greek view of human person, cf. G. E. LADD, "The Greek versus the Hebrew view of man", http://www.presenttruthmag.com/archive/XXIX/29-2.htm, Accessed on 16.7.2015; W. K. C. GUTHRIE, *A History of Greek Philosophy: The Earlier Presocratics and the Pythagoreans*, Vol.1, Cambridge 1962; J. BARR, "Athens or Jerusalem? - The Question of Distinctiveness": in idem. *Old and New in Interpretation*, New York 1966, 34-64; W. K. C. GUTHRIE, *Orpheus and the Greek Religion*, London 1952.

[3] "Even as we are conscious of the broad and very common biblical usage of the term "soul," we must be clear that scripture does not present even a rudimentarily developed theology of the soul. The creation narrative is clear that all life originates with God. Yet the Hebrew scripture offers no specific understanding of the origin of individual souls, of when and how they become attached to specific bodies, or of their potential existence, apart from the body, after death. The reason for this is that, as we noted at the beginning, the Hebrew Bible does not present a theory of the soul developed much beyond the simple concept of a force associated with respiration, hence, a life-force.", AVERY-PECK, "Soul", in Neusner, et al. (eds.), *The Encyclopedia of Judaism*, 1343 (2000).

[4] However, only in individual cases can one decide whether the choice of the word is due primarily to its association with vital force or with soul as the seat of the spirit or mind. For example, in Is10:18 the total man is denoted by the double expression *psūchê* / *sárx* but in Greek this undoubtedly suggests that the two are in juxtaposition. The Hebrew has nepēš / *baśār* and as a later text like Qoh. 5:5 shows, these words indicate only a slight distinction of meaning and not one that embraces the antithesis of body and soul. Cf. DIHLE, , *Theological Dictionary of the New Testament*, vol. IX, 632.

[5] NEYREY, "Soul", in: *Harper's Bible Dictionary* (1985), 982–983.

[6] W. A. ELWELL, s. v. "Soul", in: *Baker's Evangelical Dictionary of Biblical Theology* (1966).

[7] B. S. CHILDS, *Old Testament Theology in a Canonical Context* (Fortress, 1985), 199.

[8] For its distribution in the OT, see SEEBASS, nepēš, 502.

[9] The meanings include 1) throat Isa 5:14; 2) neck Ps 105:18; 3) breath Job 41:13; 4) living being Gen 1:20; 5) man, men, person, people a) man (i.e person)

Lev 24:17; = slaves Ezek 27:13; whoever kills a person Num 31:19; all the persons in his household Gen 36:6; one (out of every 500) Num 31:28; any person Lev 24:17, a head of cattle Lev 24:18; acquire people, rear persons (slaves?) Gen 12:5, buy a slave Lev 22:11; b) population: all persons, everyone Gen 46:15; w. numbers Genn 46:18; 6) personality, individuality: a) stressed I (myself) Gen 27:4; b) expression of reflexive, esp. stressed: like himself 1 Sam 18:3; self-humiliation, penance Num 30:14; c) every one = each one Exod 12:16, the one who, whoever Lev 7:20.27 7) life (of a person, a single life): Gen 9:5, 8. 'soul' as seat & support of feelings & sensations: a) desire (even inordinate desire): (of love) Cant 1:7; greedy (for food) Prov 23:2, greedy (for possessions) 28:25; never satisfied Eccl 6:3; b) mood, state of mind: Exod 23:9; c) feeling, taste Num 21:5; d) will: you are willing Gen 23:8; 8) someone dead, a dead person, corpse: Lev 19:28; 9) perfume-bottles Isa 3:20. For a detailed description of the meanings of *nepēš*, cf. *HALOT I*, 711-713; SEEBASS, *nepēš*, 497-519.

[10] Cf. O. JAMES, s. v. "Soul", in: *International Standard Bible Encyclopaedia*, 1915.

[11] WOLFF, *Anthropology of the OT*, 17.

[12] WESTERMANN, *nepēš*, 749.

[13] SEEBASS, *nepēš*, 511.

[14] Because "only rarely can we read the language as suggesting that ‎נפש‎ refers directly to the relationship between God and an individual (e.g., Ps 63:9[8]: "My *nepēš*, clings to Yahweh; his right hand upholds it"). For "God is in heaven, and you upon earth" (Eccl 5: 1 [2]), i.e., a direct relationship would obscure the distance between profoundly ephemeral mortals and God, whose word endures forever", SEEBASS, *nepēš*, 511.

[15] WESTERMANN, *nepēš*, 751.

[16] Ibid., 751.

[17] L. KÖHLER, *Old Testament Theology*, (Philadelphia 1957), 142.

[18] WOLFF, *Anthropology of the OT*, 10.

[19] SEEBASS, *nepēš*, *511-512*.

[20] SEEBASS, *nepēš*, 504; A series of expressions associated with *nepēš*, may presume the original meaning "maw, throat, gullet" and show the effects of both functions of the throat, swallowing and breathing (e.g. Isa 58:1 (to satiate); Isa 29:8 (to empty); Isa 29:8 and Psa 107:9 (to thirst); Prov 6:30 (to fill); Prov 3:22 (neck); Eccl 6:7 (mouth) etc. However, the concrete sense of *nepēš*, as "throat" as an organ for nourishment is rare in the OT, although it can be nuanced in certain instances (cf. Prov 28:25), cf. SEEBASS, *nepēš*, 504; WESTERMANN, *nepēš*, 745-46.

[21] A number instances show metaphorically the connection between breath and the life of the individual: cf. Gen 35:18; 1Kings 17:21-22; Jer 4:31; 15:9;

[22] For all uses and meanings of *psūchê*, see SCHWEIZER, *psūchê*, 637-656.

[23] Yet it seems at times to be employed where πνεῦμα might have been used. Thus, in Jn 19:30 we read: "Jesus gave up his πνεῦμα to the Father", and, in the same Gospel Jn10:15, "Jesus gave up his *psūchê* for the sheep", and in Mt 20:28 "he gave his *psūchê* as a ransom for many".

[24] Cf. KLEINKNECHT, *pneûma*, in: Theological dictionary of the New Testament, vol. VI, 334-339.

[25] Clearly, the word *psūchê* is used in various contexts, and it is difficult to draw any final conclusions as to what *psūchê* might be in any transcendental sense. In Matt 20:28 Jesus says that "the Son of Man did not come to be served, but to serve, and to give his life (*psūchê*) as a ransom for many", which means that Jesus' as "soul" or person died to pay for human sins. Therefore, this verse implies that the *psūchê* can be given up in death. Thus, Matt 10:28 seems to differentiate the *psūchê* from the body, and implies that the former cannot be killed by humans. However, paradoxically the same author in Matt 2:20; 20:28 says that *psūchê* can be killed. As well, one can "lose" one's "soul", and in doing so can find Jesus (cf. Matt 16:25).

[26] SCHWEIZER, *psūchê*, 644.

[27] Cf. C. Larkin, Rightly Dividing the Word, New York 2012, 86.

[28] Ibid., 644.

[29] SEEBASS, *nepēs̆*, 503-504.

Chapter 14

Concept of Mind, Body and Soul in the Sikh Scripture (SGGS)

Hardev Singh Virk

Introduction

Sri Guru Granth Sahib (SGGS), the Sikh scripture, is a unique creation in the history of world religions as it contains the sacred writings of Sikh Gurus and more than 30 saints and bards belonging to different religious and cultural traditions of India.Sikhism is a monotheistic religion and hence, believes that "God" is One, and prevails in everything, as symbolized by the symbol Ik Onkar (*one all pervading spirit*). The fundamental belief of Sikhism is that God exists, indescribable yet knowable and perceivable to anyone who surrenders his ego and Loves the Almighty. The Sikh Gurus have described God in numerous ways in their hymns included in the SGGS, the holy scripture of Sikhism, but the oneness of the deity is consistently emphasized throughout.

God is described in the MoolMantar (lit. Prime Utterance), the commencing verse in the SGGS:

ikkōankār sat(i)-nām(u) karatāpurakh(u) nirabha'uniravair(u) akālamūrat(i) ajūnīsaibhan(g) gur(a) prasād(i).

There is but one all pervading spirit, and it is called the truth, It exists in all creation, and it has no fear, It does not hate and, it is timeless, universal and self-existent! You will come to know it through the grace of the Guru.

Mind, Body and Soul connection in SGGS

The human being is comprised of three components: Mind, Body and Soul. For a healthy person, all these components need to function in an efficient and coordinated manner. Your mind, body and soul all have to work together in harmony. What is confirmed by Gurbaniin SGGS is that the body, mind and soul are three distinct and necessary components that make up a person; further, that these are all the product of God and together these three separate components function in unity to excel the human being to the highest spiritual heights.

SGGS explores the relationship between mind, body and soul. Human body is considered to be a gift of God and is obtained by good fortune after passing through a cycle of 8.4 million species as ordained in Hindu scriptures. Body needs to be nurtured as it is the abode of God. Guru Nanak considers the human body as a vehicle of soul. Prime importance is given to soul in Sikh metaphysics. Body is also called the temple of God (*HariMandir*). If a man's soul is not tuned to God, he is as good as dead.

vadai bhaagihsareerpaa-i-aa. maanasjanamsabad chit laa-i-aa.

binsabdaisabh anDh anDhayraagurmukh kisehbujhaa-idaa.

By great good fortune, I obtained this body; in this human life, I have focused my consciousness on the Word of the Shabad. Without the Shabad, everything is enveloped in utter darkness; only the Gurmukh understands.

(SGGS, M. 3, P. 1065)

jee-opaa-ay tan saaji-aarakhi-aabanat banaa-ay.

akhee daykhaijihvaabolaikanneesurat samaa-ay.

paireechalaihatheekarnaa ditaapainai khaa-ay.

jinrachrachi-aa tisehnajaanaianDhaaanDh kamaa-ay.

jaa bhajai taa theekarhovai ghaarhat gharheenajaa-ay. naanakgur
bin naahi pat pat vin paarnapaa-ay.

*He placed the soul in the body which He had fashioned. He protects the
Creation which He has created. With their eyes, they see, and with their
tongues, they speak; with their ears, they bring the mind to awareness.
With their feet, they walk, and with their hands, they work; they wear
and eat whatever is given. They do not know the One who created the
Creation. The blind fools do their dark deeds. When the pitcher of the
body breaks and shatters into pieces, it cannot be re-created again. O
Nanak, without the Guru, there is no honour; without honour, no one
is carried across.*

(SGGS, M.1, P.138)

harmandarayhusareerhaigi-aanratanpargat ho-ay.
manmukh moolnajaanneemaanasharmandarnaho-ay.

*This body is the Temple of the Lord, in which the jewel of spiritual
wisdom is revealed. The self-willed manmukhs do not know anything
at all; they do not believe that the Lord's Temple is within.*

(SGGS, M.3, P. 1346)

There are 105 hymns in SGGS where connection between mind and
body is elaborated. The mind and body are offered to the Guru by
the devotee in utter devotion. The Lord comes to dwell in the body
of the devotee and his mind and body blossom forth and flourish.
The fire of ego is extinguished and a soothing effect is produced in
both body and mind:

tan man gurpehvaychi-aa man dee-aa sir naal.
*I have sold my body and mind to the Guru,
and I have given my mind and head as well.*

(SGGS, M.1, P.20)

sabh tan man hari-aaho-i-aanaanakharvasi-aa man so-ay.
Then, the body and mind totally blossom forth and flourish;
O Nanak, the Lord comes to dwell within the mind.

(SGGS, M.4, P. 41)

chit aavaiospaarbarahmlagaina tateevaa-o.
If you come to remember the Supreme Lord God,
then your body and mind shall be cooled and soothed.

(SGGS, M.5, P. 70)

Role of Consciousness in Mind, Body and Soul:
Consciousness is the state or quality of awareness, of being aware of an external object or something within oneself. In fact, consciousness is directed outwards to objects, inwards to soul (*atma*). *Atma* is pure consciousness without any content. *Atma* is not different from *Paramatma*, the Cosmic Consciousness.BhagatKabir designated it as *Ram kians* (a by-product of *Ram*). It is the subtlest, purest essence of life.

kahokabeerihraamkeea^{N}s.
Says Kabeer, this is formed of the same essence as the Lord.

(SGGS, Bhagat Kabir, P. 871)

jin tan man dee-aasurat samo-ee.
He gave me body and mind,
and infused consciousness into my being.

(SGGS, M.1, P.1027)

adhi-aatamkaramkaray din raatee. nirmal jot nirantarjaatee.

Whoever does the deeds of the soul, day and night, sees the
immaculate Divine Light deep within.

(SGGS, M.1, P. 1039)

Human body is comprised of five elements namely air, water, fire (heat), earth and ether. After the death, these elements merge in the elements of the environs and the soul is liberated from the body for its onward journey. The birth of human is a biological process explained in SGGS, viz. from union of male sperm and female ovum.

> paa[N]ch tat ko tan rachi-o jaanhuchatursujaan.
> jih tayupji-o naankaaleen taahimaimaan.

Your body is made up of the five elements; you are clever and wise - know this well. Believe it - you shall merge once again into the One, O Nanak, from whom you originated.

(SGGS, M. 9, P. 1427)

> rakat bind kaaih tanoagneepaaspiraan.
> *This body is made of blood and semen.*
> *It shall be consigned to the fire in the end.*

(SGGS, M. 1, P. 60)

Since the body consists of five elements (*Panch Tat*); hence the soul in the body has therefore been called *Panch Bhoo Atma*, the soul of the five elements in SGGS. It means the soul is entangled in the body and has to overcome the influence of its elements.

> panch bhooaatmaaharnaamraspokhai.

The soul, the subtle essence of the five elements, cherishes the Nectar of the Naam, the Name of the Lord.

(SGGS, M. 5, P. 299)

> panch bhooaatmaa vas karahi taa tirathkarahinivaas.

If your soul overcomes the five elements, then you shall come to have a home at the true place of pilgrimage.

(SGGS, M. 3, P. 491)

Mind is considered to be an integral part of God consciousness and it needs to be awakened to realize its true potential and origin. The mind is trapped by worldly illusion called *Maya* and is afflicted by ego, desire and pride. It is led astray from God consciousness and wastes its opportunity to attain liberation from the cycle of re-incarnation. The positive and negative qualities of Mind are elaborated in SGGS.

> man too[N] jot saroophaiaapnaamoolpachhaan.
> O my mind, you are the embodiment of the Divine Light
> (consciousness) - recognize your own origin.

(SGGS, M. 3, P. 441)

> Man tũṅgārabati◦āgārabladi◦ājāhi.Mā◦i◦āmohṇīmohi◦ā
> fir firjūnībhavāhi.Garablāgājāhimugadh man
> antga◦i◦āpachhutāvhe.Ahaṅkārtisnāroglagābirthājanamgavāvhe.
> Manmukhmugadhchītėhnāhīagaiga◦i◦āpachhutāvhe.I◦okahaiNānak
> man tũṅgārabati◦āgārabladi◦ājāvhe.

O mind, you are so full of pride; loaded with pride, you shall depart. The fascinating Maya has fascinated you, over and over again, and lured you into reincarnation. Clinging to pride, you shall depart, O foolish mind, and in the end, you shall regret and repent. You are afflicted with the diseases of ego and desire, and you are wasting your life away in vain. The foolish self-willed manmukh does not remember the Lord, and shall regret and repent hereafter. Thus says Nanak: O mind, you are full of pride; loaded with pride, you shall depart.

(SGGS, M. 3, P. 441)

Mind is also considered as an entity composed of five elements in subtle form in SGGS. It is influenced by *Maya* and worldly desires. It has to be liberated by grace of God.

> ih man karmaaih man Dharmaa.ih man panch tat tayjanmaa.

This mind commits its deeds of karma, and this mind follows the Dharma. This mind is born of the five elements.

(SGGS, M. 1, P. 415)

tan jalbalmaatee bha-i-aa man maa-i-aamohimanoor.

The body is burnt to ashes; by its love of Maya, the mind is rusted through.

(SGGS, M. 1, P. 19)

The human Soul (*Atma*) and the Cosmic Soul (*Parmatma*) are intertwined and indistinguishable one from the other. Those who understand the working of their own soul are already in the realm of Supreme Soul or God. Soul (*Atma*) is also equated with the Creator God in the SGGS:

aatam meh raamraam meh aatamcheenasgurbeechaaraa.

The Lord is in the soul, and the soul is in the Lord.

This is realized through the Guru's Teachings.

(SGGS, M. 1, P. 1153)

jineeaatamcheeni-aaparmaatam

so-ee.

Those who understand their own souls, are themselves the Supreme Soul.

(SGGS, M. 1, P. 421)

The experiential realization of this identification of Soul (*Atma*) with the Supreme Soul (*Parmatma*) is the *summum bonum* of Sikh mysticism. The purpose of human birth is to reunite the *atma* with the *Parmatma* but the humans have a characteristic affliction, that of ego, which is the real cause of the gulf that is sought to be bridged. Reunion is therefore possible by giving up the ego that caused the duality and hence the separation from God:

aatmaaparaatamaaaykokarai.

antarkee dubiDhaaaantarmarai. |

His soul and the Supreme Soul become one.

The duality of the inner mind is overcome.

(SGGS, M. 1, P. 661)

Chapter 15

The Near-Death Experience

Mehra Srikhande

Near-Death experiences are the phenomena reported by a few persons who have been on the brink of death and returned to tell the tale. Typically, these people have been clinically dead after a cardiac arrest, a serious accident, a life-threatening illness, following severe allergic reactions, seizures or a problem during surgery.

After a few minutes of resuscitation these people come back to life. Description of the experience differ from person to person, but usually share some basic elements like floating out of their bodies, travelling in a tunnel at high speed and visualization of bright light at the end of the tunnel. It is found that most people who have a near- death experience or NDE are spiritually transformed for the rest of their lives and have an unshakeable belief in the existence of God and the after-life.

Although various explanations like oxygen deprivation of the brain, release of neuro-transmitters at the time of death and influence of anaesthetics have been offered, there is no conclusive evidence to explain NDEs.

Researchers like Dr.Raymond Moody, Elizabeth-Kubler-Ross, Kenneth Ring, Michael Sabom and Melvin Morse, to name a few, are of the view that NDEs are so numerous, compelling and consistent, that they cannot be dismissed casually.

Real Life Happening

1. Rupa was an uneducated, twenty two year old woman, delivering her first child in a Municipal Hospital in Mumbai, in October 1985. She had been in labour pain for 24 hours. The contractions had left her exhausted, and she had no more strength left to bear down. The baby's progress seemed to be fine, but not hers. The postpartum hemorrhage had left her drained and pale and her pulse and BP were not recordable. While her exhausted body lay on the bed, a part of Rupa'sself glided slowly upwards, and from another vantage point watched the resuscitation efforts on her body. Shortly, she heard an unpleasant ringing sound inside her head and had the sensation of being pulled through a dark tunnel at tremendous speed. At the end of the tunnel was a bright light, and in it she sensed a compassionate presence. The presence started interrogating her about her life on earth, what she had done, whether it was worth it and whether she wished to die or to return. Like most people who die young she was not prepared to leave the world and therefore chose to return.

   The return journey was much faster and she found herself re-entering the same tunnel and travelling back to her body in the labour room. She had not died after all and later found that with the exception of one doctor and a couple of nurses, no one had any interest in what she experienced during her temporary death. She recounted the episode in her own words: "After I floated out of my body I was wondering what to do. If my body was dying from shock, how was I able to see, hear and feel? Then I entered a calm dream-like state and felt very secure and loved talking to the light. The bright light did not hurt my eyes because I wasn't seeing with my physical eyes anyway."

Rupa was absolutely sure she had crossed the threshold of death and journeyed to the 'other side.' As she herself shares, "The episode has left me a more spiritual person and I am now certain of the separate existence of the spirit. Death is not final, we continue to exist in another world, a world, beyond death and sufferings."

Each has a different experience at the threshold of death. This narration is amongst a few collected by me over the years I spent talking to seriously ill patients and accident victims and others at the point of death. All their experiences cannot be explained away as possible delusions, hallucination or hoax. A surprising thing about the NDEs is that they are remarkably similar around the world, irrespective of religious beliefs and cultural background. However, most survivors are unwilling to discuss them openly in a society that isskeptical of such claims.

Some Salient Features of NDE
1. An out-of-the-body experience
2. Hearing of buzzing or unpleasant sounds
3. The tunnel experience
4. An encounter with a bung of light
5. Seeing a life review
6. Meeting departed friends and relatives
7. Arriving at a boundary or path
8. Returning to the body and
9. Spiritual transformation

1.   An out of the Body Experience
In most cases, a NDE starts with the separation of the spiritual body from the physical. Some report rising up and floating near the ceiling of the room. From a vantage point outside their body, they may see grieving relatives and observe the resuscitative efforts of the medical

team. Some report feeling calm and detached,and mention that the sensations of pain or suffocation they experienced before dying disappear. Although the sensations of sight and hearing are present in their spiritual form,they are unable to speak or influence others.

2.   Hearing Noises

Some people hear a buzzing noise or unpleasant ringing sounds. Others report hearing pleasant musical notes.

3.   The Tunnel Experience

The sensation of being pulled into a tunnel at an astonishing speed is another common feature of a NDE. Some have the feeling that they are falling into a deep dark well.

4.   The Being of Light

A fairly large number of people who undergo a NDE say they encountered a being of light at the other end of the tunnel. The light is brilliant but does not hurt the eye as the person experiencing a NDE is seeing with his/her spiritual eye, not physical. The being that projects love and compassion differs according to the religious background of the individual. A telepathic dialogue ensues with the presence asking the individual questions like "What did you do with your life? Do you have anything worthwhile to tell me? Did you regret some of the things you did? Do you want to die or return?

5.   The Life Review

People report seeing their whole life passing before them like a high speed movie, starting from childhood and depicting the important events. They often feel like spectators watching a movie of their life.

6.   Meeting Departed Friends and Relatives

They may be seen in the room where the person is lying or beyond the tunnel. They supposedly lend a helping hand in order to make the transition to the afterlife easier.

7.   Arriving at a Boundary or Path

Only a few people are able to see a stream of water,a fence, or some sort of border identified as the dividing line between life and death. Nobody crosses this border because if they do, there is no returning.

8.   Returning to the Body

Most people are reluctant to return to their earthly existence after having a glimpse of the beyond. Those who want to come back are people with small children or those who have some unfinished business. The return journey is accomplished by traversing the tunnel in the reverse direction. It may be pleasant or disturbing.

9.   Spiritual transformation

Almost all persons having faced a NDE become more spiritual, less materialistic and go on to do some charitable or humanitarian work.

The skeptics and critics, however, view NDEs in more prosaic terms. Their traditional answers are that the dying may imagine such visions because of religious beliefs, or that the stress produced by the traumatic illnesses or fatal accident may cause such experiences. They offer explanations ranging from the preposterous to those worthy of serious consideration. According to them, oxygen starvation at the time of approaching death causes failure of all the organs and tissues of the body, the eyes and brain being most sensitive to its effects. The retina due to its higher oxygen consumption is the first to fail in such a condition. The tunnel experience may be explained by oxygen starvation of the retina.

Whatever they are – hallucinations, delusions or lies – NDEs cannot be dismissed outright. They are researched and debated worldwide, and have roused a great amount of interest in the fields of psychiatry and psychology and continue to be experienced universally.

Contributors

1. **Job Kozhamthadam,** Founder-Director of Indian Institute of Science and Religion (IISR).

2. **Heidi Russell,** Institute of Pastoral Studies, Loyola University of Chicago, Chicago, USA.

3. **Vincent Braganza,** Founder-Director of Xavier Research Foundation, St. Xavvier's College Campus, Ahmedabad.

4. **Roy Pereira,** Vice-Principal and Provost, St. Xavier's College, Mumbai.

5. **FrantišekMikeš**, Saints Cyril and Methodius Faculty of Theology, Palacky University, Czech Republic

6. **Geraldine Edith Mikes**, Eastern Laboratories, Springfield, MA, USA

7. **Chacko Nadakavely,** Mary Matha Major Seminary, Thrissur, Kerala, India.

8. **Kuruvilla Pandikattu,** Jnana-DeepaVidyapeeth, Pune, India.

9. **Stephen Jayard,** Jnana-DeepaVidyapeeth, Pune, India.

10. **Sally John,** Mahatma Gandhi Institute of Medical Sciences, Sevagram, Maharashtra, India.

11. **Victor Ferrao,** Rachol Patriarchal Seminary, Goa.

12. **Ramesh Bijlanai,** All India Institute of Medical Sciences, Delhi and Sri Aurobindo Ashram, Delhi.

13. **Jijimon Alakkalam Joseph,** Fu Jen Catholic University, Taipei, Taiwan.

14. **Thomas Karimundackal,** Jnana-DeepaVidyapeeth, Pune, India.

15. **Hardev Singh Virk,** Professor of Eminence, Punjabi University, Patiala.

16. **Mehra Srikhande,** Doctor of Ophthalmology, Pune.

Index

www.ingramcontent.com/pod-product-compliance
Lightning Source LLC
Chambersburg PA
CBHW060832270525
27285CB00010B/172